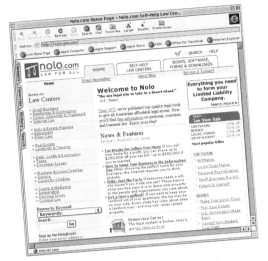

LEGAL INFORMATION ONLINE ANYTIME

24 hours a day

www.nolo.com

AT THE NOLO.COM SELF-HELP LAW CENTER, YOU'LL FIND

- Nolo's comprehensive Legal Encyclopedia filled with plain-English information on a variety of legal topics
- Nolo's Law Dictionary—legal terms <u>without</u> the legalese
- Auntie Nolo—if you've got questions, Auntie's got answers
- The Law Store—over 250 self-help legal products including Downloadable Software, Books, Form Kits and eGuides
- Legal and product updates
- Frequently Asked Questions
- NoloBriefs, our free monthly email newsletter
- Legal Research Center, for access to state and federal statutes
- Our ever-popular lawyer jokes

Quality LAW BOOKS & SOFTWARE FOR EVERYONE

Nolo's user-friendly products are consistently first-rate. Here's why:

- A dozen in-house legal editors, working with highly skilled authors, ensure that our products are accurate, up-to-date and easy to use
- We continually update every book and software program to keep up with changes in the law
- Our commitment to a more democratic legal system informs all of our work
- We appreciate & listen to your feedback. Please fill out and return the card at the back of this book.

An Important Message to Our Readers

This product provides information and general advice about the law. But laws and procedures change frequently, and they can be interpreted differently by different people. For specific advice geared to your specific situation, consult an expert. No book, software or other published material is a substitute for personalized advice from a knowledgeable lawyer licensed to practice law in your state.

3rd edition

Nolo's Law Form Kit

Personal Bankruptcy

**by Attorneys Stephen Elias, Albin Renauer,
Robin Leonard & Kathleen Michon**

Keeping Up to Date

To keep its books up to date, Nolo issues new printings and new editions periodically. New printings reflect minor legal changes and technical corrections. New editions contain major legal changes, major text additions or major reorganizations. To find out if a later printing or edition of any Nolo book is available, call Nolo at 510-549-1976 or check our website at http://www.nolo.com.

To stay current, follow the "Update" service at our website: http://www.nolo.com/update. In another effort to help you use Nolo's latest materials, we offer a 35% discount off the purchase of the new edition your Nolo book when you turn in the cover of an earlier edition. (See the "Special Upgrade Offer" in the back of the book.)

This book was last revised in: **May 2001**.

THIRD EDITION	May 2001
EDITOR	Kathleen Michon
BOOK DESIGN	Terri Hearsh
COVER DESIGN	Toni Ihara
PRODUCTION	Stephanie Harolde
PROOFREADING	Robert Wells
INDEX	Thérèse Shere
PRINTING	Consolidated Printers, Inc.

Personal bankruptcy / by Steve Elias . . . [et al.]. -- 3rd ed.
     p. cm. -- (Nolo's law form kit)
    Includes index.
    ISBN 0-87337-546-7
    1. Bankruptcy--United States Popular works. I. Elias, Stephen.
II. Series.
    KF1524.6.P47 1999
    346.7307'8--dc21   99-35065
                                          CIP

For information on bulk purchases or corporate premium sales, please contact the Special Sales Department. For academic sales or textbook adoptions, ask for Academic Sales. Call 800-955-4775 or write to Nolo, 950 Parker Street, Berkeley, CA 94710.

Table of Contents

A. How to Use This Kit

This kit was created at the request of readers of *How to File for Bankruptcy*, a detailed do-it-yourself Chapter 7 bankruptcy book also published by Nolo. Many readers conveyed that because their bankruptcy was so simple, they would have preferred a book that was less thorough and quicker to use. This kit is Nolo's response.

Rather than delving into the many legal issues that potentially surround a Chapter 7 bankruptcy, this kit focuses on the most common situations. If you have a simple and straightforward bankruptcy case, this kit should provide just the right amount of material you'll need to safely and comfortably handle it yourself.

This form kit shows you how to file your own Chapter 7 bankruptcy, which will cancel most, if not all, of your debts. Chapter 7 bankruptcy is a routine process that normally takes about four to six months, currently costs $200 in filing fees and commonly requires only one trip to the courthouse. You don't have to be a U.S. citizen to file.

If you have few assets and want to put your debt problems behind you as quickly as possible, you can use this kit to:

- figure out what property you can keep (few people lose property in Chapter 7 bankruptcy)
- determine what debts you'll get rid of forever
- find out if you have any debts that bankruptcy won't eliminate
- fill in your bankruptcy forms
- file your papers, and
- make the routine court appearance.

All you must do is pay careful attention to the instructions in this kit and use common sense. You shouldn't need to hire a lawyer to handle your case.

 Bankruptcy Law to Change for the Worse. In March, 2001, the United States Congress passed legislation that makes sweeping changes to bankruptcy law. At the time this book went to print, the legislation was in conference where congresspersons were ironing out a few minor differences between the House and Senate versions of the bill. President Bush has promised to sign the legislation into law. Once that happens, the new rules will take effect 180 days later.

The bill is backed by the credit card industry and is unfriendly to debtors. Among other things, the bill would prohibit some people from filing for bankruptcy, add to the list of debts that people cannot get rid of in bankruptcy, make it harder for people to come up with manageable repayment plans, and limit the protection from collection efforts for those who file for bankruptcy.

At the time this book is published, the legislation may have already become law. To learn about its status and details of its provisions, check Legal Updates on Nolo's website, http://www.nolo.com. The websites of the American Bankruptcy Institute at http://www.abiworld.org and Commercial Law League of America at http://www.clla.org also have up-to-date information about the legislation.

To get the best use out of this kit, we suggest you take these steps:

Step 1. Read the overview material (pages 3 through 8).

Step 2. Follow the step-by-step instructions to prepare a rough draft of your bankruptcy forms (make and use photocopies of the forms in this kit).

Step 3. Check your work. Then type your bankruptcy forms. Although you are not required to type the forms, courts prefer that you do. Many libraries have typewriters available to the public.

Step 4. Follow the step-by-step instructions for filing your documents and handling your case in court.

Look for These Icons
A caution about potential problems.
"Fast track" lets you know that you may be able to skip some material.
Information for married couples only.

B. When Not to Use This Kit

In our opinion, some situations may be too complicated for this kit—or any bankruptcy kit. The accompanying chart flags those situations and recommends whether you should consult a more detailed self-help law book or see a lawyer. We also alert you throughout the kit if a situation merits discussion beyond what we provide.

When You Need Help Beyond This Kit

Don't use this kit if...	Explanation	Where to get help
You're not sure whether to file for Chapter 7 bankruptcy.	There are often excellent alternatives to Chapter 7 bankruptcy, such as filing a different type of bankruptcy, negotiating with your creditors or simply doing nothing for the time being. Before filing, it's best to carefully assess your situation and figure out the best approach.	See *Money Troubles: Legal Strategies to Cope With Your Debts*, by Robin Leonard and Deanne Loonin (Nolo) or *Bankruptcy: Is It the Right Solution to Your Debt Problems?* by Robin Leonard (Nolo).
You want to file a different type of bankruptcy.	This kit covers only Chapter 7 bankruptcies. You'll need additional help if you want to file a different type of bankruptcy.	To file for Chapter 13 bankruptcy, see *Chapter 13 Bankruptcy: Repay Your Debts*, by Robin Leonard (Nolo). For other types of bankruptcy, you'll need to see a lawyer.
You own your house and don't want to lose it.	You might lose your house through the Chapter 7 bankruptcy process. Chapter 13 often is the better option. Before filing for any kind of bankruptcy, you should look into all options, including negotiating with your lender.	See a lawyer, *How to File for Bankruptcy*, by Elias, Renauer, Leonard and Michon (Nolo) or *Chapter 13 Bankruptcy: Repay Your Debts*, by Robin Leonard (Nolo).
You co-own a business.	If you're a partner in a business or a primary owner of a privately held corporation, Chapter 7 bankruptcy can seriously affect the business' legal and tax status.	See a lawyer.
You're married and you're not sure whether to file for bankruptcy alone or with your spouse.	Most married couples are better off filing for bankruptcy together. If, however, you are in a relatively new marriage, have not accumulated any joint (marital) property and you want to get rid of separate (premarital) debts, you are probably safe filing alone. In addition, you may want to file alone if: • your spouse owns separate, valuable property, such as a second home • you and your spouse own a house in tenancy by the entirety (look at your deed), or • you and your spouse have separated.	See a lawyer.

When You Need Help Beyond This Kit

Don't use this kit if...	Explanation	Where to get help
	Note for married couples in community property states: If you live in Arizona, California, Idaho, Louisiana, Nevada, New Mexico, Texas, Washington or Wisconsin, your share of your spouse's community property may be taken to pay your separate debts. But, your spouse's liability will be wiped out for all community (joint) debts you list on your papers, even if your spouse doesn't file with you.	
You haven't been honest with your creditors	Bankruptcy is geared towards the honest debtor who got in too deep and needs help to get a fresh start. A bankruptcy court won't help someone who unloads assets to friends or relatives, conceals property or income, has lied on a credit application or lies on the bankruptcy papers.	See a lawyer.
You don't want a codebtor to be liable for your debts.	Chapter 7 bankruptcy can relieve you from liability for your debts, but your cosigner or guarantor will be left on the hook. In Chapter 13 bankruptcy, you can repay the debt and protect your codebtor from your creditors.	See a lawyer or Chapter 13 Bankruptcy: Repay Your Debts, by Robin Leonard (Nolo).
You recently filed for bankruptcy.	You aren't eligible to file for Chapter 7 bankruptcy if: • a Chapter 7 case you filed was dismissed within the past 180 days because you violated a court order or requested a dismissal after a creditor asked for relief from the automatic stay. (The automatic stay is discussed in Section C3, below.) • you obtained a discharge of your debts under Chapter 7 or Chapter 13 in a case begun within the past six years. If, however, you obtained a Chapter 13 discharge in good faith after paying at least 70% of your unsecured debts, the six-year bar does not apply. You can file for Chapter 13 bankruptcy, however, even if you just completed a Chapter 7 case.	See a lawyer or *Chapter 13 Bankruptcy: Repay Your Debts*, by Robin Leonard (Nolo).

C. Chapter 7 Bankruptcy—an Overview

To avoid mistakes and pitfalls when you file your own Chapter 7 bankruptcy, you'll need to learn a few legal concepts and pick up a little legal terminology. Here are a few basics.

1. Chapter 7 Bankruptcy Defined

Chapter 7 bankruptcy refers to the chapter of federal statutes that contains the bankruptcy laws. Chapter 7 bankruptcy is sometimes called "straight" or "liquidation" bankruptcy. By filing for Chapter 7 bankruptcy, you ask the court to erase your debts forever. In exchange, you might have to give up some of your property. Most people, however, don't lose anything.

2. Bankruptcy Forms

To file for Chapter 7 bankruptcy, you must fill in several forms that require detailed information about your finances. You then take or mail your papers to a local bankruptcy court. You may pay the filing fee all at once or in installments.

If you need to file immediately, you can prepare and file just two forms, as long as you file the rest within 15 days. This might be a good idea if a creditor has started a wage garnishment or has threatened to take other property to satisfy a debt.

3. The Automatic Stay

Filing for bankruptcy puts into effect something called the *automatic stay.* The automatic stay is a court order that immediately stops your creditors from trying to collect what you owe them. The automatic stay does not, however, stop the government from criminally prosecuting you, your obligation to keep paying child support and alimony, or the IRS from auditing you, issuing a tax deficiency notice, demanding your tax returns, assessing taxes against you or demanding payment after an assessment.

The automatic stay is sometimes lifted as to a particular creditor to allow that creditor to proceed with a repossession or foreclosure, or to permit court proceedings that don't involve assets the bankruptcy court might want to take. Before the automatic stay is lifted for any creditor, you must get formal notice and the chance to object in court.

4. Your Bankruptcy Estate

When you file for bankruptcy, everything you own or are entitled to receive as of that date is collectively called your *bankruptcy estate.* Your bankruptcy estate becomes subject to the bankruptcy court's authority, although your property remains in your possession. Until your bankruptcy case ends, the bankruptcy court assumes legal control of the debts you owe and your bankruptcy estate. You have control of property and income you acquire after you file for bankruptcy, with a few exceptions, including property or money you were entitled to receive when you filed, as well as proceeds from a marital settlement agreement, life insurance policy or an inheritance distribution that you become entitled to receive within the six-month period immediately following your filing date.

5. Secured and Unsecured Debts

Your debts will fall into two main categories:

- **Secured debts.** A debt is secured if you've pledged property as collateral. Common examples are mortgages, car loans and home equity loans. Secured debts are also created when a creditor fixes a *lien*—or legal claim—on property. Typical examples include judgment liens, tax liens and mechanics' liens. The person or institution owed a secured debt is referred to as a *secured creditor.*

  In bankruptcy, your personal liability for a secured debt will be wiped out, unless you choose to "reaffirm" the debt or the debt is *nondischargeable.* (See **Nondischargeable Debts** sidebar below.) If your personal liability is eliminated, the creditor's right to collect the collateral or the lien, however, remains unless there is a legal way to wipe out the lien. (Secured debts are covered in more detail in Section E5, below.)
- *Unsecured debts.* These are debts that are not secured. Anyone owed an unsecured debt is an *unsecured creditor.* All unsecured debts you owe at the time you file will be wiped out in bankruptcy, unless they are *nondischargeable.* (See **Nondischargeable Debts,** below.)

Nondischargeable Debts

Several categories of debts will survive your bankruptcy intact.

Automatically Nondischargeable Debts

If the bulk of your indebtedness is from these types of debts, you will want to do more research before filing. (A detailed description of nondischargeable debts is contained in Nolo's *How to File for Bankruptcy*, by Elias, Renauer, Leonard and Michon.)

1. **Federal, state and local income taxes**, unless you filed your income tax returns for the tax year in question at least two years before filing for bankruptcy, you file for bankruptcy at least 240 days after the taxes were assessed against you, and the taxes were due at least three years before you file. Even if all of those things are true, if the IRS has filed a lien against your property and you own real estate, bankruptcy will only wipe out your personal liability to pay. The lien remains and the IRS can try to collect on it after your bankruptcy. If you borrowed money or used your credit card to pay your taxes, you cannot discharge the loan or credit card debt if the underlying tax debt is nondischargeable.

2. **Child support and alimony**, including support obligations owed to a child support collections office or the welfare department.

3. **Student loans** unless repaying would cause you undue hardship.

4. **Government-imposed fines**, such as traffic fines and restitution imposed in criminal cases.

5. **Fees imposed by a court** for the filing of a case, motion, complaint or appeal or for other costs and expenses assessed with such filing. This provision probably applies only to prisoners.

6. **Intoxicated driving debts**, if someone was injured or died. Any debts for property damage, however, will be wiped out in bankruptcy.

7. **Debts incurred prior to a previous bankruptcy filing**, if that bankruptcy was thrown out due to your fraud or misfeasance (bad acts).

8. **Debts that aren't listed on your bankruptcy forms**, unless the creditor knew about your bankruptcy.

Nondischargeable Debts If Creditor Objects

If a creditor formally objects to the discharge of a debt for one of the reasons listed below, and the court agrees with the creditor's objection, you'll still owe the debt even if you file for bankruptcy. (Again, see *How to File for Bankruptcy* for more specific information.)

1. **Debts from purposefully injuring a person or property**, such as a court judgment against you based on your getting angry at a neighbor, punching him and throwing paint on his house. But if you accidentally spilled paint on the neighbor's car, the debt would be wiped out.

2. **Debts incurred on the basis of fraud or dishonesty**. The law presumes fraud if you incur debts of more than $1,150 for luxury goods or services within 60 days before filing or obtain cash advances totaling more than $1,150 within 60 days before filing. Fraud might also include deliberately writing a bad check, lying on a credit application or using a credit card when you know you can't pay.

3. **Debts from stealing or mishandling someone else's money or property**.

4. **Debts incurred in the course of a divorce or separation or in connection with a separation agreement or divorce decree**, other than alimony and child support (which are automatically nondischargeable). If you agreed to pay certain marital debts or you owe your ex-spouse money to even up your property settlement, you can discharge the debt unless your ex-spouse or another creditor objects. If there's an objection, the court will let you discharge the debts only if you don't have the ability to repay or if the benefit you'd receive by the discharge outweighs any harm to your ex-spouse or children.

Note About Contracts: If you've signed a contract that is still in force or a lease that hasn't expired, it may be canceled unless it will produce assets for your creditors.

6. Exemptions and Nonexempt Property

On your bankruptcy papers, you must list your *exempt property*—that is, property that by law cannot be taken from you to pay your creditors. What qualifies as exempt varies from state to state. It usually includes basic items such as clothing, household furnishings, unspent Social Security payments and part of the value of a car or house.

Any *nonexempt property* may be taken or sold to pay your unsecured creditors. Used personal property often isn't bothered with, however, because the expense of court time, storage and selling the items usually exceeds the amount the sale will bring in.

7. Bankruptcy Trustee

A court-appointed person called a *bankruptcy trustee* oversees your case. The trustee sees that your unsecured creditors are paid as much as possible. The trustee is paid a percentage of the assets recovered for the creditors, so he carefully examines your bankruptcy papers. The trustee looks for nonexempt property that can be taken from you to pay your creditors. He also looks for problems in your documents—such as an undervaluation of your property or an overstatement of your expenses.

If the trustee believes that the correct information would produce more money for your unsecured creditors, he may pressure you to change your papers. If he thinks the problem would make you ineligible for Chapter 7 bankruptcy, he might even ask the bankruptcy court to dismiss your bankruptcy case. If you carefully follow the instructions in this kit and are honest in your bankruptcy papers, you need not worry that the trustee will take such drastic steps.

8. Creditors' Meeting

Approximately a month after you file your papers, you'll go to court for a *creditors' meeting*, so named because creditors are invited to attend and ask you questions about the information in your bankruptcy papers. In most parts of the country they usually don't attend unless they want to challenge the dischargeability of a debt or an exemption you claimed.

The trustee will, however, ask you questions about your bankruptcy papers and will try to identify any nonexempt property that can be taken from you. If you've been honest with your creditors and in your bankruptcy papers, the creditors' meeting should go smoothly. A typical creditors' meeting lasts five minutes.

9. Ending Your Bankruptcy

If you change your mind after you file for bankruptcy, you can ask the court to *dismiss* your case. If your case is dismissed, your creditors are free to go after you for payments; it's as though your bankruptcy was never started. A court generally will dismiss a Chapter 7 bankruptcy case as long as the dismissal isn't unfair to your creditors. Usually, you can file again if you want to. (How to dismiss a bankruptcy case is covered in *How to File for Bankruptcy*.)

On the other hand, if you go through the entire bankruptcy process, the court will grant you a *discharge*. At the end of the bankruptcy process, your debts that qualify for cancellation are wiped out—discharged—by the court. If you complete your bankruptcy and are granted a discharge, you can't file for Chapter 7 bankruptcy again for another six years from the date of your filing.

D. Before You Fill in the Forms

These steps will help you get the information you need to file for bankruptcy.

Step 1: Find the Bankruptcy Court

You must file your papers in a federal bankruptcy court. Normally, you file in the bankruptcy court for the federal judicial district where you've lived during the greater part of the last six months. If you conduct a business, you can choose to file in the district where your principal place of business has been located during the previous 180 days, or where the business' principal assets have been located during that period. To find the appropriate bankruptcy court, look in the government listings in your white pages, call directory assistance or find it on the Federal Judiciary's website at http://www.uscourts.gov (most, but not all, courts are listed).

Step 2: Get Information and Local Court Forms

Before filling in the bankruptcy forms, you'll want to get copies of any local forms required by your court. These are generally self-explanatory cover sheets or summaries of information you provide in the official forms. Call and ask for any local forms required or information available for an individual filing a Chapter 7 bankruptcy. If you can't get through on the phone, visit the court. Or, visit the court's website—many have forms and filing instructions. (Again, look for your court's website on the Federal Judiciary's website, at http://www.uscourts.gov.)

You should have little problem getting any necessary forms. In large cities, however, the bankruptcy court clerk's office may be bureaucratic. If necessary, be prepared to request help from a supervisor if you are stymied by the clerk.

⚠ **Be sure to contact the court.** You could skip contacting the court before you file, but you may face some frustrating hurdles when you file your papers.

Step 3: Decide Whether to Make an Emergency Filing

If you want to file for bankruptcy to get the immediate protection of the automatic stay and stop your creditors' collection activities, you can file a few short forms now and the rest within 15 days. Here's how:

1. Fill in Form 1—Voluntary Petition. (See Section E2.)
2. Check with the court to find out exactly what additional forms must be submitted for an emergency filing.
3. On a Mailing Matrix (or whatever form is required by your court), list all your creditors, as well as collection agencies, sheriffs, attorneys and others who are seeking to collect debts from you. (See Section E6.)
4. Fill in any additional forms the court requires.
5. File your emergency papers with the court along with the required number of copies, a self-addressed envelope and either the fee or an application for payment of fee in installments. (See Section F for filing papers and paying in installments.)
6. File all other required forms within 15 days.

⚠ **Don't miss the filing deadline.** If you don't file the rest of your forms within the 15 days allotted, your bankruptcy case may be dismissed. Depending on the circumstance, you may be prevented from filing again for 180 days and from discharging the debts you owed prior to your emergency filing.

E. How to Fill in the Bankruptcy Forms

The instructions that follow will take you through the entire process of preparing your Chapter 7 bankruptcy forms.

If You Need Help With the Forms

Nonlawyer businesses known as bankruptcy petition preparers provide services such as:
- typing your bankruptcy papers under your direction, and
- helping you find the information you need to fill out the forms.

Using a bankruptcy petition preparer can be a relatively inexpensive way to get your forms prepared for filing in court. Bankruptcy petition preparers may not, however, give legal advice, answer legal questions or represent you in court—only lawyers may do those things. So, if you aren't sure about important details of your bankruptcy, a bankruptcy petition preparer is not advisable.

In most major cities, you can find bankruptcy petition preparers listed in ads or in the Yellow Pages under "paralegal" or "typing services." Some bankruptcy petition preparers also offer their services over the Internet. Here are a few tips to help you get your money's worth. Reputable bankruptcy petition preparers often have been in business for quite a while. Most good businesses will be more than happy to provide a list of satisfied customers you can contact for references. If the bankruptcy petition preparer tries to give you legal advice (which, by law, they can't do), use another service. Always sign a written contract. Finally, be sure that the advertised or quoted price includes everything you think it does.

1. Guidelines for Completing Forms

Here are some general tips which will make filling in your forms easier and the whole bankruptcy process smoother.

Photocopy the blank forms. The forms in this kit are slightly under regulation size. You must photocopy at least two sets of the forms on 8½-by-11-inch paper. Photocopies must be one-sided. Or, print the forms off of the Federal Judiciary's website at http://www.uscourts.gov/bankform.

Prepare drafts. You'll need to type or neatly hand write your final forms, so you're wise to start with drafts and make corrections along the way.

Use continuation pages if you run out of room. A few forms come with pre-formatted continuation pages. If you need more room and there is no continuation form, put "see continuation page" next to the question. Then prepare a continuation page using a piece of regular white 8½-by-11-inch paper. Label continuation pages with your name, and the form name, and indicate "Continuation Page 1," "Continuation Page 2" and so on. Enter the additional information on the continuation page.

Respond to every question. Most forms have a box to check if your answer is "none." If a question doesn't have a "none" box and the question doesn't apply to you, fill in "N/A" for "not applicable."

Be thorough and honest. It's fine to give too much information or even to put it in the wrong place. But if you leave creditors off the forms, the debts you owe these creditors might not be discharged. And if you don't list all your property, or inaccurately describe your recent property transactions, the court may deny your bankruptcy discharge or take some property that you might otherwise have kept.

Know whether or not you live in a community property state. On many of the forms, married couples will need to indicate whether or not they live in a community property state.

Community Property States

Arizona	Louisiana	Texas
California	Nevada	Washington
Idaho	New Mexico	Wisconsin

All other states are common law property states.

2. Form 1—Voluntary Petition

Court Name. At the top of the first page, fill in the first two blanks with the name of the judicial district you're filing in, such as the "Central District of California" or "Northern District of Ohio, Eastern Division."

Name of Debtor. Enter your full name (last name first), in capital letters, as used on your checks, driver's license and other formal documents. If you and your spouse are filing jointly, designate one of you as the debtor and the other as the spouse.

Name of Joint Debtor (Spouse). If you are married and filing jointly with your spouse, put your spouse's name (last name first) in the joint debtor box. Use the name that appears on formal documents. If you are unsure of your marital status or whether you should file jointly with your spouse, see a lawyer. If you are filing alone, type "N/A" anywhere in the box.

All Other Names. If you have been known by any other name in the last six years, list it here. If you operated a business as a sole proprietor any time during the previous six years, include your trade name (fictitious or assumed business name). But you don't need to include minor variations in spelling or form. If you're uncertain, list all names you may have used with creditors so that they'll know who you are when they receive notice of your bankruptcy filing. Do the same for your spouse if you are filing jointly.

Soc. Sec./Tax I.D. No. Enter your Social Security number. If you have a taxpayer's I.D. number, enter it as well. Do the same for your spouse if you are filing jointly.

Street Address of Debtor. Enter your current street address, even if you get your mail at a post office box. Do the same for your spouse if you are filing jointly—even if it's the same address.

County of Residence. Enter the county in which you live. Do the same for your spouse if you are filing jointly.

Mailing Address of Debtor. Enter your mailing address if it is different from your street address. If it isn't, put "N/A." Do the same for your spouse if you are filing jointly—again, even if it's the same address.

Location of Principal Assets of Business Debtor. If you—or your spouse if you are filing jointly—have been self-employed or operated a business as a sole proprietor within the last two years, you'll be considered a "business debtor." If your business owns any assets—such as tools, machines, computers, bank accounts and the like—list their primary location. If they are all located at your street or

(Official Form 1) (9/97)

FORM 1. VOLUNTARY PETITION

UNITED STATES BANKRUPTCY COURT __Northern__ DISTRICT OF __Ohio, Eastern Division__	**Voluntary Petition**

Name of Debtor (if individual, enter Last, First, Middle):	Name of Joint Debtor (Spouse) (Last, First, Middle):
MAYTAG, MOLLY MARIA	MAYTAG, JONATHAN

All Other Names used by the Debtor in the last 6 years (include married, maiden, and trade names):	All Other Names used by the Joint Debtor in the last 6 years (include married, maiden, and trade names):
Johnson, Molly Maria	dba Maytag Delicatessen

Soc. Sec./Tax I.D. No. (if more than one, state all):	Soc. Sec./Tax I.D. No. (if more than one, state all):
999-99-9999	000-00-0000

Street Address of Debtor (No. & Street, City, State & Zip Code):	Street Address of Joint Debtor (No. & Street, City, State & Zip Code):
21 Scarborough Road South Cleveland Heights, OH 41118	21 Scarborough Road South Cleveland Heights, OH 41118

County of Residence or of the Principal Place of Business: Cuyahoga	County of Residence or of the Principal Place of Business: Cuyahoga

Mailing Address of Debtor (if different from street address):	Mailing Address of Joint Debtor (if different from street address):
N/A	N/A

Location of Principal Assets of Business Debtor
(if different from street address above):

N/A

Information Regarding the Debtor (Check the Applicable Boxes)

Venue (Check any applicable box)

☒ Debtor has been domiciled or has had a residence, principal place of business, or principal assets in this District for 180 days immediately preceding the date of this petition or for a longer part of such 180 days than in any other District.

☐ There is a bankruptcy case concerning debtor's affiliate, general partner, or partnership pending in this District.

Type of Debtor (Check all boxes that apply)		**Chapter or Section of Bankruptcy Code Under Which the Petition is Filed** (Check one box)	
☒ Individual(s) ☐ Railroad		☒ Chapter 7 ☐ Chapter 11 ☐ Chapter 13	
☐ Corporation ☐ Stockbroker		☐ Chapter 9 ☐ Chapter 12	
☐ Partnership ☐ Commodity Broker		☐ Sec. 304 – Case ancillary to foreign proceeding	
☐ Other _____			

Nature of Debts (Check one box)	**Filing Fee** (Check one box)
☒ Consumer/Non-Business ☐ Business	☒ Full Filing Fee attached
	☐ Filing Fee to be paid in installments. (Applicable to individuals only.) Must attach signed application for the court's consideration certifying that the debtor is unable to pay fee except in installments. Rule 1006(b). See Official Form No. 3.

Chapter 11 Small Business (Check all boxes that apply)

☐ Debtor is a small business as defined in 11 U.S.C. § 101   N/A
☐ Debtor is and elects to be considered a small business under 11 U.S.C. §1121(e) (Optional)

Statistical/Administrative Information (Estimates only)	THIS SPACE FOR COURT USE ONLY
☒ Debtor estimates that funds will be available for distribution to unsecured creditors.	
☐ Debtor estimates that, after any exempt property is excluded and administrative expenses paid, there will be no funds available for distribution to unsecured creditors.	

Estimated Number of Creditors	1-15	16-49	50-99	100-199	200-999	1000-over
	☐	☒	☐	☐	☐	☐

Estimated Assets								
$0 to $50,000	$50,001 to $100,000	$100,001 to $500,000	$500,001 to $1 million	$1,000,001 to $10 million	$10,000,001 to $50 million	$50,000,001 to $100 million	More than $100 million	
☐	☐	☒	☐	☐	☐	☐	☐	

Estimated Debts								
$0 to $50,000	$50,001 to $100,000	$100,001 to $500,000	$500,001 to $1 million	$1,000,001 to $10 million	$10,000,001 to $50 million	$50,000,001 to $100 million	More than $100 million	
☐	☐	☒	☐	☐	☐	☐	☐	

mailing address listed above, enter "N/A." You can use this kit if you own your own business; you'll just have to answer a few additional questions about your business.

Venue. Check the top box, which states why you're filing in this particular bankruptcy court.

Type of Debtor. Check the first box—"Individual(s)"—even if you have been self-employed or operated a sole proprietorship during the previous two years. (If you are filing as a corporation, partnership or other type of business entity, you shouldn't be using this kit.)

Nature of Debts. Check "Non-Business/Consumer" if you aren't in business and haven't been for the previous two years. If you're self-employed or in business as a sole proprietor, and most of your debts are owed personally—not by your business—check "Non-Business/Consumer." If the bulk of your indebtedness is owed by your business or you're not sure, check "Business."

Chapter 11 Small Business. Type "N/A" anywhere in the box.

Chapter or Section of Bankruptcy Code Under Which the Petition is Filed. Check "Chapter 7."

Filing Fee. If you will attach the entire fee (currently $200), check the first box. If you plan to ask the court for permission to pay in installments, check the second box.

Statistical/Administrative Information. Here you estimate information about your creditors, debts and assets. If you plan to make an emergency filing, do your best to arrive at correct estimates. Otherwise, wait until you've completed the other forms before providing this information. But remember to come back and check the appropriate boxes before filing. You may want to put a checkmark on the sheet next to the blank boxes as a reminder.

Voluntary Petition—Second Page
Name of Debtors. Enter your name and your spouse's name if you are filing jointly.

Prior Bankruptcy Case Filed Within Last Six Years. If you—or your spouse if you're filing jointly—haven't filed a bankruptcy case within the previous six years, type "N/A" in the boxes. Otherwise, see a bankruptcy lawyer before filing.

Pending Bankruptcy Case Filed. If your spouse has a bankruptcy case pending anywhere in the country, enter the requested information. Otherwise, type "N/A" in the boxes; the rest of this item deals with partnerships and corporations.

Signature(s) of Debtor(s) (Individual/Joint). You—and your spouse if you are filing jointly—must sign and date where indicated. If you are filing singly, type "N/A" on the joint debtor signature line. Include your telephone number and the date.

Signature(s) of Debtor(s) (Corporation/Partnership). Type "N/A" on the first line.

Signature of Attorney. Type "N/A" on the first line.

Exhibit "B." Type "N/A" on the signature line.

Signature of Non-Attorney Petition Preparer. If you hire a bankruptcy petition preparer to complete your forms, that person must fill in the information here and sign this form. Otherwise, type "N/A" on the first line.

(Official Form 1) (9/97)

Voluntary Petition *(This page must be completed and filed in every case.)*	Name of Debtor(s): Maytag, Molly & Jonathan	**Form 1, Page 2**

Prior Bankruptcy Case Filed Within Last 6 Years (If more than one, attach additional sheet)

Location Where Filed: N/A	Case Number:	Date Filed:

Pending Bankruptcy Case Filed by any Spouse, Partner or Affiliate of this Debtor (If more than one, attach additional sheet)

Name of Debtor: N/A	Case Number:	Date Filed:
District:	Relationship:	Judge:

Signatures

Signature(s) of Debtor(s) (Individual/Joint)

I declare under penalty of perjury that the information provided in this petition is true and correct.

[If petitioner is an individual whose debts are primarily consumer debts and has chosen to file under chapter 7] I am aware that I may proceed under chapter 7, 11, 12 or 13 of title 11, United States Code, understand the relief available under each such chapter, and choose to proceed under chapter 7.

I request relief in accordance with the chapter of title 11, United States Code, specified in this petition.

X *Molly Maytag*
   Signature of Debtor

X *Jonathan Maytag*
   Signature of Joint Debtor

   (216) 555-7373
   Telephone Number (If not represented by attorney)

   July 13, 20XX
   Date

Signature of Debtor (Corporation/Partnership)

I declare under penalty of perjury that the information provided in this petition is true and correct and that I have been authorized to file this petition on behalf of the debtor.

The debtor requests relief in accordance with the chapter of title 11, United States Code, specified in this petition.

X N/A
   Signature of Authorized Individual

   Printed Name of Authorized Individual

   Title of Authorized Individual

   Date

Signature of Attorney

X N/A
   Signature of Attorney for Debtor(s)

   Printed Name of Attorney for Debtor(s)

   Firm Name

   Address

   Telephone Number

   Date

Signature of Non-Attorney Petition Preparer

I certify that I am a bankruptcy petition preparer as defined in 11 U.S.C. § 110, that I prepared this document for compensation, and that I have provided the debtor with a copy of this document.

   N/A
   Printed Name of Bankruptcy Petition Preparer

   Social Security Number

   Address

Names and Social Security numbers of all other individuals who prepared or assisted in preparing this document:

If more than one person prepared this document, attach additional sheets conforming to the appropriate official form for each person.

Exhibit A

(To be completed if debtor is required to file periodic reports (e.g., forms 10K and 10Q) with the Securities and Exchange Commission pursuant to Section 13 or 15(d) of the Securities Exchange Act of 1934 and is requesting relief under chapter 11.)

☐ Exhibit A is attached and made a part of this petition.

Exhibit B

(To be completed if debtor is an individual whose debts are primarily consumer debts.)

I, the attorney for the petitioner named in the foregoing petition, declare that I have informed the petitioner that [he or she] may proceed under chapter 7, 11, 12, or 13 of title 11, United States Code, and have explained the relief available under each such chapter.

X N/A
   Signature of Attorney for Debtor(s)   Date

X
   Signature of Bankruptcy Petition Preparer

   Date

A bankruptcy petition preparer's failure to comply with the provisions of title 11 and the Federal Rules of Bankruptcy Procedure may result in fines or imprisonment or both. 11 U.S.C. § 110; 18 U.S.C. § 156.

Other Bankruptcy Options

When you sign the Petition, you are declaring that you're aware of the other bankruptcy sections, but you have chosen Chapter 7 bankruptcy.

Chapter 13 Bankruptcy lets you pay off your debts over a three- to five-year period without giving up any property. Unlike Chapter 7, which is available every six years, Chapter 13 bankruptcy is available any time.

Chapter 13 is most beneficial when you're threatened with a foreclosure on a mortgage or you have a large tax debt that cannot be wiped out in Chapter 7. By filing for Chapter 13, you can make up the mortgage arrears or force the IRS into a repayment plan.

To qualify for Chapter 13, you must have steady income in an amount sufficient to pay your unsecured creditors the value of your nonexempt property. "Income" includes wages as well as receipts from independent contractors, Social Security benefits, pension payments, alimony, and other sources of income. To qualify for Chapter 13, your unsecured debts can't exceed $290,525 and your secured debts can't be more than $871,550.

Chapter 12 Bankruptcy is specially designed for family farmers and provides a way to keep the farm while paying off debts over time. It's similar to Chapter 13. As of June 30, 2000, this option has been unavailable. Legislation in 2001 is likely to reauthorize the program and allow farmers who have filed another type of bankruptcy to convert to a Chapter 12. In the meantime, most family farmers can file a Chapter 11 or Chapter 13 instead.

Chapter 11 Bankruptcy allows debtors with debts in excess of Chapter 13's limits to reorganize their financial affairs and keep operating. Chapter 11 bankruptcy is generally very complex, used by corporations and partnerships, and is rarely beneficial to individuals or sole proprietors. A streamlined Chapter 11 bankruptcy allows small businesses with debts under $2 million to reorganize.

3. Form 6—Schedules

Form 6 refers to a series of schedules that provide the trustee and court with a picture of your current financial situation. Many of our instructions cover one column at a time. You'll probably find it easier, however, to list one item and complete all columns for that item before moving on to the next item.

To complete the schedules correctly, you'll need to know the specifics of your financial life.

Step 1: Locate Your Financial Records

Gather together all of your bills, bank and brokerage statements, canceled checks, pay stubs, tax returns, public benefit statements, insurance policies, trust documents, retirement plan statements, title documents, court papers and any other financial documents you have.

Step 2: Understand What Will Be in Your Bankruptcy Estate

Your entire bankruptcy estate will be available to pay your creditors, with the exception of your exempt property. For that reason, it's essential that you understand what your bankruptcy estate will include:

- **property you own and possess.** Examples include your clothing, books, TV, stereo system, furniture, tools, car, real estate and stock certificates.
- **property you own but don't have in your possession.** For instance, you may own a share of a vacation cabin or car that someone else uses. Another example is a security deposit held by a landlord or utility company.
- **property you've recently given or had taken away.** Property given away or paid out within 90 days before you file for bankruptcy (or within one year if payment was to a relative, friend or business associate) is still part of your bankruptcy estate, and the trustee has legal authority to get it back.
- **property you're entitled to receive but don't yet possess.** Common examples are wages you have earned but have not yet been paid, a tax refund that is legally due you but which you haven't yet received and a lawsuit you've filed that hasn't been settled.
- **proceeds from property of the bankruptcy estate.** If property of your bankruptcy estate earns income or otherwise produces money after you file for bank-

ruptcy, this money is also part of your bankruptcy estate. The one exception to this rule is money you earn from providing personal services after filing for bankruptcy.

- **certain property acquired within 180 days after you file for bankruptcy.** If you receive, or become entitled to receive, an inheritance, property from a marital settlement agreement or divorce decree, death benefits or life insurance policy proceeds within 180 days of when you file your bankruptcy papers, the property becomes part of your bankruptcy estate.

Retirement Plans Note: Many retirement plans are not part of your bankruptcy estate (see **Special Rules for Retirement Plans** in Section c, below). Even so, you should list them on Schedule B and write, "This retirement plan is not part of the bankruptcy estate."

Step 3: Don't Leave Anything Out

Remember to include everything that you could possibly list on these schedules. By listing debts you dispute that you owe, you're not admitting that you owe them. You are, however, ensuring that all dischargeable debts will be discharged. If you and your spouse are filing jointly, supply information for both of you.

⚠ Unlisted debts probably won't be discharged. Inadvertent errors or omissions on your schedules can come back to haunt you. A debt you owe to a creditor you forget to list probably won't be discharged in bankruptcy if the creditor doesn't otherwise learn of your bankruptcy filing. It's equally as important to list the creditor's full address, including zip code, and the account number on your papers. Otherwise, the creditor may never learn of your filing, and your debts won't be discharged.

a.　Schedule A—Real Property

Here you list all the real property—land and things permanently attached to land—you own as of the date you file the petition. Real property includes houses, unimproved land, vacation cabins, condominiums, duplexes, rental property, business property, mobile home park spaces, agricultural land, airplane hangars and any other buildings permanently attached to land.

Lease Note: If you hold a lease in real property, don't list it on Schedule A.

⚠ You risk losing your house. If you own your house, see a lawyer, *How to File for Bankruptcy*, by Elias, Renauer, Leonard and Michon or *Chapter 13 Bankruptcy: Repay Your Debts*, by Robin Leonard before you file a Chapter 7 bankruptcy.

In re. Type your name and the name of your spouse if you're filing jointly.

Case No. If you made an emergency filing, fill in the case number assigned by the court. Otherwise, leave this blank.

 If you own no real property. Type "N/A" anywhere in the first column and proceed to Schedule B.

Description and Location of Property. For each piece of property, list its type (for example, house, farm or unimproved lot) and street address or location.

Nature of Debtor's Interest in Property. Specify the nature of your interest in the real estate. Your ownership is called "fee simple" if you own the property outright, even if you owe a bank or other lender, as long as you have the right to sell the house, leave it to your heirs and make alterations. If your ownership is not fee simple, but you have no idea what it is, put "Don't know."

Husband, Wife, Joint or Community. If you're not married, put "N/A." If you are married, indicate whether the real estate is owned by husband (H), by wife (W), jointly by husband and wife in a common law property state (J), or jointly by husband and wife in a community property state (C). (Community property states are listed in Section E.1, above.)

Current Market Value of Debtor's Interest in Property... Enter the current fair market value of your real estate ownership interest. Don't deduct any mortgages, liens or exemptions.

If you own property with someone else who is not filing for bankruptcy, put only your ownership share in this column. For example, if you and your brother own a home as joint tenants (each owns 50%), split the current market value in half.

See **Evaluating Market Value of Real Estate,** for information on how to arrive at realistic market values.

If your interest is intangible—for example, you are a beneficiary of real estate held in trust that won't be distributed for many years—provide an estimate or state "Don't know," explaining why you can't be more precise.

FORM B6A (6/90)

In re ___Maytag, Molly and Jonathan_____ ,   Case No._____
                   Debtor   (If known)

SCHEDULE A—REAL PROPERTY

Except as directed below, list all real property in which the debtor has any legal, equitable, or future interest, including all property owned as a co-tenant, community property, or in which the debtor has a life estate. Include any property in which the debtor holds rights and powers exercisable for the debtor's own benefit. If the debtor is married, state whether husband, wife, or both own the property by placing an "H," "W," "J," or "C" in the column labeled "Husband, Wife, Joint, or Community." If the debtor holds no interest in real property, write "None" under "Description and Location of Property."

Do not include interests in executory contracts and unexpired leases on this schedule. List them in Schedule G—Executory Contracts and Unexpired Leases.

If an entity claims to have a lien or hold a secured interest in any property, state the amount of the secured claim. See Schedule D. If no entity claims to hold a secured interest in the property, write "None" in the column labeled "Amount of Secured Claim."

If the debtor is an individual or if a joint petition is filed, state the amount of any exception claimed in the property only in Schedule C—Property Claimed as Exempt.

DESCRIPTION AND LOCATION OF PROPERTY	NATURE OF DEBTOR'S INTEREST IN PROPERTY	HUSBAND, WIFE, JOINT, OR COMMUNITY	CURRENT MARKET VALUE OF DEBTOR'S INTEREST IN PROPERTY WITHOUT DEDUCTING ANY SECURED CLAIM OR EXEMPTION	AMOUNT OF SECURED CLAIM
House at 21 Scarborough Road South Cleveland Heights OH 44118	Fee Simple	J	$95,000	$75,000 mortgage
				$12,000
			second	mortgage
				$2,000 judgment lien
Unimproved lot at 244 Highway 50 Parma, OH 44000	Fee Simple	H	$5,000	none
		Total ➡ $	$100,000	

(Report also on Summary of Schedules.)

Evaluating Market Value of Real Estate

As a general rule, the lower the fair market value of your property, the better off you'll be in bankruptcy. If your property isn't worth much, you'll have a better chance of keeping it. It's okay to be wrong as long as your estimate is an honest one and reasonably close to real market conditions. To get an estimate of your real estate's market value, contact a local real estate agent or appraiser. If your real estate is unusual—for example, it is used for growing crops—enter the amount that it would bring in a forced sale. You can look through newspaper ads or real estate listings to find prices of comparable property.

Total. Add the amounts in the fourth column and enter the total in the box at the bottom of the page.

Amount of Secured Claim. Enter separately the amount of each outstanding mortgage, deed of trust, home equity loan or lien claimed against the property. If there is no secured claim of any type on the item of real estate, enter "None."

If you don't know the balance on a mortgage or other loan, call the lender. To find out the values of liens, visit the county recorder of deeds or order a title search through a real estate attorney or title insurance company. If you own several pieces of real estate and there is one lien on file against all of them, list the full amount of the lien for each separate property item. Don't worry if the total value of secured claims on a property item is higher than the value of the property; it's quite common. If you can't find out any of this information, enter "unknown."

b. Schedule B—Personal Property

Here you must list and evaluate all of your personal property—everything you own other than real property. It doesn't matter if the property isn't worth much, is security for a debt or is exempt.

In re and **Case No.** Follow the instructions for Schedule A.

Type of Property. The form already lists general categories of personal property. Leave this as is.

None. If you don't own property that fits in a category listed in the first column, enter an "X."

Description and Location of Property. List specific items that fall in each general category. Separately list all items worth $50 or more. Combine small items such as spatulas and pots and pans into broad categories, such as kitchen cookware, whenever reasonable. While some specificity is called for, separating your forks from your spoons is not.

When listing cash or deposit accounts, explain the source of the funds—for instance wages, Social Security payments or child support. This may help you later in determining if any of your money qualifies as exempt property.

If most of your personal property is at your residence, write a sentence at the top of the form to that effect and indicate specifically when the facts are different. If someone else holds property for you, for example, you loaned your aunt your color TV, put that person's name and address in this column.

Remember to include money owed to you and not yet paid. For example, if you've obtained a judgment against someone but haven't been paid, list the defendant's name, the date of judgment, the court that issued the judgment, the judgment amount and the kind of case, such as car accident.

A few items ask for you to "give particulars." Simply provide enough information to identify the property and its value.

Husband, Wife, Joint or Community. If you're not married, put "N/A" at the top of the column.

If you are married and own all or most of your personal property jointly with your spouse, note whichever one of the following statements applies on the top or bottom of the form:

- **Common law property state.** Enter the words, "All property is jointly owned unless otherwise indicated." Then note when a particular item is owned by only H or W.

- **Community property state.** Enter the words, "All property is owned jointly in a community property state unless otherwise indicated." Then note when a particular item is owned by only H or W. (Community property states are listed in Section E.1, above.)

If, however, you are married and many items are owned separately, for each item specify: husband (H), wife (W), jointly by husband and wife in a common law property state (J), or jointly by husband and wife in a community property state (C).

Current Market Value of Debtor's Interest in Property. Put the current market value of the property, regardless of what you owe on it.

See **Evaluating Market Value of Personal Property** below, for information on how to arrive at realistic market values.

If you don't know how to arrive at a value, fill in "don't know." If you've prepared continuation pages in addition to the preprinted forms, remember to evaluate the property listed on those pages.

Total. Add the amounts in this column and put the total in the box at the bottom of the last page. If you used any continuation pages in addition to the preprinted ones, remember to attach those pages and include the amounts from those pages in this total.

Evaluating Market Value of Personal Property

As long as your estimates are honest and reasonable, the lower the value you place on property, the more of it you will probably be allowed to keep. Enter actual values for cash on hand, financial deposits, security deposits, interest in insurance, annuities, pensions, stock and interest in corporations, partnerships, bonds, accounts receivable, support to which you are entitled, tax refunds, non-contingent claims and other liquid debts owed you.

Here are some suggestions for valuing specific items:

Cars. Start with the low *Kelly Blue Book* price. You can find a copy of the book at the public library or visit http://www.kbb.com on the Internet and select "Used Cars" to get the value. If the car needs substantial repair, reduce the value by the amount it would cost you to fix the car.

Older goods. Want ads in a local flea market or penny-saver newspaper are a good place to look for prices. If an item isn't listed, use the garage sale value—that is, begin with the price you paid and then deduct about 20% for each year you've owned the item. For example, if you bought a camera for $400 three years ago, subtract $80 for the first year (down to $320), $64 for the second year (down to $256) and $51 for the third year (down to $205).

Life insurance. Put the current cash surrender value here (ask your agent). Term life insurance has a cash surrender value of zero. Don't put the amount of benefits the policy will pay unless you're the beneficiary of an insurance policy and the insured person has died.

Stocks, bonds, securities. Call your broker or check the current price in a newspaper business section.

Jewelry, antiques or other collectibles. For valuable items, call an appraiser.

FORM B6B (10/89)

In re ___Maytag, Molly and Jonathan_____ ,   Case No._____
                          Debtor   (If known)

SCHEDULE B—PERSONAL PROPERTY

Except as directed below, list all personal property of the debtor of whatever kind. If the debtor has no property in one or more of the categories, place an "X" in the appropriate position in the column labeled "None." If additional space is needed in any category, attach a separate sheet properly identified with the case name, case number, and the number of the category. If the debtor is married, state whether husband, wife, or both own the property by placing an "H," "W," "J," or "C" in the column labeled "Husband, Wife, Joint, or Community." If the debtor is an individual or a joint petition is filed, state the amount of any exemptions claimed only in Schedule C—Property Claimed as Exempt.

Do not include interests in executory contracts and unexpired leases on this schedule. List them in Schedule G—Executory Contracts and Unexpired Leases.

If the property is being held for the debtor by someone else, state that person's name and address under "Description and Location of Property."

TYPE OF PROPERTY	NONE	* All property is located at our residence unless otherwise noted. DESCRIPTION AND LOCATION OF PROPERTY	HUSBAND, WIFE, JOINT, OR COMMUNITY	CURRENT MARKET VALUE OF DEBTOR'S INTEREST IN PROPERTY, WITHOUT DEDUCTING ANY SECURED CLAIM OR EXEMPTION
1. Cash on hand.		Cash from wages	J	100
2. Checking, savings or other financial accounts, certificates of deposit, or shares in banks, savings and loan, thrift, building and loan, and homestead associations, or credit unions, brokerage houses, or cooperatives.		Checking account #12345, Ameritrust, 10 Financial Way, Cleveland Hts, OH 44118 (from wages)	J	250
		Savings account #98765, Shaker Savings, 44 Trust Street, Cleveland Hts, OH 44118 (from wages)	J	400
		Checking account #058-118061, Ohio Savings, 1818 Lakeshore Dr., Cleveland, OH 44123	H	100
3. Security deposits with public utilities, telephone companies, landlords, and others.	X			
4. Household goods and furnishings, including audio, video, and computer equipment.		Stereo system	J	300
		Washer/Dryer set	J	150
		Refrigerator	J	250
		Stove	J	150
		Household furniture	J	600
		Minor appliances	J	75
		Antique desk	J	250
		Vacuum	J	30
		Bed & bedding	J	500
		Television	J	135
		VCR	J	75
		Lawnmower	J	100
		Swingset, children's toys	J	180
		Snowblower	J	100
		Oriental rug	J	2,500

FORM B6B (10/89) continued

In re ___Maytag, Molly and Jonathan_____,   Case No._____
                    Debtor   (If known)

SCHEDULE B—PERSONAL PROPERTY
(Continuation Sheet)

TYPE OF PROPERTY	NONE	DESCRIPTION AND LOCATION OF PROPERTY	HUSBAND, WIFE, JOINT, OR COMMUNITY	CURRENT MARKET VALUE OF DEBTOR'S INTEREST IN PROPERTY, WITHOUT DEDUCTING ANY SECURED CLAIM OR EXEMPTION
5. Books, pictures and other art objects, antiques, stamp, coin, record, tape, compact disc, and other collections or collectibles.		Books	J	50
		Stamp collection	J	75
6. Wearing apparel.		Clothing	J	625
7. Furs and jewelry.		Wedding rings	J	225
		Diamond necklace	W	325
		Watches	J	50
8. Firearms and sports, photographic, and other hobby equipment.		Mountain bike	J	165
		Camera	J	125
		Sword collection	W	1,485
9. Interests in insurance policies. Name insurance company of each policy and itemize surrender or refund value of each.		Life insurance policy, Lively Ins. Co., 120 Manhattan St.,NY, NY 10012, Policy #14-171136	H	120
		Life insurance policy, Live-a-long-time Co., 52 Mitchell Ave., Hartford, CT 06434. Policy #33-19195WY17	W	65
10. Annuities. Itemize and name each issuer.	X			
11. Interests in IRA, ERISA, Keogh, or other pension or profit sharing plans. Itemize.		Cleveland Builder's Pension, 100 Chester Way, Cleveland, OH 44114	H	6,612
		IRA, Basic Bank, 9712 Smitco Creek Blvd., , Columbus, OH 45923	J	3,400
12. Stock and interests in incorporated and unincorporated businesses. Itemize.		Trusso Corp. stock, #3711. 50 shares @ $20 each	J	1,000
		Investco Ltd. stock, #1244711, 5 shares @ $100 each	J	500
		Rayco Co. stock, #RC53, 20 shares @ $40 each	J	800
		All certificates at Ameritrust, 10 Financial Way, Cleveland Hts, OH 44118		
13. Interests in partnerships or joint ventures. Itemize.	X			

FORM B6B (10/89) continued

In re ___Maytag, Molly and Jonathan___ ,   Case No._____
                          Debtor   (If known)

SCHEDULE B—PERSONAL PROPERTY
(Continuation Sheet)

TYPE OF PROPERTY	NONE	DESCRIPTION AND LOCATION OF PROPERTY	HUSBAND, WIFE, JOINT, OR COMMUNITY	CURRENT MARKET VALUE OF DEBTOR'S INTEREST IN PROPERTY, WITHOUT DEDUCTING ANY SECURED CLAIM OR EXEMPTION
14. Government and corporate bonds and other negotiable and non-negotiable instruments.		US Savings Bonds, located at Ameritrust, 10 Financial Way, Cleveland Hts, OH 44118	J	1,000
		Promissory note from Jonathan Maytag's sister, Trini Maytag Ellison, dated 11/3/XX	J	500
15. Accounts receivable.	X			
16. Alimony, maintenance, support, and property settlements to which the debtor is or may be entitled. Give particulars.	X			
17. Other liquidated debts owing debtor including tax refunds. Give particulars.		Wages for 6/XX from Cleveland Builder Wages for 6/1/XX to 6/30/XX from Typing Circles	H W	1,900 100
18. Equitable or future interest, life estates, and rights or powers exercisable for the benefit of the debtor other than those listed in Schedule of Real Property.	X			
19. Contingent and noncontingent interests in estate of a decedent, death benefit plan, life insurance policy, or trust.	X			
20. Other contingent and unliquidated claims of every nature, including tax refunds, counter claims of the debtor, and rights to setoff claims. Give estimated value of each.	X			
21. Patents, copyrights, and other intellectual property. Give particulars.	X			
22. Licenses, franchises, and other general intangibles. Give particulars.	X			

FORM B6B (10/89) continued

In re ___Maytag, Molly and Jonathan___ ,   Case No._____
           Debtor   (If known)

SCHEDULE B—PERSONAL PROPERTY
(Continuation Sheet)

TYPE OF PROPERTY	NONE	DESCRIPTION AND LOCATION OF PROPERTY	HUSBAND, WIFE, JOINT, OR COMMUNITY	CURRENT MARKET VALUE OF DEBTOR'S INTEREST IN PROPERTY, WITHOUT DEDUCTING ANY SECURED CLAIM OR EXEMPTION
23. Automobiles, trucks, trailers, and other vehicles and accessories.		1988 Honda Motorcycle	W	1,000
24. Boats, motors, and accessories.		Sailboard, docked at Lake Erie Dock, Cleveland, OH	J	1,250
25. Aircraft and accessories.	X			
26. Office equipment, furnishings, and supplies.		Computer (for business)	J	1,100
		Typewriter (for business)	J	125
		Fax Machine (for business)	J	500
27. Machinery, fixtures, equipment, and supplies used in business.		Carpentry tools	J	150
28. Inventory.	X			
29. Animals.		Poodles (2)	J	200
30. Crops—growing or harvested. Give particulars.	X			
31. Farming equipment and implements.	X			
32. Farm supplies, chemicals, and feed.	X			
33. Other personal property of any kind not already listed, such as season tickets. Itemize.	X			
			Total ➡ $	29,692

___0___ continuation sheets attached

(Include amounts from any continuation sheets attached. Report total also on Summary of Schedules.)

c. Schedule C—Property Claimed As Exempt

Some of your property is exempt—protected by law from being taken to pay your creditors. You may keep all of your exempt property through the bankruptcy process. If you own any property that is not exempt, however, the bankruptcy trustee may take it—or its value in cash—to pay your unsecured creditors.

Carefully follow the steps set out below to determine which of your property is exempt.

Step 1: Determine If You Must Choose an Exemption System

Each state has laws that determine which items of property are exempt in bankruptcy. The states in the accompanying chart allow their residents to choose between two sets of exemptions.

If you don't have a choice. If your state isn't listed in **States Where You Must Choose Your Bankruptcy Exemption System** below, only your state's exemption system is available to you; skip to Step 3.

Step 2: Choose the Better Set of Exemptions

If you must choose between two exemption systems, locate these exemption lists from the Appendix:

- the federal bankruptcy exemptions list (see the end of the Appendix), and
- your state's exemptions list plus the federal *non-bankruptcy* exemptions list (the federal *non-bankruptcy* exemptions list is at the end of the Appendix).

If you are filing in California, look at the System 1 exemptions list, the System 2 exemptions list and the federal *non-bankruptcy* exemptions list.

Your goal is to exempt all—or most—of your property. Compare each exemption set with the property you listed on Schedules A and B. You'll want to choose the set of exemptions that will produce the better result in your situation. Bear in mind that you can't select some exemptions from one system and some from the other. Follow the **Guidelines for Claiming Exemptions** on the next page.

You can't mix and match. If a married couple jointly files for bankruptcy, both must select the same system. In other words, one spouse cannot choose the federal bankruptcy exemptions while the other chooses the state exemptions.

States Where You Must Choose Your Bankruptcy Exemption System

	You may choose either: • the federal bankruptcy exemptions or • your state's bankruptcy exemptions	You may choose either: • your state's System 1 exemptions or • your state's System 2 exemptions
Arkansas	X	
California		X
Connecticut	X	
District of Columbia	X	
Hawaii	X	
Massachusetts	X	
Michigan	X	
Minnesota	X	
New Hampshire	X	
New Jersey	X	
New Mexico	X	
Pennsylvania	X	
Rhode Island	X	
Texas	X	
Vermont	X	
Washington	X	
Wisconsin	X	

Guidelines for Claiming Exemptions

These tips should help you exempt as much property as possible:

- **Give yourself the benefit of the doubt.** If it appears that a particular exemption covers all or part of a property item, claim it. The bankruptcy trustee must favor your selection in close cases.
- **Use your equity amount to determine exemptions.** Exemptions with monetary limits are based on your equity in property—that is, the value you personally own in the property. To figure your equity, start with the property's fair market value. Then subtract any debts or liens against the property, such as mortgages, auto loans, tax liens, judgment liens and the like. The balance is your equity. From your equity, deduct your exemption and the approximate cost of sale. If the balance is greater than zero, you may lose the item.
- **Apply the wild card exemption, if available.** A wild card exemption is a general-purpose exemption that is available in many exemption systems. It consists of a set dollar amount that can be applied to any type of property or split among several items. You can use a wild card exemption to exempt property whose value exceeds the exemption limit, or to exempt items that ordinarily aren't exempt.
- **Use federal non-bankruptcy exemptions, if available.** If you use your state exemptions—this includes all Californians—you may also select from a list of federal *non-bankruptcy* exemptions, mostly military and other federal benefits, as well as 75% of earned but unpaid wages. You cannot, however, stack your exemptions if the federal *non-bankruptcy* exemptions duplicate your state's exemptions. For example, if you're using your state's exemptions and your state exempts 75% of unpaid wages, that's all you can claim.
- **Double your exemptions if you're married and doubling isn't prohibited.** Bankruptcy rules allow married couples to double all exemptions unless your state expressly prohibits it. If you're using the federal bankruptcy exemptions, you may double all exemptions. If your state's chart doesn't say doubling is prohibited, go ahead and double.

Step 3: Fill In Schedule C

This may be your most important form. It's where you claim all property you think is legally exempt from being taken to pay your creditors. In the overwhelming majority of Chapter 7 bankruptcies filed by individuals, all—or virtually all—of the debtor's property is exempt.

Your exemption claims will be examined by the trustee and possibly a creditor or two, although few creditors monitor Chapter 7 consumer bankruptcy proceedings. In close cases, bankruptcy laws require the trustee to honor your exemption claims.

To complete this form, have in front of you:

- your draft of Schedule A
- your draft of Schedule B
- the list of state or federal bankruptcy exemptions you'll be using, provided in the Appendix
- if you're using your state's exemptions, the additional *non-bankruptcy* federal exemptions, provided in the Appendix.

In re and **Case No.** Follow the instructions for Schedule A.

Debtor elects the exemptions… If you're using the federal bankruptcy exemptions, check the top box. If you're using your state exemptions along with the federal *non-bankruptcy*, exemptions (this includes all California debtors), check the lower box.

 Here's a shortcut. If you are married and doubling your exemptions, put a note to this effect on the form.

The following instructions cover one column at a time. But rather than listing all your exempt property in the first column and then completing the second column before moving on to the third column, list one exempt item and complete all columns for that item before moving on to the next exempt item.

Description of Property. Use the same descriptions that you used in Column 1 of Schedule A and Column 3 of Schedule B.

If an exemption is limited to a certain amount, you may have to make some decisions. If more than one item falls into the category, rank the items from the ones you most want to keep to those you're most willing to part with. Start from the top and add the items' values one at a time. When you've reached the exemption amount, stop; those items are the ones you can claim as exempt. The others will have to be surrendered to the trustee unless they're worth too little for the trustee to bother with, or a wild card exemption can be used. (For an explanation of wild card exemptions, see **Guidelines for Claiming Exemptions**, above.)

In evaluating whether or not your cash on hand and deposits of money are exempt, look to the source of the money. For example, if wages are exempt and the money in your bank account is from your last pay check, indicate the source and claim the exemption.

Exempt property that secures a debt. The rules change if your exempt property is security for a debt. You will probably have to give up the property unless you use one of the remedies outlined in the instructions for Form 8 (see Section E5).

Specify Law Providing Each Exemption. Citations to the specific laws that create exemptions are in the state and federal exemption lists provided in this kit.

Start by citing anywhere on the form the law noted at the top of the exemption list. For example, "All law references are to the Florida Statutes Annotated unless otherwise noted." If you use any other reference, such as federal *non-bankruptcy* exemptions or a case, remember to list the entire reference.

For each item of property, list the specific law that creates the exemption, as set out on the exemption list. If you are combining part or all of a wild card exemption with a regular exemption, list both citations. If the wild card and the regular exemption have the same citation, list the citation twice and put "wild card" next to one of the citations.

Value of Claimed Exemption. Claim the exemption amount allowed according to the exemption list, up to the value of the item.

If you are using part or all of a wild card exemption in addition to a regular exemption, list both amounts. For example, if the regular exemption for an item of furniture is $200, and you plan to exempt it to $500 using $300 from your state's wild card exemption, list $200 across from the citation you listed for the regular exemption, and the $300 across from the citation you listed for the wild card exemption (or across from the term "wild card").

Current Market Value of Property Without Deducting Exemption. Enter the fair market value of the item you are claiming as exempt. You should have already listed this information on Schedule A or Schedule B.

Special Rules for Retirement Plans

If your retirement plan is covered by the federal law called ERISA (Employee Retirement Income Security Act), pay special attention to these rules.

Rule 1: Your ERISA retirement plan is exempt if you use the federal bankruptcy exemption system.

Rule 2: Your ERISA retirement plan is exempt if you use a state exemption system, even if your state exemption list doesn't refer to ERISA retirement plans. The reason is somewhat complex, involving both ERISA law and bankruptcy law. But the upshot for you is that you don't even need to list your ERISA retirement plan in Schedule C, because it's not considered to be part of your bankruptcy estate. (*Patterson v. Shumate*, 504 U.S. 753 (1992).)

If your retirement plan is not covered by ERISA (ask your employer's personnel officer), it is exempt only if:
- you use your state's exemptions, and
- the plan is listed in either your state exemption list or the federal non-bankruptcy exemption list.

Some retirement plans that are not ERISA-qualified may still be exempt. If it looks like you might lose your retirement plan in bankruptcy, see a lawyer before filing.

Limits on exemptions. Don't claim more than you need for any particular item. For instance, if you're allowed household furniture up to a total amount of $2,000, don't inflate the value of each item of furniture, simply to get to $2,000. Use the value as stated on Schedule B.

Step 4: Reevaluate Filing for Bankruptcy

At this point, you should have a good idea of what property, if any, you'll have to give up in the bankruptcy process. Any items of value that are not listed as exempt in Schedule C can be taken by the bankruptcy trustee to pay your creditors.

If you stand to lose a lot of nonexempt property by filing for bankruptcy, you may want to hold off, at least for a while. There are some techniques for converting nonexempt property into exempt property that may be available to you. (Those techniques are covered in Nolo's *How to File for Bankruptcy*.)

FORM B6C (6/90)

In re ___Maytag, Molly and Jonathan_____ ,   Case No._____
                        Debtor   (If known)

SCHEDULE C—PROPERTY CLAIMED AS EXEMPT

Debtor elects the exemptions to which debtor is entitled under:

(Check one box)

☐ 11 U.S.C. § 522(b)(1):   Exemptions provided in 11 U.S.C. § 522(d). **Note: These exemptions are available only in certain states.**

☒ 11 U.S.C. § 522(b)(2):   Exemptions available under applicable nonbankruptcy federal laws, state or local law where the debtor's domicile has been located for the 180 days immediately preceding the filing of the petition, or for a longer portion of the 180-day period than in any other place, and the debtor's interest as a tenant by the entirety or joint tenant to the extent the interest is exempt from process under applicable nonbankruptcy law.

DESCRIPTION OF PROPERTY	SPECIFY LAW PROVIDING EACH EXEMPTION	VALUE OF CLAIMED EXEMPTION	CURRENT MARKET VALUE OF PROPERTY WITHOUT DEDUCTING EXEMPTIONS
Real Property House at 21 Scarborough Road South, Cleveland Hts, OH 44118	2329.66(A)(1)	10,000	95,000
Cash on hand Cash from wages	2329.66(A)(13)	100	100
Money deposits Ameritrust checking account #12345	2329.66(A)(4)(a)	250	250
Shaker Savings account #98765	2329.66(A)(4)(a)	400	400
Ohio Savings account #058-118061	1775.24(A)(4)(a)	100	100
Household goods Stereo System	2329.66(A)(17) (wildcard)	300	300
Washer/Dryer set	2329.66(A)(4)(b)	150	150
Refrigerator	2329.66(A)(3)	250	250
Stove	2329.66(A)(3)	150	150
Household furniture	2329.66(A)(4)(b)	600	600
Minor appliances	2329.66(A)(4)(b)	75	75
Antique desk	2329.66(A)(4)(b)	250	250
Vacuum	2329.66(A)(4)(b)	30	30
Beds & bedding	2329.66(A)(3)	500	500
Television	2329.66(A)(4)	135	135
VCR	2329.66(A)(4)	75	75
Lawnmower	2329.66(A)(4)	100	100
Swingset, children's toys	2329.66(A)(4)	180	180
Snowblower	2329.66(A)(4)	100	100
Books, pictures, etc. Stamp collection	2329.66(A)(4)(b)	75	75
Lithograph	2329.66(A)(4)(b)	50	50

Because we are married, we each claim a full set of exemptions to the extent permitted by law. All references are to Ohio Revised Code unless otherwise noted.

In re <u>Maytag, Molly and Jonathan</u>

SCHEDULE C—PROPERTY CLAIMED AS EXEMPT

(Continuation Sheet)

DESCRIPTION OF PROPERTY	SPECIFY LAW PROVIDING EACH EXEMPTION	VALUE OF CLAIMED EXEMPTION	CURRENT MARKET VALUE OF PROPERTY WITHOUT DEDUCTING EXEMPTIONS
<u>Wearing Apparel</u>			
Clothing	2329.66(A)(3)	625	625
<u>Furs & jewelry</u>			
Wedding rings	2329.66(A)(4)(c)	225	225
Diamond necklace	2329.66(A)(4)(c)	325	325
Watches	2329.66(A)(4)(c)	50	50
<u>Insurance</u>			
Lively Insurance Co., life insurance policy #14-171136	3911.12	120	120
Live-a-long-time Co., life insurance policy #33-19195WY17	3911.14	65	65
<u>IRA, Pensions, Etc.</u>			
Cleveland Builder Pension	2329.66(A)(10)(a)	6,612	6,612
IRA	2329.66(A)(10)(b)	3,400	3,400
<u>Firearms, sports equipment</u>			
Mountain bike	2329.66(A)(4)(b)	165	165
Camera	2329.66(A)(4)(b)	125	125
<u>Other liquidated debts</u>			
Wages from Cleveland Builder	2329.66(A)(13)	1,900	1,900
Wages from Typing Circles	2329.66(A)(13)	100	100
<u>Vehicles</u>			
1988 Honda motorcycle	2329.66(A)(2)	1,000	1,000
<u>Animals</u>			
2 Poodles	2329.66(A)(4)(b)	200	200
<u>Office equipment</u>			
Computer (for business)	2329.66(A)(5)	1,100	1,100
Typewriter (for business)	2329.66(A)(5)	125	125
Fax (for business)	2329.66(A)(17) (wildcard)	500	500
<u>Tools of trade</u>			
Carpentry tools	2329.66(A)(5)	150	150

d. Schedule D—Creditors Holding Secured Claims

A debt is **secured** if any of the following applies:

- **You've pledged property as collateral for a loan.** Examples include mortgages, home equity loans, most motor vehicle loans and most loans from finance companies. Loans obtained from consumer loan businesses, like Beneficial Finance, are secured loans if you were required to pledge collateral for them. If you signed a security agreement with a retailer when making a major purchase, those loans are also secured.

- **A creditor has fixed a lien—that is, a legal claim—on your property.** Typical examples include: notices of tax liens filed by the IRS or your state or local taxing authority, judgment liens created by people who won court judgments against you, mechanics' liens created by a contractor who worked on your real property or a mechanic who worked on your vehicle and child support liens.

- **You signed a document granting a security interest in the outcome of your lawsuit.** This applies if a doctor or lawyer worked on a lawsuit on your behalf and you signed a document that provided that the collection of her fees would be postponed until you win or settle the case. The fees would be paid out of the expected court judgment.

To completely eliminate a secured debt in bankruptcy, you might have to give up the property that is security for the debt, or pay its market value. (How to deal with secured debts is covered in Section E5.)

In Schedule D you simply list all creditors who hold claims secured by your property. Here's how.

In re and **Case No.** Follow the instructions for Schedule A.

☐ **Check this box…** Check the box following the form's instructions if you have no secured creditors. Then proceed to Schedule E.

Creditor's Name and Mailing Address. List all secured creditors, preferably in alphabetical order. For each, fill in the account number, if you know it, and the creditor's name and complete mailing address, including zip code. If you have more than one creditor for a given secured debt (such as the original creditor, a collection agency and an attorney), list the original creditor first and then immediately list the other creditors. If you get to the end and discover that you've missed a few creditors, simply add them

at the end. If your creditors don't all fit on the first page of Schedule D, use copies of the preprinted continuation page. (The sample does not show completed continuation pages.)

Codebtor. If someone else can be legally forced to pay your debt to a listed secured creditor, enter an "X" in this column. (You'll also list the codebtor as a creditor in Schedule F and as a codebtor on Schedule H; instructions are below.)

The most common codebtors are:

- cosigners and guarantors—people who guarantee payment of a loan, credit card or other debt (you could either be the main signator or the cosigner or guarantor)

- ex-spouses with whom you jointly incurred debts before divorcing

- non-filing spouses in non-community property states

- joint owners of real estate or other property, and

- co-parties in a lawsuit.

Husband, Wife, Joint or Community. If you are married, identify who is indebted to the secured creditor: husband (H), wife (W), husband and wife jointly in a common law property state (J), or husband and wife jointly in a community property state (C). If in doubt, put (J) or (C).

Date Claim Was Incurred… Here you give information about the secured claim. If you have more than one creditor for a given secured claim (for example, the original lender and a collection agency), list the debt only for the original creditor and put ditto marks (") for each subsequent creditor. Let's take these one at a time.

Date Claim Incurred. Enter the date the secured claim was incurred. For most claims, this is the date you signed a security agreement. If you didn't sign a security agreement with the creditor, the date is most likely the date a creditor recorded a lien against your property. If there are two or more creditors on the same secured claim, put the same date for both.

Nature of Lien. Here are the possibilities:

- **Purchase-money security interest.** The debt or loan was incurred to purchase property that was pledged as collateral for that debt or loan, as with a mortgage or car note.

- **Nonpossessory nonpurchase-money security interest.** The debt was incurred for a purpose other than buying the collateral, as with home equity loans, loans from finance companies or secured credit cards (where you pledged property or cash as security).

FORM B6D (6/90)

In re ___Maytag, Molly and Jonathan_____ ,   Case No._____
                  Debtor   (If known)

SCHEDULE D—CREDITORS HOLDING SECURED CLAIMS

State the name, mailing address, including zip code, and account number, if any, of all entities holding claims secured by property of the debtor as of the date of filing of the petition. List creditors holding all types of secured interest such as judgment liens, garnishments, statutory liens, mortgages, deeds of trust, and other security interests. List creditors in alphabetical order to the extent practicable. If all secured creditors will not fit on this page, use the continuation sheet provided.

If any entity other than a spouse in a joint case may be jointly liable on a claim, place an "X" in the column labeled "Codebtor," include the entity on the appropriate schedule of creditors, and complete Schedule H—Codebtors. If a joint petition is filed, state whether husband, wife, both of them, or the marital community may be liable on each claim by placing an "H," "W," "J," or "C" in the column labeled "Husband, Wife, Joint, or Community."

If the claim is contingent, place an "X" in the column labeled "Contingent." If the claim is unliquidated, place an "X" in the column labeled "Unliquidated." If the claim is disputed, place an "X" in the column labeled "Disputed." (You may need to place an "X" in more than one of these three columns.)

Report the total of all claims listed on this schedule in the box labeled "Total" on the last sheet of the completed schedule. Report this total also on the Summary of Schedules.

☐   Check this box if debtor has no creditors holding secured claims to report on this Schedule D.

CREDITOR'S NAME AND MAILING ADDRESS INCLUDING ZIP CODE	CODEBTOR	HUSBAND, WIFE, JOINT, OR COMMUNITY	DATE CLAIM WAS INCURRED, NATURE OF LIEN, AND DESCRIPTION AND MARKET VALUE OF PROPERTY SUBJECT TO LIEN	CONTINGENT	UNLIQUIDATED	DISPUTED	AMOUNT OF CLAIM WITHOUT DEDUCTING VALUE OF COLLATERAL	UNSECURED PORTION, IF ANY
ACCOUNT NO. 64-112-1861 Ameritrust 10 Financial Way Cleveland Hts, OH 44118		J	9/12/XX; purchase-money secured debt; mortgage on residence VALUE $ 95,000				75,000	-0-
ACCOUNT NO. 64-112-8423 Ameritrust 10 Financial Way Cleveland Hts, OH 44118		J	8/9/XX; nonpurchase-money secured debt; second mortgage on residence VALUE $ 95,000				12,000	-0-
ACCOUNT NO. N/A Computers for Sale P.O. Box 1183 San Ramon, CA 94000		J	8/12/XX; purchase-money secured interest, computer VALUE $ 1,100				2,000	900
ACCOUNT NO. 521129 Quality Collection Agency 21 Main Drive West Cleveland Hts, OH 44115	"		" VALUE $				"	"

___1___ continuation sheets attached

Subtotal ➡ (Total of this page) $ 89,000

Total ➡ (Use only on last page) $

(Report total also on Summary of Schedules)

- **Possessory nonpurchase-money security interest.** You own property that has been pledged to (and impounded by) a pawnshop.
- **Judgment lien.** The creditor sued you, obtained a court judgment and recorded a lien against your property. (List the lien even if you don't currently own property in the county where the lien was recorded.)
- **Tax lien.** A taxing authority recorded a notice of tax lien against your property because you owe delinquent taxes.
- **Child support lien.** You owe child support and your child's other parent has recorded a lien against your property.
- **Mechanics' or materialmen's liens.** These liens may be created when someone performs work on real property, a vehicle or other property and isn't paid.
- **Don't know.** You don't know. You might also try describing the lien in your own words.

Description of Property. Describe each item that is collateral for the secured debt. Use the same description you used on Schedule A, for real property, or Schedule B, for personal property.

Market Value. The amount you put here must be the same as what you put on Schedules A, B and C. If you previously put the total value for a group of items, you must now get more specific. For instance, if a department store has a secured claim against your washing machine, and you listed your "washer/dryer set" on Schedules B and C, now you must provide the washer's specific market value. (If the claim is against both the washer and dryer, you can list them together.)

Contingent, Unliquidated, Disputed. Indicate whether the creditor's secured claim is contingent, unliquidated or disputed. Check all that apply; here's what the terms mean:

- **Contingent.** The claim depends on some event that hasn't yet occurred and may never occur. For example, if you cosigned a secured loan, you won't be liable unless the principal debtor defaults.
- **Unliquidated.** This means that a debt may exist, but the exact amount hasn't been determined. For example, you've sued someone for injuries you suffered

in an auto accident, but the case isn't over. Your lawyer has taken the case under a contingency fee agreement—he'll get a third of the recovery if you win, and nothing if you lose—and has a security interest in the final recovery amount. The debt to the lawyer is unliquidated because you don't know what the final recovery will be. The debt is also contingent because you won't owe the lawyer anything if you lose.

- **Disputed.** You and the creditor disagree about the existence or amount of the debt. For instance, the IRS says you owe $10,000 and has put a notice of federal tax lien on your property, and you say you owe $5,000.

Amount of Claim Without Deducting Value of Collateral. For each secured creditor, put the amount it would take to pay off its secured claim, regardless of what the property is worth. If you can't get the information, such as by checking with the lender, fill in "don't know."

If you have more than one creditor for a given secured claim (for example, the original lender and a collection agency), list the debt only for the original creditor and put ditto marks (") for each subsequent creditor. Also, if one creditor has liens on multiple items of property, list the amount once, and fill in "see amount listed above for (name of creditor)" on additional items of property.

Subtotal/Total. Total the amounts in the Amount of Claim column for each page. Do not include amounts represented by the ditto marks or "see above" notations. On the final page of Schedule D (which may be the first page or a preprinted continuation page), enter the total of all secured claims. (The sample does not show the completed continuation page.)

Unsecured Portion, If Any. If the market value of the collateral is equal to or greater than the amount of the claim, enter "0," meaning that the creditor's claim is fully secured. If the market value of the collateral is less than the amount of the claim(s) listed, enter the difference here.

e. Schedule E—Creditors Holding Unsecured Priority Claims

Schedule E identifies certain creditors who are entitled to be paid first—by the trustee—out of your nonexempt assets.

In re and **Case No.** Follow the instructions for Schedule A.

☐ **Check this box...** Many people can check this box. You won't know, however, until you go through the first page of Schedule E.

Types of Priority Claims. Read the description of each of the six categories of priority of debts listed on the form and check only those boxes for which you owe a debt in that category. They are self-explanatory, with the following clarification.

- **Taxes and certain other debts owed to governmental units.** This applies if you owe back taxes, including payroll deposits, or other debts to the government such as moving violation fines. If you owe the IRS, the IRS has recorded a Notice of Federal Tax lien and you own real estate, your tax debt is secured and should be on Schedule D, not here.

If you didn't check any of the priority debt boxes, go back and check the first box following the instructions. Then skip ahead to Schedule F.

f. Schedule E—Continuation Sheet

Make as many photocopies of the continuation page as the number of priority debt boxes you checked; you must complete a separate page for each type. Then complete each page as follows:

In re and **Case No.** Follow the instructions for Schedule A.

Type of Priority. Identify one of the types of priority you checked on the first page of this schedule.

Creditor's Name and Mailing Address. List the name and complete mailing address, including zip code, of each priority creditor, as well as the account number if you know it. You may have more than one priority creditor for a given debt, such as an original creditor and collection agency.

Codebtor. If a codebtor is liable to a listed priority creditor, enter an "X" in this column. (You'll also list the codebtor as a creditor on Schedule F and also on Schedule H; instructions are below.) Common codebtors are listed above in the instructions for Schedule D.

Husband, Wife, Joint or Community. If you are married, identify who is indebted to the priority creditor: husband (H), wife (W), husband and wife jointly in a common law property state (J), or husband and wife jointly in a community property state (C). If in doubt, put (J) or (C).

Date Claim Was Incurred and Consideration for Claim. State the date you incurred the debt—this may be a specific date or a period of time. Also briefly state what the debt is for. For example, "goods purchased," "hours worked for me" or "deposit for my services."

Contingent, Unliquidated, Disputed. Indicate whether the creditor's secured claim is contingent, unliquidated or disputed. These terms are defined in the instructions for Schedule D in Section d, above.

Total Amount of Claim. For each priority creditor (other than tax creditors), put the amount it would take to pay off the debt in full, even if it's over the priority limit. For taxes, list only the amount that is unsecured (the amount that is secured goes on Schedule D). If the amount isn't determined, make an estimate and note this next to the amount.

Subtotal/Total. Total the amounts in the Total Amount of Claim column on each page. If you use continuation pages for additional priority debts, enter the total of all priority debts on the final page.

Amount Entitled to Priority. If the priority claim is larger than the maximum indicated on the first page of Schedule E, insert the maximum here. If the claim is less than the maximum, put the amount you entered in the Total Amount of Claim column.

B6E (Rev. 4/98)

In re _____Maytag, Molly and Jonathan_____,   Case No._____
           Debtor   (If known)

SCHEDULE E—CREDITORS HOLDING UNSECURED PRIORITY CLAIMS

A complete list of claims entitled to priority, listed separately by type of priority, is to be set forth on the sheets provided. Only holders of unsecured claims entitled to priority should be listed in this schedule. In the boxes provided on the attached sheets, state the name and mailing address, including zip code, and account number, if any, of all entities holding priority claims against the debtor or the property of the debtor, as of the date of the filing of the petition.

If any entity other than a spouse in a joint case may be jointly liable on a claim, place an "X" in the column labeled "Codebtor," include the entity on the appropriate schedule of creditors, and complete Schedule H—Codebtors. If a joint petition is filed, state whether husband, wife, both of them, or the marital community may be liable on each claim by placing an "H," "W," "J," or "C" in the column labeled "Husband, Wife, Joint, or Community."

If the claim is contingent, place an "X" in the column labeled "Contingent." If the claim is unliquidated, place an "X" in the column labeled "Unliquidated." If the claim is disputed, place an "X" in the column labeled "Disputed." (You may need to place an "X" in more than one of these three columns.)

Report the total of all claims listed on each sheet in the box labeled "Subtotal" on each sheet. Report the total of all claims listed on this Schedule E in the box labeled "Total" on the last sheet of the completed schedule. Repeat this total also on the Summary of Schedules.

  ☐   **Check this box if debtor has no creditors holding unsecured priority claims to report on this Schedule E.**

TYPES OF PRIORITY CLAIMS (Check the appropriate box(es) below if claims in that category are listed on the attached sheets)

☐   **Extensions of credit in an involuntary case**

Claims arising in the ordinary course of the debtor's business or financial affairs after the commencement of the case but before the earlier of the appointment of a trustee or the order for relief. 11 U.S.C. § 507(a)(2).

☐   **Wages, salaries, and commissions**

Wages, salaries, and commissions, including vacation, severance, and sick leave pay owing to employees and commissions owing to qualifying independent sales representatives up to $4,000* per person, earned within 90 days immediately preceding the filing of the original petition, or the cessation of business, whichever occurred first, to the extent provided in 11 U.S.C. § 507(a)(3).

☐   **Contributions to employee benefit plans**

Money owed to employee benefit plans for services rendered within 180 days immediately preceding the filing of the original petition, or the cessation of business, whichever occurred first, to the extent provided in 11 U.S.C. § 507(a)(4).

☐   **Certain farmers and fishermen**

Claims of certain farmers and fishermen, up to a maximum of $4,000* per farmer or fisherman, against the debtor, as provided in 11 U.S.C. § 507(a)(5).

☐   **Deposits by individuals**

Claims of individuals up to a maximum of $1,800* for deposits for the purchase, lease, or rental of property or services for personal, family, or household use, that were not delivered or provided. 11 U.S.C. § 507(a)(6).

☐   **Alimony, Maintenance, or Support**

Claims of a spouse, former spouse, or child of the debtor for alimony, maintenance, or support, to the extent provided in 11 U.S.C. § 507(a)(7).

☐   **Taxes and Certain Other Debts Owed to Governmental Units**

Taxes, customs, duties, and penalties owing to federal, state, and local governmental units as set forth in 11 U.S.C. § 507(a)(8).

☐   **Commitments to Maintain the Capital of an Insured Depository Institution**

Claims based on commitments to the FDIC, RTC, Director of the Office of Thrift Supervision, Comptroller of the Currency, or Board of Governors of the Federal Reserve system, or their predecessors or successors, to maintain the capital of an insured depository institution. 11 U.S.C. § 507 (a)(9).

* Amounts are subject to adjustment on April 1, 2001, and every three years thereafter with respect to cases commenced on or after the date of adjustment.

_____1_____ continuation sheets attached

B6E (10/98) continued

In re _Maytag, Molly and Jonathan_____, Case No._____
          Debtor   (If known)

SCHEDULE E—CREDITORS HOLDING UNSECURED PRIORITY CLAIMS
(Continuation Sheet)

Taxes
_____
TYPE OF PRIORITY

CREDITOR'S NAME AND MAILING ADDRESS INCLUDING ZIP CODE	CODEBTOR	HUSBAND, WIFE, JOINT, OR COMMUNITY	DATE CLAIM WAS INCURRED AND CONSIDERATION FOR CLAIM	CONTINGENT	UNLIQUIDATED	DISPUTED	TOTAL AMOUNT OF CLAIM	AMOUNT ENTITLED TO PRIORITY
ACCOUNT NO. N/A IRS Cincinnati, OH 42111		J	April 15, 20XX, Tax Liability				2,200	2,200
ACCOUNT NO. N/A Ohio Dept. of Tax P.O. Box 1460 Cincinnati, OH 43266-0106		J	April 15, 20XX, Tax Liability				800	800
ACCOUNT NO.								
ACCOUNT NO.								
ACCOUNT NO.								

Subtotal ➡ (Total of this page) $ 3,000

Total ➡ (Use only on last page) $ 3,000

Sheet no. _1_ of _1_ sheets attached to
Schedule of Creditors Holding Unsecured Priority Claims

(Report total also on Summary of Schedules)

g. Schedule F—Creditors Holding Unsecured Nonpriority Claims

In this schedule, list all creditors you haven't listed in Schedules D or E. Photocopy and use as many preprinted continuation pages as you need. For purposes of completing Schedule F, it doesn't matter that the debt might be nondischargeable—such as a student loan. It also doesn't matter that you believe that you don't owe the debt.

Unsecured Debts Defined

An unsecured debt is not secured by any particular property you possess. Failure to repay the debt does not entitle the creditor to repossess or foreclose on your property to satisfy the debt. Unless a creditor has a judgment and has recorded a judgment lien against you, debts are unsecured, including most: bank credit card debts, medical and legal bills, accountants' bills, unsecured personal loans, utility bills and store revolving charge accounts. Unsecured debts are almost always canceled by bankruptcy.

It's essential that you list every creditor to whom you owe, or possibly owe, money. Even if you want to repay a particular creditor, list the debt, get it discharged and pay voluntarily.

In re and **Case No.** Follow the instructions for Schedule A.

☐ **Check this box…** Check this box if you have no unsecured debts (this would be very rare).

Creditor's Name and Mailing Address. List, preferably in alphabetical order, the name and complete mailing address (including zip code) of each unsecured creditor, as well as the account number if you know it. If you have more than one unsecured creditor for a given debt, list the original creditor first and then immediately list the other creditors, such as an attorney or collection agency. If you get to the end and discover that you left a creditor off, just add the creditor at the end. If your creditors don't all fit on the first page of Schedule F, use the preprinted continuation page.

Codebtor. If a codebtor is liable to a listed creditor, enter an "X" in this column. You'll also list the codebtor as a creditor in this schedule and on Schedule H (instructions are below). Common codebtors are listed in Section d, above.

Easy-to-Overlook Creditors

One debt may involve several different creditors. Remember to include:
- anyone who has cosigned or guaranteed a note, loan or credit application for you
- the primary debtor of a note or loan you cosigned or guaranteed, and
- anyone who has sued you or may sue you because of a car accident, business dispute or the like.

Husband, Wife, Joint or Community. If you are married, identify who is indebted to the unsecured creditor: husband (H), wife (W), husband and wife jointly in a common law property state (J), or husband and wife jointly in a community property state (C). If in doubt, put (J) or (C).

Date Claim Was Incurred… State when the debt was incurred. It may be one date or a period of time. If there is more than one creditor for a single debt, list the same date for each creditor. With credit card debts, put the approximate time over which you ran up the charges unless the unpaid charges were made on one or two specific dates. Then state what the debt was for. You can be general ("clothes," "household furnishings" or "vacation") or more specific ("refrigerator" or "teeth capping").

If you are entitled to a **setoff** against the debt—that is, the creditor owes you some money as well—give the amount and reason for the setoff.

Contingent, Unliquidated, Disputed. Indicate whether the creditor's claim is contingent, unliquidated or disputed. These terms are defined in the instructions for Schedule D, in Section d, above.

Amount of Claim. List the amount of the debt. Even if you dispute the amount claimed by the creditor, put in the amount the creditor claims. That way, it will all be wiped out if it's dischargeable. If there's more than one creditor for a single debt, put the debt amount across from the original creditor and put ditto marks (") across from each subsequent creditor you have listed.

FORM B6F (9/97)

In re ___Maytag, Molly and Jonathan_____ ,   Case No._____
                          Debtor   (If known)

SCHEDULE F—CREDITORS HOLDING UNSECURED NONPRIORITY CLAIMS

State the name, mailing address, including zip code, and account number, if any, of all entities holding unsecured claims without priority against the debtor or the property of the debtor as of the date of filing of the petition. Do not include claims listed in Schedules D and E. If all creditors will not fit on this page, use the continuation sheet provided.

If any entity other than a spouse in a joint case may be jointly liable on a claim, place an "X" in the column labeled "Codebtor," include the entity on the appropriate schedule of creditors, and complete Schedule H—Codebtors. If a joint petition is filed, state whether husband, wife, both of them, or the marital community may be liable on each claim by placing an "H," "W," "J," or "C" in the column labeled "Husband, Wife, Joint, or Community."

If the claim is contingent, place an "X" in the column labeled "Contingent." If the claim is unliquidated, place an "X" in the column labeled "Unliquidated." If the claim is disputed, place an "X" in the column labeled "Disputed." (You may need to place an "X" in more than one of these three columns.)

Report the total of all claims listed on this schedule in the box labeled "Total" on the last sheet of the completed schedule. Report this total also on the Summary of Schedules.

☐ Check this box if debtor has no creditors holding unsecured nonpriority claims to report on this Schedule F.

CREDITOR'S NAME AND MAILING ADDRESS INCLUDING ZIP CODE	CODEBTOR	HUSBAND, WIFE, JOINT, OR COMMUNITY	DATE CLAIM WAS INCURRED AND CONSIDERATION FOR CLAIM. IF CLAIM IS SUBJECT TO SETOFF, SO STATE	CONTINGENT	UNLIQUIDATED	DISPUTED	AMOUNT OF CLAIM
ACCOUNT NO. N/A Alan Accountant 5 Green St. Cleveland, OH 44118		J	4/XX, tax preparation				250
ACCOUNT NO. 4189000026113 American Allowance P.O. Box 1 New York, NY 10001		J	1/XX to 4/XX, VISA credit card charges			X	5,600
ACCOUNT NO. Patricia Washington, Esq. Washington & Lincoln Legal Plaza, Suite 1 Cleveland, OH 44114		"	"		"		"
ACCOUNT NO. 845061-86-3 Citibank 200 East North Columbus, OH 43266		J	20XX , student loan charges				10,000

_____2_____ continuation sheets attached

Subtotal ➡ (Total of this page) $ 15,850

Total ➡ (Use only on last page) $ N/A

(Report total also on Summary of Schedules)

Total the amounts in the last column for this page. Do not include the amounts represented by the ditto marks. On the final page, which may be the first page or a pre-printed continuation page, enter the total of all unsecured claims. (The sample does not show completed continuation pages.)

h. Schedule G—Executory Contracts and Unexpired Leases

In this form, you list every executory contract or unexpired lease that you're a party to. *Executory* means the contract is still in force—somebody is still obligated to do something under it. Similarly, *unexpired* means that the lease period hasn't run out, so it is still in effect.

Common examples of executory contracts and unexpired leases are:

- car, residence and business leases or rental agreements
- service contracts
- business contracts
- time-share contracts or leases
- contracts for sale of real estate
- copyright and patent license agreements
- real estate leases to harvest timber, minerals or oil
- homeowners' association fee requirements
- agreements for boat docking privileges, and
- insurance contracts.

If you are behind in payments. The delinquency should also be listed as a debt on Schedule D, E or F. The sole purpose of this schedule is to identify existing contractual obligations that you still owe or that someone owes you.

In re and **Case No.** Follow the instructions for Schedule A.

☐ **Check this box…** Check this box if it applies; otherwise, complete the form.

Name and Mailing Address… Provide the name and full mailing address, including zip code, of each party—other than yourself—to each lease or contract. These parties are either people who signed agreements or the companies for whom these people work. If you're unsure about whom to list, include the person who signed an agreement, any com-pany whose name appears on the agreement and anybody who might have an interest in having the contract or lease enforced. If you still aren't sure, put "don't know."

Description of Contract or Lease… For each lease or contract, give:

- a description of the basic type, for instance, insurance contract, residential lease, non-residential real estate lease, commercial lease, car lease, business obligation, copyright license
- the date the contract or lease was signed
- the date the contract is to expire, if there is a date
- a summary of each party's rights and obligations under the lease or contract, and
- the contract number, if the contract is with any government body.

The trustee is likely to terminate all leases and contracts unless:

- you want the lease or contract to continue, as you might for an insurance contract or apartment lease, provided that your creditors won't be adversely affected, or
- the lease or contract will produce assets for your creditors.

If the trustee terminates a lease or contract, you and the other parties to the agreement are cut loose from any obligations unless you agree otherwise.

i. Schedule H—Codebtors

In Schedules D, E and F you identified those debts for which you have codebtors. You must also list those codebtors here. In a Chapter 7 bankruptcy, your codebtors will be wholly responsible for your debts unless they, too, declare bankruptcy.

In re and **Case No.** Follow the instructions for Schedule A.

☐ **Check this box…** Check this box if it applies; otherwise, complete the form.

Name and Address of Codebtor. List the name and complete address (including zip code) of each codebtor.

Name and Address of Creditor. List the name and address of each creditor (as listed on Schedule D, E or F) to which each codebtor is indebted.

FORM B6G (10/89)

In re <u>Maytag, Molly and Jonathan</u>   ,
          Debtor

Case No._____
                                (If known)

SCHEDULE G—EXECUTORY CONTRACTS AND UNEXPIRED LEASES

Describe all executory contracts of any nature and all unexpired leases of real personal property. Include any timeshare interests.

State nature of debtor's interest in contract, i.e., "Purchaser," "Agent," etc. State whether debtor is the lessor or lessee of a lease.

Provide the names and complete mailing addresses of all other parties to each lease or contract described.

NOTE: A party listed on this schedule will not receive notice of the filing of this case unless the party is also scheduled in the appropriate schedule of creditors.

☐ Check this box if debtor has no executory contracts or unexpired leases.

NAME AND MAILING ADDRESS, INCLUDING ZIP CODE, OF OTHER PARTIES TO LEASE OR CONTRACT	DESCRIPTION OF CONTRACT OR LEASE AND NATURE OF DEBTOR'S INTEREST. STATE WHETHER LEASE IS FOR NONRESIDENTIAL REAL PROPERTY. STATE CONTRACT NUMBER OF ANY GOVERNMENT CONTRACT
Scarborough Road South Homeowners Association 1 Scarborough Road South Cleveland Hts, OH 41118	Homeowner's Association Contract for residential property, signed 10/XX, expires 12/XX. Provides for maintenance, gardening and repairs of property.

FORM B6H (6/90)

In re ___Maytag, Molly and Jonathan___,   Case No._____
                Debtor   (If known)

SCHEDULE H—CODEBTORS

Provide the information requested concerning any person or entity, other than a spouse in a joint case, that is also liable on any debts listed by debtor in the schedules of creditors. Include all guarantors and co-signers. In community property states, a married debtor not filing a joint case should report the name and address of the nondebtor spouse on this schedule. Include all names used by the nondebtor spouse during the six years immediately preceding the commencement of this case.

☐ Check this box if debtor has no codebtors.

NAME AND ADDRESS OF CODEBTOR	NAME AND ADDRESS OF CREDITOR
Bonnie Johnson 40 Mayfield University Hts, OH 44118	Fanny's Furniture 14–4th Street Cleveland, OH 44114

j. Schedule I—Current Income of Individual Debtor(s)

The bankruptcy trustee screens each set of forms for possible abuse of the bankruptcy system. If you have enough disposable income to pay a substantial majority of your unsecured debts over a three- to five-year period, the bankruptcy court will probably pressure you to convert your case to Chapter 13 bankruptcy or dismiss your case if you refuse.

Your disposable income is computed by subtracting your reasonable expenditures from your take-home income. Expenditures for items the trustee considers luxuries, such as expensive cars, investment property or high credit card bills for non-necessities, may be disregarded.

Most of the questions on the form are self-explanatory. We provide detailed information for questions that are not.

 Don't forget your spouse! Married couples filing jointly should fill in information for both spouses.

Debtor's Marital Status. You are divorced only if you have received a final judgment of divorce from a court.

Dependents of Debtor and Spouse. List the names, ages and relationships of all persons for whom you and your spouse (if you're married) provide at least 50% of support.

Employment. If you are retired, unemployed or disabled, state that and indicate how long and where you last worked.

Payroll Deductions. Additional possible deductions are state disability taxes, wages withheld or garnished for child support, credit union payments or perhaps payments on a student loan or a car.

Regular income from operation of business or profession or farm. If you are self-employed or operate a sole proprietorship, enter your monthly income from that source here. If it's been fairly steady for at least one calendar year, divide the amount you entered on your most recent tax return (IRS Schedule C) by 12 for a monthly amount. If your income hasn't been steady for at least one calendar year, enter the average net income from your business or profession for the past three months. In either case you must attach a statement of your income. Use either your most recent IRS Schedule C or a worksheet of your business records.

Social Security or other government assistance. Enter the total monthly amount you receive in Social Security, SSI, public assistance, disability payments, veterans' benefits, workers' compensation, unemployment compensation or any other government benefit. If you receive food stamps, include their monthly value. Specify the source of the benefits.

Pension or retirement income. Enter the total monthly amount of all pension, annuity, IRA, Keogh or other retirement benefits you currently receive.

Other monthly income. Specify any other income (such as royalty payments or payments from a trust) you receive on a regular basis and enter the monthly amount here. Divide by 3, 6 or 12 if you receive the payments quarterly, semiannually or annually.

Describe any increase or decrease of more than 10%... Identify any changes in your pay or other income—in excess of 10%—that you expect in the coming year. For instance, if recent layoffs mean you probably won't be working overtime, which will reduce your net monthly income by more than 10%, say so.

FORM B6I (6/90)

In re ___Maytag, Molly and Jonathan_____,   Case No._____
                    Debtor   (If known)

SCHEDULE I—CURRENT INCOME OF INDIVIDUAL DEBTOR(S)

The column labeled "Spouse" must be completed in all cases filed by joint debtors and by a married debtor in a Chapter 12 or 13 case whether or not a joint petition is filed, unless the spouses are separated and a joint petition is not filed.

DEBTOR'S MARITAL STATUS:	DEPENDENTS OF DEBTOR AND SPOUSE		
	NAMES	AGE	RELATIONSHIP
Married	Sara Maytag	14	daughter
	Harold Maytag	12	son

Employment:	DEBTOR	SPOUSE
Occupation	Clerk/typist	Construction Worker
Name of Employer	Typing Circles	Cleveland Builder
How long employed	1 1/2 years	4 years
Address of Employer	40 Euclid Drive Cleveland, OH 44112	100 Chester Way Cleveland, OH 44114

INCOME: (Estimate of average monthly income)	DEBTOR	SPOUSE
Current monthly gross wages, salary, and commissions (pro rate if not paid monthly)	$ 1,450	$ 3,000
Estimated monthly overtime	$ 0	$ 0
SUBTOTAL	$ 1,450	$ 3,000
LESS PAYROLL DEDUCTIONS		
a. Payroll taxes and Social Security	$ 350	$ 600
b. Insurance	$ N/A	$ 250
c. Union dues	$ N/A	$ 50
d. Other (Specify: _____)	$ N/A	$ N/A
SUBTOTAL OF PAYROLL DEDUCTIONS	$ 350	$ 900
TOTAL NET MONTHLY TAKE HOME PAY	$ 1,100	$ 2,100
Regular income from operation of business or profession or farm (attach detailed statement)	$ N/A	$ N/A
Income from real property	$ N/A	$ N/A
Interest and dividends	$ 100	$ 100
Alimony, maintenance or support payments payable to the debtor for the debtor's use or that of dependents listed above	$ N/A	$ N/A
Social Security or other government assistance (Specify:_____)	$ N/A	$ N/A
Pension or retirement income	$ N/A	$ N/A
Other monthly income	$ N/A	$ N/A
(Specify:_____)	$ N/A	$ N/A
	$ N/A	$ N/A
TOTAL MONTHLY INCOME	$ 1,200	$ 2,200

TOTAL COMBINED MONTHLY INCOME $ _____3,400_____   (Report also on Summary of Schedules)

Describe any increase or decrease of more than 10% in any of the above categories anticipated to occur within the year following the filing of this document:

N/A

k. Schedule J—Current Expenditures of Individual Debtor(s)

In this form, you list your family's monthly expenditures, even if you are married and filing alone. Be ready to provide proof of the amounts you enter on this form, especially when they are higher than average. Photocopy bills that are unusually large and attach them to Schedule J.

Be careful of fraud claims. Creditors sometimes try to use the information on these forms to claim that you committed fraud when you applied for credit and therefore should not be allowed to discharge your debt in bankruptcy. If accuracy on this form will substantially contradict information you previously gave a creditor, see a bankruptcy attorney before filing.

Most of the questions on the form are self-explanatory. We provide detailed information for questions that are not.

☐ **Check this box…** If you and your spouse are filing jointly, but maintain separate households, check this box and make sure that you each fill in a separate Schedule J.

Expenditures. For each listed item, fill in your monthly expenses. Prorate any payments that are made biweekly, quarterly, semiannually or annually.

- Do not list payroll deductions you listed on Schedule I.
- Utilities—Other: This includes garbage and cable TV service.
- Installment payments—Other: For credit card payments, fill in "credit card accounts" on one line and enter your total monthly payments for them. Put the average amount you actually pay, even if it's less than it should be. For loan payments (except auto loans), put "loans" and enter your total payments.

For Chapter 12 and Chapter 13 Debtors Only. Type "N/A" anywhere in this section.

l. Summary of Schedules

This form helps the bankruptcy trustee and judge get a quick look at your bankruptcy filing.

Court name. Copy this information from Form 1—Voluntary Petition.

In re and **Case No.** Follow the instructions for Schedule A.

Name of Schedule. This lists the schedules. Don't add anything.

Attached (Yes/No). You should have completed all of the schedules, so type "Yes" in this column for each schedule.

Number of Sheets. Enter the number of pages you completed for each schedule. Remember to count continuation pages. Enter the total at the bottom of the column.

Amounts Scheduled. For each column—Assets, Liabilities and Other—copy the totals from Schedules A, B, D, E, F, I and J and enter them where indicated. Add up the amounts in the Assets and Liabilities columns and enter their totals at the bottom.

m. Declaration Concerning Debtor's Schedules

In this form, you are required to swear that everything you have said on your schedules is true and correct. Deliberate lying is a major sin in bankruptcy, and could cost you your bankruptcy discharge, a fine of up to $500,000 and up to five years in prison.

In re and **Case No.** Follow the instructions for Schedule A.

Declaration Under Penalty of Perjury by Individual Debtor. Enter the total number of pages in your schedules (the number on the Summary of Schedules plus one). Enter the date and sign the form. Be sure that your spouse signs and dates the form if you are filing jointly.

Certification and Signature of Non-Attorney Bankruptcy Petition Preparer. If you hire a bankruptcy petition preparer to complete your forms, that person must fill in the information here and sign this form. Otherwise, type "N/A" anywhere in the box.

Declaration Under Penalty of Perjury on Behalf of Corporation or Partnership. Enter "N/A" anywhere in this section.

FORM B6J (6/90)

In re ___Maytag, Molly and Jonathan___,   Case No._____
                    Debtor   (If known)

SCHEDULE J—CURRENT EXPENDITURES OF INDIVIDUAL DEBTOR(S)

Complete this schedule by estimating the average monthly expenses of the debtor and the debtor's family. Pro rate any payments made bi-weekly, quarterly, semi-annually, or annually to show monthly rate.

☐ Check this box if a joint petition is filed and debtor's spouse maintains a separate household. Complete a separate schedule of expenditures labeled "Spouse."

Rent or home mortgage payment (include lot rented for mobile home)	$ 650
Are real estate taxes included? Yes _X_ No _____	
Is property insurance included? Yes _X_ No _____	
Utilities: Electricity and heating fuel	$ 245
Water and sewer	$ 40
Telephone	$ 85
Other ___garbage___	$ 15
Home maintenance (repairs and upkeep)	$ 175
Food	$ 550
Clothing	$ 125
Laundry and dry cleaning	$ 50
Medical and dental expenses	$ 400
Transportation (not including car payments)	$ 80
Recreation, clubs and entertainment, newspapers, magazines, etc.	$ 30
Charitable contributions	$ 50
Insurance (not deducted from wages or included in home mortgage payments)	
Homeowner's or renter's	$ 120
Life	$ N/A
Health	$ N/A
Auto	$ 60
Other _____	$ N/A
Taxes (not deducted from wages or included in home mortgage payments)	
(Specify: ___income taxes to IRS & Ohio Dept. of Tax___)	$ 200
Installment payments: (In Chapter 12 and 13 cases, do not list payments to be included in the plan)	
Auto	$ N/A
Other ___credit card accounts___	$ 400
Other ___loans___	$ 550
Alimony, maintenance, and support paid to others	$ 600
Payments for support of additional dependents not living at your home	$ N/A
Regular expenses from operation of business, profession, or farm (attach detailed statement)	$ N/A
Other _____	$ N/A
TOTAL MONTHLY EXPENSES (Report also on Summary of Schedules)	$ 4,425

[FOR CHAPTER 12 AND CHAPTER 13 DEBTORS ONLY]
Provide the information requested below, including whether plan payments are to be made bi-weekly, monthly, annually, or at some other regular interval.

A. Total projected monthly income N/A	$ _____
B. Total projected monthly expenses	$ _____
C. Excess income (A minus B)	$ _____
D. Total amount to be paid into plan each _____	$ _____
(interval)	

FORM B6 (6/90) continued

United States Bankruptcy Court

Northern _____ District of ___ Ohio, Eastern Division ___

In re ___ Maytag, Molly and Jonathan _____ ,   Case No._____
                        Debtor   (If known)

SUMMARY OF SCHEDULES

Indicate as to each schedule whether that schedule is attached and state the number of pages in each. Report the totals from Schedules A, B, D, E, F, I and J in the boxes provided. Add the amounts from Schedules A and B to determine the total amount of the debtor's assets. Add the amounts from Schedules D, E and F to determine the total amount of the debtor's liabilities.

NAME OF SCHEDULE		ATTACHED (YES/NO)	NUMBER OF SHEETS	AMOUNTS SCHEDULED		
				ASSETS	LIABILITIES	OTHER
A	Real Property	Yes	1	$ 100,000		
B	Personal Property	Yes	4	$ 29,692		
C	Property Claimed as Exempt	Yes	2			
D	Creditors Holding Secured Claims	Yes	2		$ 92,200	
E	Creditors Holding Unsecured Priority Claims	Yes	2		$ 3,000	
F	Creditors Holding Unsecured Nonpriority Claims	Yes	3		$ 52,450	
G	Executory Contracts and Unexpired Leases	Yes	1			
H	Codebtors	Yes	1			
I	Current Income of Individual Debtor(s)	Yes	1			$ 3,400
J	Current Expenditures of Individual Debtor(s)	Yes	1			$ 4,425

Total Number of Sheets of All Schedules ➡ **18**

Total Assets ➡ $ **129,692**

Total Liabilities ➡ $ **147,650**

FORM B6 (12/94) continued

In re ___Maytag, Molly and Jonathan_____, Case No._____
          Debtor   (If known)

DECLARATION CONCERNING DEBTOR'S SCHEDULES

DECLARATION UNDER PENALTY OF PERJURY BY INDIVIDUAL DEBTOR

I declare under penalty of perjury that I have read the foregoing summary and schedules consisting of _____19_____ sheets, and that they are true and correct to the best of my knowledge, information, and belief.

(Total shown on summary page plus 1)

Date___July 3, 20XX_____   Signature___*Molly Maytag*_____
                                                        Debtor

Date___July 3, 20XX_____   Signature___*Jonathan Maytag*_____
                                                     (Joint Debtor, if any)

[If joint case, both spouses must sign.]

CERTIFICATION AND SIGNATURE OF NON-ATTORNEY BANKRUPTCY PETITION PREPARER (See 11 U.S.C. § 110)

I certify that I am a bankruptcy petition preparer as defined in 11 U.S.C. § 110, that I prepared this document for compensation, and that I have provided the debtor with a copy of this document.

N/A

_____   _____
Printed or Typed Name of Bankruptcy Petition Preparer   Social Security No.

_____

_____
Address

Names and Social Security numbers of all other individuals who prepared or assisted in preparing this document:

If more than one person prepared this document, attach additional signed sheets conforming to the appropriate Official Form for each person.

X_____   _____
Signature of Bankruptcy Petition Preparer   Date

A bankruptcy petition preparer's failure to comply with the provisions of Title 11 and the Federal Rules of Bankruptcy Procedure may result in fine or imprisonment or both. 11 U.S.C. § 110; 18 U.S.C. § 156.

DECLARATION UNDER PENALTY OF PERJURY ON BEHALF OF CORPORATION OR PARTNERSHIP

I, the _____ [the president or other officer or an authorized agent of the corporation or a member or an authorized agent of the partnership] of the _____ [corporation or partnership] named as debtor in this case, declare under penalty of perjury that I have read the foregoing summary and schedules, consisting of _____ sheets, and that they are true and correct to the best of my knowledge, information, and belief.
(Total shown on summary page plus 1)

Date_____   Signature_____

                                                   _____
                                                   [Print or type name of individual signing on behalf of debtor]

[An individual signing on behalf of a partnership or corporation must indicate position or relationship to debtor.]

Penalty for making a false statement or concealing property: Fine of up to $500,000, imprisonment for up to 5 years, or both. 18 U.S.C. §§ 152 and 3571.

4. Form 7—Statement of Financial Affairs

This form asks for information about your recent economic transactions such as payments to creditors, sales, gifts and the like. Under certain circumstances, the trustee may be entitled to recapture property or money that you transferred to others prior to filing for bankruptcy, and use it to pay your unsecured creditors.

Most of the questions on the form are self-explanatory. We provide detailed information only for questions (or portions of questions) that are not. If you have no information for a particular item, check the "none" box. If you fail to answer a question and don't check the "none" box, you will have to amend your papers down the line. Add your own continuation sheets if necessary. (There is no sample of the Statement of Financial Affairs in this kit.)

1. Income from employment or operation of business. Gross income means the total income before taxes and other payroll deductions or business expenses are removed.

2. Income other than from employment or operation of business. Include interest, dividends, royalties, worker's compensation and other government benefits, and child support and alimony.

3. Payments to creditors. There are two kinds of creditors—regular and insiders. An *insider*—defined on the first page of the Statement of Financial Affairs—is essentially a relative or close business associate. All other creditors are *regular* creditors.

If you have paid a regular creditor during the 90 days before you file or paid an insider creditor during the year before you file, the trustee can demand that the creditor turn over the amount to the court, so the trustee can use it to pay your other unsecured creditors. The trustee may ask you to produce written evidence of any payments you list here.

4. Suits, executions, garnishments and attachments. Include personal injury cases, small claims suits, contract disputes, divorces, paternity actions, support or custody modification actions and the like.

5. Repossessions, foreclosures and returns. Include any property you voluntarily return to a creditor because you couldn't keep up the payments.

6. Assignments and receiverships. An *assignment* is where you legally transfer your right to receive benefits or property to someone else. Examples: assigning a percentage of your wages to a creditor or assigning a portion of a personal injury award to an attorney. A *receivership* is where a court-appointed person, agency or institution receives payments from you and forwards them to your creditor. Include child support payments made directly to a court or social service agency.

7. Gifts. The bankruptcy court and trustee want this information to make sure you haven't improperly unloaded any property before filing for bankruptcy. Be sure to include any loans you have forgiven, as well as loans for which you're charged no interest or interest substantially below market rate. Other gifts include giving a car or prepaid trip to a business associate. If anything you've done for someone has economic value and could conceivably be considered a gift by the bankruptcy trustee or judge, describe it here.

8. Losses. If the loss was for an exempt item, many states let you keep the insurance proceeds up to the limit of the exemption. If the item was not exempt, the trustee is entitled to the proceeds. In either case, list any proceeds you've received or expect to receive.

9. Payments related to debt counseling or bankruptcy. List all payments made by you or by someone else on your behalf to anyone who counseled you about your debts or helped you file your bankruptcy papers. If you paid an improperly high fee to an attorney, bankruptcy petition preparer, debt consultant or debt consolidator, the trustee may try to get some of it back to distribute to your creditors.

10. Other transfers. List all real and personal property that you've sold or used as collateral for a secured debt during the year before you file for bankruptcy. Some examples are selling or junking a car, pledging your house as security for a loan or trading property.

Don't include any gifts you listed in Item 7. Also, don't list property you spent as regular home or business expenses, such as your phone bill, utilities or rent.

13. Setoffs. A setoff is when a creditor uses money in a customer's account to pay a debt owed to the creditor by that customer.

14. Property held for another person. Describe all property you've borrowed from, are storing for or hold in trust for someone. Examples are funds in an irrevocable trust controlled by you and property you hold as executor or administrator of an estate. Don't describe all of your property as being in trust or otherwise belonging to someone else, hoping to escape giving it to the trustee; include only property you truly hold for others.

➡ **Only business debtors must complete questions 19–25.** A business debtor is anyone who operated a profession or business, or who was otherwise self-employed, anytime during the six years before filing for bankruptcy. If you are not a business debtor, fill in "N/A" before question 19 and go to the signature page.

19. Books, records and financial statements.

c. Usually, you, your bookkeeper, accountant, tax attorney, ex-business associate or possibly an ex-mate will have business records. If any are missing, explain. The more the loss of your records was beyond your control, the better off you'll be. Conversely, if you recklessly threw records away, the trustee or bankruptcy court may become suspicious.

d. You may have prepared a financial statement if you applied for a loan or line of credit. If you're self-employed and applied for a personal loan to purchase a car or house, you probably submitted a financial statement as evidence of your ability to repay. Financial statements include:

- balance sheets (compares assets with liabilities)
- profit and loss statements (compares income with expenses)
- financial statements (provides an overall financial description of a business).

20. Inventories. If your business doesn't have an inventory because it's a service business, check "none." If your business does deal in products, but you were primarily the middle person or original manufacturer, put "no inventory required" or "materials purchased for each order as needed." If you have an inventory, fill in the information requested in items "a" and "b."

21. Current partners, officers, directors and shareholders. Check "none" for "a" and "b."

22. Former partners, officers, directors and shareholders. Check "none" for "a" and "b."

23. Withdrawals from a partnership or distributions by a corporation. Check "none."

24. Tax consolidation group. Check "None."

25. Pension funds. Check "None."

[If completed by an individual or individual and spouse]. Sign and date this section. If you're filing jointly, be sure your spouse dates and signs it as well.

[If completed on behalf of a partnership or corporation]. Type "N/A."

Certification and Signature of Non-Attorney Bankruptcy Petition Preparer. If you hire a bankruptcy petition preparer to complete your forms, that person must fill in the information here and sign this form. Otherwise, type "N/A" anywhere in the box.

Be sure to insert the number of continuation sheets, if any.

5. Form 8—Chapter 7 Individual Debtor's Statement of Intention

➡ **This form is for debtors with secured debts.** If you don't have any secured debts, skip to Step 2. Secured debts are defined in Section C5, above.

This form is very important if you owe any secured debts. Bankruptcy's effect on secured debts is different than on other kinds of debts, because a secured debt consists of two parts:

- **your personal liability for the debt.** This is your obligation to pay the debt to the creditor. Bankruptcy wipes out this part of a secured debt, if the debt is dischargeable. Once your personal liability is eliminated, the creditor cannot take any action, including suing you, to collect the debt.

- **the creditor's legal claim, called a lien or security interest.** This gives the creditor the right to take or repossess the property that is collateral for the debt, or force its sale, if you do not pay the debt. The creditor has this right even if the property is exempt, and even if the underlying debt has been discharged in bankruptcy. Bankruptcy, by itself, does not eliminate liens. But sometimes during bankruptcy you can take additional steps to eliminate, or at least reduce, liens on secured property.

Secured Debts and Bankruptcy

Unless you reaffirm your obligation to repay the debt, bankruptcy eliminates personal liability for secured debts, but the creditor's lien remains. Sometimes you can take further steps in bankruptcy to eliminate or reduce a lien.

| Unsecured Debt | Secured Debt | Secured Debt After Bankruptcy |

The Statement of Intention tells your creditors how you plan to deal with your secured debts. You have these choices:

- surrender the property in exchange for cancellation of the lien
- keep an item in one of the ways permitted by the bankruptcy laws, or
- get rid of the creditor's lien in a manner allowed by the bankruptcy laws.

The trustee will go over this form with you at the creditor's meeting. By law, you must carry out your stated intentions within 45 days of the date you file the form—but there are no apparent penalties if you don't.

Step 1: Understand Your Options

Read the chart, **How to Deal With Secured Debts**, on the following pages. The chart covers each of the options listed in the Statement of Intention Form.

Note that although you have several methods to handle your secured debts, this kit gives step-by-step instructions for only the simplest.

If you need help beyond the kit to handle your secured debts, seek it. It could mean the difference between keeping property and losing it altogether. Consult *How to File for Bankruptcy*, by Elias, Renauer, Leonard and Michon (Nolo), or see a lawyer.

Step 2: Complete Statement of Intention Form

Spouses file only one form. If you're filing jointly, use one form for both spouses, even though the form says "Individual Debtor's Statement of Intention."

Court name. Copy this information from Form 1—Voluntary Petition.

In re and **Case No.** Follow the instructions for Schedule A. **Chapter.** Type in "7."

Skip ahead if you have no secured debts. If you don't have any secured creditors, fill in "N/A" (not applicable) anywhere on the form, and skip ahead to the Mailing Matrix.

Section a, Property to Be Surrendered. If you've decided to give up any (or all) property you've pledged as collateral for a secured debt, or the property has already been taken and you don't want to get it back, complete this section.

Description of Property. Identify the collateral, such as "1989 Volvo" or "house at 316 Maiden Lane, Miami Beach, Florida."

Creditor's Name. List on a separate line the name of each secured creditor listed in the first column.

Section b, Property to Be Retained. If you plan to claim property as exempt, redeem property or reaffirm a debt, you'll need help beyond this kit.

Proceed cautiously! If you reaffirm a debt or redeem property, it's not wise to rely on papers a creditor drafts for you—they're unlikely to be to your advantage. (See Nolo's *How to File for Bankruptcy*, by Elias, Renauer, Leonard and Michon.)

If your district lets you retain property by keeping your payments current without reaffirming or redeeming (see **How to Deal With Secured Debts**) and you want to use this method, fill in a description of the property in the first column. In the second column, fill in the creditor's name, followed by the words, "intend to retain property by keeping payments current on contract with creditor." Do not check any of the last three columns. If your district doesn't specifically allow this method but the creditor has informally agreed to let you retain the property by keeping your payments current, complete Section a, Property to Be Surrendered, by following the above instructions.

How to Deal With Secured Debts

Option/What It Is	How to Do It	Important Considerations
Surrender the property You allow the creditor to repossess (take) the item or foreclose on the lien. This completely frees you from the debt—the lien is satisfied by your surrender of the property and your personal liability is discharged by the bankruptcy.	You list the property as surrendered on your Statement of Intention and send a copy of the form to the creditor. It's then up to the creditor to contact you to arrange a time to pick up the property. If the creditor never takes the property, it's yours to keep.	Although this is a quick and easy way to completely rid yourself of a secured debt, the disadvantage is that you lose the property. You should only surrender property that you don't need or would cost too much to keep.
Reaffirm a debt You agree in writing to repay the debt in full. In exchange the creditor agrees that you can keep the property. If you default on your payments, the creditor can repossess the collateral and, depending on state law, can probably sue you for any unpaid balance.	On your Statement of Intention you indicate that the property will be reaffirmed. You and the creditor draw up an agreement that sets out the amount you owe and the terms of the repayment. If possible, you should try to get the creditor to accept less than the full amount you owe as full payment of the debt. It's unwise to reaffirm a debt for more than the property is worth. This kit does not provide samples or instructions. If you want a more detailed discussion and step-by-step instructions, see *How to File for Bankruptcy*, by Elias, Renauer, Leonard and Michon (Nolo).	For some types of property, such as automobiles and houses, reaffirmation may be the only practical way to keep the item. Also, reaffirmation can be a sensible way to keep property worth significantly more than what you owe on it. But beware! Both the creditor's lien on the collateral and your personal liability survive bankruptcy intact—as if you never filed for bankruptcy. You'll still be legally bound to pay the agreed-upon amount even if the property is damaged or destroyed. And because you can't file for Chapter 7 bankruptcy again until six years from the date of your discharge, you'll be stuck with the debt. If you don't pay, the creditor can usually sue you.
Redeem property You pay the creditor the property's current market value, usually in a lump sum. You then own the property free and clear, regardless of how much you owe on it, and all liens are eliminated. You have the right to redeem only tangible personal property (not real estate) that was bought for personal (non-business) use. The property must be either: • exempt, or • abandoned by the trustee. A trustee will abandon property that has little or no nonexempt value beyond the amount of the liens. If property is abandoned, you'll receive notice in the mail.	On your Statement of Intention, you indicate that the property will be redeemed. You and the creditor must agree on the value of the property and draft and sign a redemption agreement. This kit does not provide samples or instructions. If you want a more detailed discussion and step-by-step instructions, see *How to File for Bankruptcy*, by Elias, Renauer, Leonard and Michon (Nolo).	Redemption is a great option if you owe more than the property is worth, because the creditor must accept the current value of the item as payment in full. One downside to redemption is that it generally requires an immediate lump-sum payment of the value of the item; it may be difficult to come up with that much cash on short notice. You can try to get the creditor to accept your redemption payments in installments (and if you do, you'll probably have to pay some interest), but few courts require a creditor to accept installment payments.

How to Deal WIth Secured Debts

Option/What It Is	How to Do It	Important Considerations
Retain property without reaffirming or redeeming Some bankruptcy courts let you keep secured property as long as you remain current on your payments under your contract with the creditor. If you fall behind, the creditor can repossess the property, but your personal liability for the debt is wiped out by the bankruptcy. 　Other courts limit your options for retaining property to those listed on the form. In those districts, if you do not use these methods, the creditor may repossess the property at any time, regardless of whether you are current on your payments.	In those districts that allow it (noted to the right), you indicate on your Statement of Intention that you plan to retain the property by keeping current on your obligations under the contract. Be sure you understand that your obligation may include monthly payments, insurance coverage and more. 　In those districts that do not allow this method of retaining property, you can ask the creditor to informally agree to let you keep the property as long as you keep current on your contractual obligations. On the Statement of Intention, however, you indicate that you are surrendering the property. If you default, the creditor's only recourse is to repossess the property. But the creditor doesn't have to wait for you to default. Because you indicated you are surrendering your property on the Statement of Intention, the creditor can repossess at any time.	Any court not listed below has not ruled on this matter. **Where method is allowed (as of 12/00):**

Where method is allowed (as of 12/00):

Alaska	North Carolina
Arizona	Ohio (Northern District)
Arkansas	Oklahoma
(Western District)	Oregon
California	Pennsylvania (Eastern
Colorado	and Western Districts)
Connecticut	South Carolina
Hawaii	Tennessee
Idaho	(Western District)
Kansas	Utah
Maryland	Vermont
Montana	Virginia
Nevada	Washington
New Mexico	West Virginia
New York	Wyoming

Where method is prohibited (as of 12/00):

Alabama	Massachusetts
Arkansas	Michigan (Western District)
(Eastern District)	Mississippi
Florida	Missouri (Western District)
Georgia	New Hampshire
Illinois	Rhode Island
Indiana	Tennessee (Eastern District)
Louisiana	Texas
Maine	Wisconsin

　In districts that have not ruled on the question, consult a bankruptcy practitioner as to the local custom in your area. But because this is an unsettled and changing area of the law, even if your district is listed above, you may want to consult a bankruptcy practitioner to see if there's been a change.

How to Deal With Secured Debts

Option/What It Is	How to Do It	Important Considerations

Avoid (eliminate) liens on exempt property
 	
You formally ask the bankruptcy court to "avoid"—eliminate or reduce—certain types of liens on your exempt property. How much of a lien is avoided depends on the amount of the lien, value of the property and the exemption amount.
 	
Lien avoidance has several important restrictions:
1. The property must be exempt.
2. You must have owned the property before the lien was created.
3. The lien must be either (definitions are in Section d, above):
  • **a judgment lien** (unless it secures a debt owed a spouse, former spouse or child for alimony or child support), which can be removed from any exempt property, or
  • **a nonpossessory nonpurchase-money security interest**, which can be avoided only on personal household property, health aids professionally prescribed for you or a dependent, and implements, professional books or tools used in a trade.
4. The total of the lien you want to avoid, all other liens on the property and your exemption amount must exceed the market value of the property.
5. If you choose your state exemptions and your state limits or bars you from avoiding liens on exempt property, you cannot avoid a lien on implements, professional books or tools used in a trade that are worth more than $5,000.
	On your Statement of Intention, you indicate that the lien will be avoided. You type and file a document called a "motion." Although it may sound complicated, lien avoidance is a routine procedure that involves just a little time.
	
	This kit does not provide samples or instructions. If you want a more detailed discussion and step-by-step instructions, see *How to File for Bankruptcy*, by Elias, Renauer, Leonard and Michon (Nolo).
		Lien avoidance costs nothing, involves only a moderate amount of paperwork and allows you to keep property without paying anything. It is the best and most powerful tool to get rid of liens that are avoidable.

Signature. Date and sign the form. If you're married and filing jointly, your spouse must also date and sign the form.

Certification and Signature of Non-Attorney Bankruptcy Petition Preparer. If you hire a bankruptcy petition preparer to complete your forms, that person must fill in the information here and sign this form. Otherwise, type "N/A" anywhere in the box.

6. Mailing Matrix

The mailing matrix is a blank page divided into approximately 30 boxes. You type in the names and addresses of your creditors, which you've already listed on the forms you've completed. The trustee photocopies the page to create mailing labels. Some courts don't require a Mailing Matrix, while other courts have their own forms or require a specific type face or spacing. If you need to provide a Matrix, but your court doesn't have its own, you can use the form in this kit. Here's how to fill it out:

Step 1. On a separate piece of paper, make a list of all your creditors, in alphabetical order. You can copy them off Schedules D, E, F and H. Be sure to include cosigners and joint debtors other than your spouse, if you are filing jointly. Include collection agencies or attorneys, if you've been sued. If you're seeking to discharge marital debts you assumed during a divorce, include both your ex-spouse and the creditors.

Step 2. Make enough copies of the Mailing Matrix form to list all of your creditors.

Step 3. In the top left-hand box on the form, enter your name and address. Then enter the names and addresses of each creditor, one per box and in alphabetical order (or in the order required by your local bankruptcy court). Use as many sheets as you need.

F. Filing Your Bankruptcy Forms

You're ready to take the final steps necessary to file for bankruptcy.

1. Check Over Your Papers

Check over your completed forms and fill in any missing information. Make sure that you have done all of the following:

- filled in the Statistical/Administration Information boxes on Form 1—Voluntary Petition
- signed and dated each form where required (your spouse must sign and date too, if you're filing a joint petition)
- indicated the number of continuation pages and attached them to the appropriate forms. Look at the lower left-hand corner of each form and fill in any missing page numbers. Make sure that the first page of each form contains the number of attached continuation sheets, if requested (Schedules B, D, E and F and Form 7—Statement of Financial Affairs)
- completed any forms required by your local bankruptcy court (see Section D), and
- completed all documents fully, and neatly typed or printed the finals.

2. Paying in Installments

If you need time to pay the fee. Skip this section if you can afford to pay the $200 filing fee all at once when you file your bankruptcy papers with the court.

You must pay $45 of the fee when you file your petition. You can pay the remaining $155 filing fee in up to four installments over 120 days with only these restrictions:

- You can't apply for permission to pay in installments if you've already paid an attorney or typing service to help you with your bankruptcy.
- You can't pay anyone for help with your case until you've paid all the installments.

To qualify to pay in installments, complete the Application to Pay Filing Fee in Installments. Here's how.

District, In re and **Case No.** Follow the instructions for Form 1. Include your name and your spouse's name if you're filing jointly.

Chapter. Fill in "7."

Item 1. Enter the amount of the entire filing fee—$200.

Items 2 and 3. You don't add anything here.

Item 4. On the first line, enter the amount you plan to pay when you file your papers. In the next three lines, specify the amounts and dates you propose for each installment payment.

Type "N/A" on the attorney signature line. Then you, and your spouse if you're filing jointly, must sign and date the Application. If you use a bankruptcy petition preparer to type your forms, that person must complete the middle section. Otherwise, type "N/A" in that section.

On the second page of the form, fill in the top of the form just as you did with the first page (name of court, debtor, chapter "7"). Leave the rest blank. The judge will either approve the Application or modify it. The court will notify you of the judge's decision.

3. Copy and File Your Papers

Filing your papers should be simple. Here's how to do it.

Step 1. Make the number of copies required by the court, plus:

- two additional copies of all forms—one set for the clerk to file-stamp and give or send back to you when you file the papers, and one set in the event your papers are lost in the mail (if you plan to file by mail)
- one extra copy of the Statement of Intention for each creditor listed on that form as well as one extra copy for the trustee.

Step 2. Use a standard two-hole punch (copy centers have them) to punch holes into the top/center of all your bankruptcy papers. Don't staple together any forms.

Step 3. Put complete sets of all your bankruptcy forms in the order required by the court (or listed in the court's local rules).

Step 4. Call the court clerk and verify the amount of the fees. If you can pay the fee in full, clip or staple a money order, payable to "U.S. Bankruptcy Court," to your original set of papers. If you want to pay in installments, attach the papers you prepared.

Step 5. Take or mail the original and copies of your papers to the bankruptcy court. In some cases (see Steps 6 and 7, below), you won't file the Statement of Intention until you mail it to the trustees and creditor. If you want the automatic stay to go into effect right away, you'll want to take your papers to the court in person. That way, you can also correct any problems that might arise, such as an overlooked signature or missing pages. If you mail your documents, include a large self-addressed envelope so the clerk can send you a file-stamped set of your papers.

Step 6. In some courts, you may be required to send the Statement of Intention to your creditors. If you must, ask the court clerk the name and address of the trustee assigned to your case. Then have a friend or relative (other than your spouse if you are filing jointly) over the age of 18 mail, by first class, a copy of your Statement of Intention to the bankruptcy trustee and to all the creditors listed on that form. Be sure to keep the original. You are required to do this within 30 days of filing your papers, but should do it sooner.

Step 7. Make sure you have several copies of the Proof of Service by Mail form—a copy is provided in this kit. On one copy, enter the name and complete address of the trustee and all creditors to whom your friend or relative sent your Statement of Intention. If you need more room than the form allows, fill in the words "See Continuation Page" in the space allotted for the names and addresses. Then attach the list to the Proof of Service by Mail form. (See Section E.1 for guidelines on preparing continuation pages.) Have that person sign and date the form.

Step 8. Make copies of the original Statement of Intention and the Proof of Service by Mail your friend or relative signed. Staple the original Proof of Service By Mail to the original Statement of Intention, and send or take the originals to the bankruptcy clerk.

4. Effect of Filing

Once you file your bankruptcy papers, the automatic stay immediately goes into effect. The automatic stay stops any lawsuit filed against you and most actions against your property by a creditor, collection agency or government entity.

Creditors won't know to stop their collection efforts until they receive notice of your bankruptcy filing, which may take several weeks. If you want quicker results, send your own notice (in the form of a letter or copy of the filed petition) to creditors, bill collectors, their attorneys, landlords, sheriffs, social workers and the like.

Here is how the automatic stay affects some common emergencies.

- **Wage garnishments.** Stops garnishments dead in their tracks. Not only will you take home a full salary, but you may be able to discharge the debt in bankruptcy.
- **Utility disconnections.** Prevents disconnections for at least 20 days. After 20 days, a utility company can disconnect service unless you provide adequate assurance that your future bills will be paid, which generally means you'll need to come up with a security deposit. Bankruptcy will probably discharge past due debts for utility service. If your service was disconnected before you file for bankruptcy, the utility company must restore it within 20 days after you file.
- **Foreclosure.** Temporarily stops the proceedings, but the creditor usually successfully petitions the court to remove the stay and is often able to proceed with the house foreclosure.
- **Eviction.** Can buy you a few days or a few weeks, depending on the court. But if the landlord asks the court to lift the stay and let the eviction proceed, which landlords usually do, the court will probably allow it.
- **Enforcement action for child support or alimony.** Will not interrupt your obligation to make current payments. Nor will it stop proceedings to establish paternity, establish or modify a support order or to collect support you owe.
- **Public benefit overpayments.** Prevents agency from collecting overpayment out of your future checks. The overpayment you owe is dischargeable unless the agency convinces the court it resulted from fraud on your part.
- **Loss of driver's license because of liability for damages.** In some states, your driver's license may be suspended until you pay a court judgment for damages resulting from an automobile accident. The automatic stay can prevent this suspension if it hasn't already occurred.

Your property is under the supervision of the bankruptcy court. Don't throw out, give away, sell or otherwise dispose of any property unless and until the bankruptcy trustee says otherwise. You can make day-to-day purchases such as groceries, personal effects and clothing with the income you earn after filing. If you have any questions about this, ask the bankruptcy trustee.

G. Handling Your Case in Court

Shortly after you file for bankruptcy, a trustee appointed by the court reads your bankruptcy forms. The trustee decides, based on your papers, whether you have any nonexempt property that can be sold to raise cash to pay your creditors. The trustee then sends notice of your bankruptcy filing to all the creditors you listed and informs them that the automatic stay is in effect. The notice also tells creditors whether or not they should file claims—that is, request to be paid. If you don't have significant nonexempt assets, they are advised not to file claims. If you have nonexempt assets that can be sold, they are entitled to file claims. The notice gives a date for the meeting of creditors, usually several weeks later. Within 60 days after the meeting, your creditors must file their claims.

1. Attend the Meeting of Creditors

For most people, the creditors' meeting (also called the "341(a) meeting") is brief—no more than five minutes. The trustee and any creditors who show up can ask you questions related to your bankruptcy—that is, about your debts, your property and your financial transactions for the year or two preceding your filing date.

If you're married and you file jointly, both you and your spouse must attend. If you don't show up, you may be fined. Even worse, your case may be dismissed. If you know in advance that you can't attend the scheduled creditors' meeting, contact the court clerk and try to reschedule the meeting.

Some people become anxious at the prospect of attending the creditor's meeting alone. But if you were honest in preparing your bankruptcy papers, you should have no trouble. On the other hand, if you think you've been dishonest with a creditor or the court, see a lawyer before you go to court (preferably, before you file).

The night before the creditors' meeting, review the papers you filed with the bankruptcy court. If you discover mistakes, make careful note of them. You'll probably have to correct your papers after the meeting—an easy process.

Bring to the hearing a copy of every paper you've filed with the bankruptcy court. Also bring copies of documents that describe your debts and property, such as bills, deeds, contracts and licenses. Some courts also require you to bring financial records, such as tax returns and checkbooks.

Your answers to all questions should be both truthful and consistent with your bankruptcy papers. If you discovered any errors in your papers, bring them to the trustee's attention before the trustee begins asking questions. If you don't admit mistakes voluntarily, and they're discovered during questioning, the trustee may suspect that you're hiding something. If you discover while you're being questioned that your papers were in error, give the correct answer in your testimony and immediately point out to the trustee that your papers are incorrect and need to be amended.

The trustee is likely to ask questions about nonexempt property, such as anticipated tax refunds, any possible right that you have to sue someone, a valuable car or recent large payments to creditors or relatives. These items could produce cash for your creditors.

The trustee will also question you about your familiarity with Chapter 7 bankruptcy, including:

- the consequences of filing, including the effect on your credit
- the possibility of filing a different type of bankruptcy (see **Other Bankruptcy Options** in Section E2)
- the effect of receiving a discharge of your debts, and
- the effect of reaffirming any debts.

Creditors may ask you questions about your financial situation. Occasionally, creditors use the meeting as a forum to intimidate you. For example, a credit card company may try to show that you incurred a debt without intending to pay it and threaten to challenge your entire bankruptcy case on the basis of fraud, unless you agree to reaffirm the debt.

2. Deal With Property

After the meeting of creditors, the trustee is entitled to collect all of your nonexempt property and have it sold to pay off your creditors. The trustee will most likely "abandon"— that is, not bother with—any nonexempt property unlikely to yield a profit. For example, she'll probably abandon an old typewriter and stereo system, even if they aren't exempt.

The trustee may be willing to let you keep nonexempt property if you volunteer to trade exempt property of equal value. If you really want to keep certain nonexempt items and can come up with some cash, the trustee will usually be happy to accept cash for the item. But bear in mind that if you suddenly have an enormous amount of cash on hand, the trustee may want to reappraise your bankruptcy estate.

Secured property should be dealt with in the manner set out in your Statement of Intention. (See Section E5.) Remember, the law says you must carry out your intentions within 45 days of the date you filed the Statement. If you're surrendering property, it's up to the creditor to arrange to pick it up.

3. Attend the Discharge Hearing, If Required

Most debtors never have to return to the bankruptcy court after the creditors' meeting. In rare situations, you may have to attend a brief court hearing, called a discharge hearing. At the hearing, the judge explains the effects of discharging (eliminating) your debts in bankruptcy and lectures you about staying clear of debt. Most judges require discharge hearings only when a person without a lawyer agrees to reaffirm a debt. In such a case, the judge must approve the agreement.

Shortly after the hearing—or instead of it—you'll receive a final discharge notice in the mail and your bankruptcy will be over. (See Section H.)

4. Special Situations

While your bankruptcy case is open, some of the following issues may arise.

a. Amending Your Bankruptcy Papers

If you made a mistake on papers you've filed and haven't yet received your discharge, you can easily correct the problem. (If you've already received your discharge, see Section

H.) If your mistake means that notice of your bankruptcy filing must be sent to additional creditors (for instance, you inadvertently left off a creditor), you'll have to pay a small fee. If your mistake doesn't require new notice (for example, you add information about an income tax refund you expect to receive soon), there's no additional fee.

If you amend your schedules to add creditors before the meeting of creditors, you'll usually be required to provide the newly listed creditors with notice of the meeting as well as with notice of your amendment.

If you become aware of debts or property that you should have included in your papers, amending your papers will avoid any suspicion that you're trying to conceal things from the trustee. If you don't amend your papers after discovering this kind of information, your bankruptcy petition may be dismissed or one or more of your debts not discharged.

To make an amendment, take these steps:

Step 1. Type an Amendment Cover Sheet if no local form is required (a blank copy is included with this kit). Otherwise, use the local form. Then make copies of all forms affected by your amendment.

Step 2. Review the information you received from the court or ask the court clerk whether you must re-type the whole form to make the correction, or if you can just type the new information on another blank form. If you can't find the answer, ask a local bankruptcy lawyer or a non-attorney bankruptcy petition preparer. If it's acceptable to just type the new information, precede the information you're typing with the appropriate description:

  • ADD:
  • CHANGE:
  • DELETE:

At the bottom of the form, type "AMENDED" in capital letters.

Step 3. If your amendment involves adding a creditor, follow this step—otherwise, go on to Step 4.

If the creditors' meeting hasn't yet been held, include with the amended papers you are preparing a copy of the Notice of the Meeting of Creditors you received from the court.

If the meeting of creditors occurred before you file your amendment, the court is likely to schedule another one.

Step 4. Call or visit the court and ask what order the papers must be in and how many copies it needs. Then make the needed number of copies, plus one copy for yourself, one for the trustee and one for any creditor you must notify.

Step 5. Have a friend or relative mail, first class, a copy of your amended papers to the bankruptcy trustee and to any creditor affected by your amendment.

Step 6. Complete a Proof of Service by Mail. Enter the name and complete address of every new creditor who was sent copies of your amended papers. Also enter the name and address of the bankruptcy trustee. Then have the person who mailed the amended papers sign and date the Proof of Service by Mail. (See Section F3, for guidelines on preparing a Proof of Service by Mail.)

Step 7. Mail or take the original amendment and Proof of Service by Mail and copies to the bankruptcy court. Enclose or take a money order for the filing fee, if required.

b. Filing a Change of Address

If you move while your bankruptcy case is still open, you must give the court, the trustee and your creditors your new address. Here's how:

Step 1. Fill in the self-explanatory Notice of Change of Address form. (A blank form is included with this kit.)

Step 2. Make the required number of copies and have a friend or relative mail a copy of the Notice of Change of Address to the trustee and to each creditor listed in Schedules D, E and F (or use the list of creditors on your Mailing Matrix, if you prepared one).

Step 3. Have the friend or relative complete and sign a Proof of Service by Mail form, listing the bankruptcy trustee and the names and addresses of all creditors the Notice was mailed to.

Step 4. File the original Notice of Change of Address and original Proof of Service by Mail with the bankruptcy court.

c. Handling Problems With Your Bankruptcy

If you want to fight any problems that crop up during your bankruptcy, you'll need to see a lawyer. Here are some of the more common problems:

- **A creditor asks the court to lift the automatic stay.** The automatic stay lasts for the length of your bankruptcy case unless the court lifts the stay for a particular creditor. To get the stay lifted, a creditor must make the request in writing, in a document called a motion. The court will schedule a hearing, and you'll be notified.
- **The trustee or creditors dispute claimed exemptions.** After the meeting of creditors, the trustee and creditors have 30 days to object to the exemptions you claimed. Written objections must be filed with the bankruptcy court, and you and the trustee must be given copies. Unless you wish to contest the objections, you don't have to respond or even show up at the scheduled hearing unless required by local rules or a court order.
- **A creditor objects to the discharge of a debt.** To object formally to the discharge of a debt, a creditor must file a written complaint and have copies served on you and the trustee. To defend against the objection, you'll need to file a written response and be prepared to argue your case in a court hearing. If the debt isn't large enough to justify an attorney's fee, you're probably better off not responding.

H. Life After Bankruptcy

Your final discharge is set out in a court order, which merely says all debts that are legally dischargeable have been discharged. The discharge order does not, however, actually list your discharged debts. So how do you know what debts have been discharged and which debts must still be paid? Here's the general rule: All debts you listed in your bankruptcy papers are discharged unless a creditor successfully objected to the discharge of a particular debt in the bankruptcy court, or the debt falls under the following categories:

- income taxes that became due within the past three years
- child support and alimony
- student loans, unless the court ruled it would cause you undue hardship to repay them
- fines and penalties
- court fees
- debts related to intoxicated driving
- condominium or cooperative association dues
- debts not discharged in a previous bankruptcy because of fraud or misfeasance.

If creditors go after discharged debts. Creditors sometimes incorrectly claim that the debts you owe them cannot be wiped out in bankruptcy. In fact, most leases contain unenforceable clauses stating that if you're unable to complete the lease period, you can't eliminate the balance of the debt in bankruptcy. Nonsense. Be confident that the only debts you can't discharge in bankruptcy are the ones the Bankruptcy Code lists as nondischargeable (see Section C5). Don't let your creditors intimidate you into thinking otherwise.

After you receive your final discharge and your case is closed, you can enjoy the fresh start that bankruptcy offers. If you are worried that you'll have trouble getting or keeping a job or finding a place to live, or will suffer other discrimination, be aware that there are laws against discrimination by private employers and all government entities.

Although a bankruptcy discharge remains on your credit record for ten years, in a few years you can probably rebuild your credit to the point that you won't be turned down for a major credit card or loan. Most major creditors look for steady employment and a history, since bankruptcy, of making and paying for purchases on consumer credit. And many creditors disregard bankruptcy after only three years. For more information on rebuilding your credit, see *Credit Repair*, by Robin Leonard and Deanne Loonin (Nolo).

If You Left Off a Debt

Debts you didn't list in your bankruptcy papers are not discharged unless the creditor actually knew you filed for bankruptcy and had an opportunity to file a claim with the court or object to the discharge. If, after your bankruptcy is closed, you discover that you left a creditor off your papers, with a lawyer's help you may be able to reopen your bankruptcy case, amend your papers and discharge the debt.

1. When to Notify the Trustee After Discharge

After your discharge, it's your legal responsibility to notify the bankruptcy trustee if:

- you omitted nonexempt property from your bankruptcy papers, or
- you receive or become entitled to receive, within 180 days of filing for bankruptcy, an inheritance, property from a divorce settlement, or proceeds of a life insurance policy or death benefit plan.

You can simply notify the trustee by letter.

 Beware if any of the new property or newly discovered property is valuable and nonexempt. The trustee may reopen your case, take the property and have it sold to pay your creditors. If either your bankruptcy discharge or valuable property is at stake, find a bankruptcy lawyer to defend your interests in court. If, however, the amount at stake is something you can stand to lose, you'll probably be better off simply consenting to what the trustee wants.

■

Appendix 1: State and Federal Exemption Tables

Using the Exemption Tables

Every state lets people who file for bankruptcy keep certain property, called exemptions. Ch. 2, *Your Property and Bankruptcy*, Section B6, discusses exemptions in detail.

1. What This Appendix Contains

- lists of each state's exemptions
- list of the federal bankruptcy exemptions (available as a choice in 14 states and the District of Columbia)
- list of the federal non-bankruptcy exemptions (available as additional exemptions when the state exemptions are chosen), and
- glossary defining exemption terms.

Each list is divided into three columns. Column 1 lists the major exemption categories: homestead, insurance, miscellaneous, pensions, personal property, public benefits, tools of the trade, wages and wild card. (These categories differ on the federal non-bankruptcy exemptions chart.)

Column 2 gives the specific property that falls into each large category with noted limitations.

For example, the federal bankruptcy exemptions allow married couples filing jointly to each claim a full set of exemptions. This is called "doubling." Many state exemption systems do not allow doubling or do not allow doubling for certain types of property, such as the homestead exemption (which exempts equity in your residence). In some states, the legislature has expressly allowed or prohibited doubling. In others, the courts have allowed or prohibited doubling. In still others, neither the courts nor the legislature has addressed the issue. If that is the case, doubling is probably allowed. In Column 2, we've noted whether a court or state legislature has expressly allowed or prohibited doubling. If the chart doesn't say, it is probably safe to double. However, keep in mind that this area of the law changes rapidly—legislation or court decisions regarding doubling issued after the publication date of this book will not be reflected in the chart.

Column 3 lists the applicable law, which must be included on Schedule C.

2. Choosing Between State and Federal Exemptions

Each state chart indicates whether the federal exemptions are available for that state. The list of federal exemptions follows Wyoming.

3. Houses and Pensions

With pensions, some states exempt only the money building up in the pension fund, and a few exempt only payments actually being received. Most exempt both. If the pension listing doesn't indicate otherwise, it means the state exempts both.

4. Wages, Benefits and Other Payments

Many states exempt insurance proceeds, pension payments, alimony and child support payments, public benefits or wages. This means that payments you received before filing are exempt if you haven't mixed them with other money or, if you have mixed them, you can trace the exempt portion back to its source.

If, when you file for bankruptcy, you're entitled to receive an exempt payment but haven't yet received it, you can exempt the payment when it comes in by amending Schedules B (personal property you own or possess) and C (property you claim as exempt).

Alabama

Federal Bankruptcy Exemptions not available. All law references are to Alabama Code.

ASSET	EXEMPTION	LAW
homestead	Real property or mobile home to $5,000; property cannot exceed 160 acres (husband & wife may double)	6-10-2
	Must record homestead declaration before attempted sale of home	6-10-20
insurance	Annuity proceeds or avails to $250 per month	27-14-32
	Disability proceeds or avails to an average of $250 per month	27-14-31
	Fraternal benefit society benefits	27-34-27
	Life insurance proceeds or avails	6-10-8; 27-14-29
	Life insurance proceeds or avails if clause prohibits proceeds from being used to pay beneficiary's creditors	27-15-26
	Mutual aid association benefits	27-30-25
miscellaneous	Property of business partnership	10-8-72(b)(3)
pensions	IRAs and other retirement accounts	19-3-1
	Judges (only payments being received)	12-18-10(a), (b)
	Law enforcement officers	36-21-77
	State employees	36-27-28
	Teachers	16-25-23
personal property	Books (husband and wife may double)	6-10-6
	Burial place	6-10-5
	Church pew	6-10-5
	Clothing (husband and wife may double)	6-10-6
	Family portraits or pictures	6-10-6
public benefits	Aid to blind, aged, disabled, public assistance	38-4-8
	Coal miners' pneumoconiosis benefits	25-5-179
	Crime victims' compensation	15-23-15(e)
	General public assistance	38-4-8
	Southeast Asian War POWs' benefits	31-7-2
	Unemployment compensation	25-4-140
	Workers' compensation	25-5-86(b)
tools of trade	Arms, uniforms, equipment that state military personnel are required to keep	31-2-78
wages	75% of earned but unpaid wages; bankruptcy judge may authorize more for low-income debtors	6-10-7
wild card	$3,000 of any personal property, except wages (husband and wife may double)	6-10-6

Alaska

Alaska law states that only the items found in Alaska Statutes §§ 9.38.010, 9.38.015(a), 9.38.017, 9.38.020, 9.38.025 and 9.38.030 may be exempted in bankruptcy. In *In re McNutt*, 87 B.R. 84 (9th Cir. 1988), however, an Alaskan debtor used the federal bankruptcy exemptions. All law references are to Alaska Statutes.

ASSET	EXEMPTION	LAW
homestead	$250,000 (joint owners may each claim a portion, but total can't exceed $250,000)	09.38.010(a)
insurance	Disability benefits	09.38.015(b), 09.38.030(e)(1),(5)
	Fraternal benefit society benefits	21.84.240
	Life insurance or annuity contract[s], total aggregate cash surrender value to $250,000	09.38.017, 09.38.025
	Life insurance proceeds payable to beneficiary	09.38.025(c)
	Medical, surgical or hospital benefits	09.38.015(a)(3)
miscellaneous	Alimony, to extent wages exempt	09.38.030(e)(2)
	Child support payments made by collection agency	09.38.015(b)
	Liquor licenses	09.38.015(a)(7)
	Permits for limited entry into Alaska Fisheries	09.38.015(a)(8)
	Property of business partnership	09.38.100(b)
pensions	Elected public officers (only benefits building up)	09.38.015(b)
	ERISA-qualified benefits deposited more than 120 days before filing bankruptcy	09.38.017
	Judicial employees (only benefits building up)	09.38.015(b)
	Public employees (only benefits building up)	09.38.015(b); 39.35.505
	Roth & traditional IRAs, medical savings accounts	09.38.010(e)(3)
	Teachers (only benefits building up)	09.38.015(b)
	Other pensions, to extent wages exempt (only payments being received)	09.38.030(e)(5)
personal property	Books, musical instruments, clothing, family portraits, household goods & heirlooms to $3,600 total	09.38.020(a)
	Building materials	34.35.105
	Burial plot	09.38.015(a)(1)
	Cash or other liquid assets to $8,075	09.38.020(f)
	Deposit in apartment or condo owners association	09.38.010(e)
	Health aids	09.38.015(a)(2)
	Jewelry to $1,200	09.38.020(b)
	Motor vehicle to $3,360; vehicle's market value can't exceed $24,000	09.38.020(e)
	Personal injury recoveries, to extent wages exempt	09.38.030(e)(3)
	Pets to $1,200	09.38.020(d)
	Proceeds for lost, damaged or destroyed exempt property	09.38.060
	Tuition credits under an advance college tuition payment contract	09.38.015(a)(9)
	Wrongful death recoveries, to extent wages exempt	09.38.030(e)(3)
public benefits	Adult assistance to elderly, blind, disabled	47.25.550
	Alaska longevity bonus	09.38.015(a)(5)
	Crime victims' compensation	09.38.015(a)(4)
	Federally exempt public benefits paid or due	09.38.015(a)(6)
	General relief assistance	47.25.210
	Public assistance	47.25.395
	45% of permanent fund dividends	43.23.065
	Unemployment compensation	09.38.015(b); 23.20.405
	Workers' compensation	23.30.160
tools of trade	Implements, books & tools of trade to $3,360	09.38.020(c)
wages	Weekly net earnings to $420; for sole wage earner in a household, $660; if you don't receive weekly, or semi-monthly pay, can claim $1,680 in cash or liquid assets paid any month; for sole wage earner in household, $2,640	9.38.030(a),(b), 9.38.050(b)
wild card	None	

Arizona

Federal Bankruptcy Exemptions not available. All law references are to Arizona Revised Statutes unless otherwise noted. **Note:** Doubling is permitted for noted exemptions by Arizona Revised Statutes § 33-1121.01.

ASSET	EXEMPTION	LAW
homestead	Real property, an apartment or mobile home you occupy to $100,000; sale proceeds exempt 18 months after sale or until new home purchased, whichever occurs first (husband & wife may not double)	33-1101(A)
	Must record homestead declaration before attempted sale of home	33-1102
insurance	Fraternal benefit society benefits	20-881
	Group life insurance policy or proceeds	20-1132
	Health, accident or disability benefits	33-1126(A)(4)
	Life insurance cash value or proceeds to $25,000 total (husband & wife may double)	20-1131(D) 33-1126(A)(6)
	Life insurance proceeds to $20,000 if beneficiary is spouse or child	33-1126(A)(1)
miscellaneous	Alimony, child support needed for support	33-1126(A)(3)
	Minor child's earnings, unless debt is for child	33-1126(A)(2)
	Property of business partnership	29-225(B)
pensions *also see wages*	Board of regents members	15-1628(I)
	District employees	48-227
	ERISA-qualified benefits deposited more than 120 days before filing bankruptcy	33-1126(C)
	IRAs	*In re Herrscher,* 121 B.R. 29 (D. Ariz. 1990)
	Firefighters	9-968
	Police officers	9-931
	Public safety personnel	38-850(C)
	Rangers	41-955
	State employees	38-792
personal property *husband & wife may double all personal property exemptions*	2 beds & bedding; 1 living room chair per person; 1 dresser, table, lamp; kitchen table; dining room table & 4 chairs (1 more per additional person); living room carpet or rug; couch; 3 lamps; 3 coffee or end tables; pictures, paintings, personal drawings, family portraits; refrigerator, stove, washer, dryer, vacuum cleaner; TV, radio, stereo, alarm clock to $4,000 total	33-1123
	Bank deposit to $150 in one account	33-1126(A)(8)
	Bible; bicycle; sewing machine; typewriter; burial plot; rifle, pistol or shotgun to $500 total	33-1125
	Books to $250; clothing to $500; wedding & engagement rings to $1,000; watch to $100; pets, horses, milk cows & poultry to $500; musical instruments to $250	33-1125
	Food & fuel to last 6 months	33-1124
	Funeral deposits	32-1391.04
	Health aids	33-1125
	Motor vehicle to $1,500 ($4,000, if disabled)	33-1125(8)
	Prepaid rent or security deposit to lesser of $1,000 or 1 ½ times rent, in lieu of homestead	33-1126(D)
	Proceeds for sold or damaged exempt property	33-1126(A)(5),(7)
public benefits	Unemployment compensation	23-783(A)
	Welfare benefits	46-208
	Workers' compensation	23-1068(B)
tools of trade	Arms, uniforms & accoutrements profession or office requires by law	33-1130(3)
	Farm machinery, utensils, seed, instruments of husbandry, feed, grain & animals to $2,500 total (husband & wife may double)	33-1130(2)
	Library & teaching aids of teacher	33-1127
	Tools, equipment, instruments & books to $2,500	33-1130(1)
wages	Minimum 75% of earned but unpaid wages, pension payments; bankruptcy judge may authorize more for low-income debtors	33-1131
wild card	None	

Arkansas

Federal Bankruptcy Exemptions available. All law references are to Arkansas Code Annotated unless otherwise noted.

ASSET	EXEMPTION	LAW
homestead *choose option 1 or 2, not both*	1. For married person or head of family: unlimited exemption on real or personal property to ¼ acre in city, town, or village, or 80 acres elsewhere, used as residence; if property is between ¼ -1 acre in city, town or village, or 80-160 acres elsewhere, additional limit is $2,500; homestead may not exceed 1 acre in city, town or village, or 160 acres elsewhere (husband & wife may not double)	Constitution 9-3, 9-4, 9-5; 16-66-210, 16-66-218(b)(3),(4) *In re Stevens,* 829 F. 2d 693 (8th Cir. 1987)
	2. Real or personal property used as residence to $800 if single; $1,250 if married	16-66-218(a)(1)
insurance	Annuity contract	23-79-134
	Disability benefits	23-79-133
	Fraternal benefit society benefits	23-74-403
	Group life insurance	23-79-132
	Life, health, accident or disability cash value or proceeds paid or due to $500	16-66-209; Constitution 9-1, 9-2 *In re Holt,* 97 B.R. 997 (W.D. Ark. 1988)
	Life insurance proceeds if clause prohibits proceeds from being used to pay beneficiary's creditors	23-79-131
	Life insurance proceeds or avails if beneficiary isn't the insured	23-79-131
	Mutual assessment life or disability benefits to $1,000	23-72-114
	Stipulated insurance premiums	23-71-112
miscellaneous	Property of business partnership	4-42-502
pensions	Disabled firefighters	24-11-814
	Disabled police officers	24-11-417
	Firefighters	24-10-616
	IRA deposits to $20,000 if deposited over 1 year before filing for bankruptcy	16-66-218(b)(16)
	Police officers	24-10-616
	School employees	24-7-715
	State police officers	24-6-202, 24-6-205, 24-6-223
personal property	Burial plot to 5 acres, if choosing Federal homestead exemption (option 2)	16-66-207, 16-66-218(a)(1)
	Clothing	Constitution 9-1, 9-2
	Motor vehicle to $1,200	16-66-218(a)(2)
	Wedding rings	16-66-219
public benefits	Crime victims' compensation	16-90-716(e)
	Unemployment compensation	11-10-109
	Welfare assistance grants	20-76-430
	Workers' compensation	11-9-110
tools of trade	Implements, books & tools of trade to $750	16-66-218(a)(4)
wages	Earned but unpaid wages due for 60 days; in no event under $25 per week	16-66-208, 16-66-218(b)(6)
wild card	$500 of any personal property if married or head of family; $200 if not married	Constitution 9-1, 9-2; 16-66-218(b)(1),(2)

California—System 1

Federal Bankruptcy Exemptions not available. California has two systems; you must select one or the other. All law references are to California Code of Civil Procedure unless otherwise noted.

ASSET	EXEMPTION	LAW
homestead	Real or personal property you occupy including mobile home, boat, stock cooperative, community apartment, planned development or condo to $50,000 if single & not disabled; $75,000 for families if no other member has a homestead (if only one spouse files, may exempt one-half of amount if home held as community property and all of amount if home held as tenants in common); $125,000 if 65 or older, or physically or mentally disabled; $125,000 if 55 or older, single & earn under $15,000 or married & earn under $20,000 & creditors seek to force the sale of your home; sale proceeds received exempt for 6 months after (husband & wife may not double)	704.710, 704.720, 704.730 *In re McFall*, 112 B.R. 336 (9th Cir. B.A.P. 1990)
	May file homestead declaration	704.920
insurance	Disability or health benefits	704.130
	Fidelity bonds	Labor 404
	Fraternal unemployment benefits	704.120
	Homeowners' insurance proceeds for 6 months after received, to homestead exemption amount	704.720(b)
	Life insurance proceeds if clause prohibits proceeds from being used to pay beneficiary's creditors	Ins. 10132, Ins. 10170, Ins. 10171
	Matured life insurance benefits needed for support	704.100(c)
	Unmatured life insurance policy loan value to $8,000 (husband & wife may double)	704.100(b)
miscellaneous	Business or professional licenses	695.060
	Inmates' trust funds to $1,000 (husband and wife may not double)	704.090
	Property of business partnership	Corp. 16501-04
pensions	County employees	Gov't 31452
	County firefighters	Gov't 32210
	County peace officers	Gov't 31913
	Private retirement benefits, including IRAs & Keoghs	704.115
	Public employees	Gov't 21201
	Public retirement benefits	704.110
personal property	Appliances, furnishings, clothing & food	704.020
	Bank deposits from Social Security Administration to $2,000 ($3,000 for husband and wife)	704.080
	Building materials to repair or improve home to $2,000 (husband and wife may not double)	704.030
	Burial plot	704.200
	Health aids	704.050
	Homeowners' Association Assessments	Civil 1366(c)
	Jewelry, heirlooms & art to $5,000 total (husband and wife may not double)	704.040
	Motor vehicles to $1,900, or $1,900 in auto insurance for loss or damages (husband and wife may not double)	704.010
	Personal injury & wrongful death causes of action	704.140(a), 704.150(a)
	Personal injury & wrongful death recoveries needed for support; if receiving installments, at least 75%	704.140(b), (c),(d), 704.150(b), (c)

ASSET	EXEMPTION	LAW
public benefits	Aid to blind, aged, disabled, public assistance	704.170
	Financial aid to students	704.190
	Relocation benefits	704.180
	Unemployment benefits	704.120
	Union benefits due to labor dispute	704.120(b)(5)
	Workers' compensation	704.160
tools of trade	Tools, implements, materials, instruments, uniforms, books, furnishings & equipment to $5,000 total ($10,000 total if used by both spouses in same occupation)	704.060
	Commercial vehicle (Vehicle Code § 260) to $4,000 ($8,000 total if used by both spouses in same occupation)	704.060
wages	Minimum 75% of wages	704.070
	Public employees vacation credits; if receiving installments, at least 75%	704.113
wild card	None	

California—System 2

Federal Bankruptcy Exemptions not available. All law references are to California Code of Civil Procedure unless otherwise noted.

Note: Married couples may not double any exemptions (*In re Talmadge*, 832 F.2d 1120 (9th Cir. 1987); *In re Baldwin*, 70 B.R. 612 (9th Cir. B.A.P. 1987).

ASSET	EXEMPTION	LAW
homestead	Real or personal property, including co-op, used as residence to $15,000; unused portion of homestead may be applied to any property	703.140 (b)(1)
insurance	Disability benefits	703.140 (b)(10)(C)
	Life insurance proceeds needed for support of family	703.140 (b)(11)(C)
	Unmatured life insurance contract accrued avails to $8,000	703.140 (b)(8)
	Unmatured life insurance policy other than credit	703.140 (b)(7)
miscellaneous	Alimony, child support needed for support	703.140 (b)(10)(D)
pensions	ERISA-qualified benefits needed for support	703.140 (b)(10)(E)
personal property	Animals, crops, appliances, furnishings, household goods, books, musical instruments & clothing to $400 per item	703.140 (b)(3)
	Burial plot to $15,000, in lieu of homestead	703.140 (b)(1)
	Health aids	703.140 (b)(9)
	Jewelry to $1,000	703.140 (b)(4)
	Motor vehicle to $2,400	703.140 (b)(2)
	Personal injury recoveries to $15,000 (not to include pain & suffering; pecuniary loss)	703.140(b)(11)(D),(E)
	Wrongful death recoveries needed for support	703.140 (b)(11)(B)
public benefits	Crime victims' compensation	703.140 (b)(11)(A)
	Public assistance	703.140 (b)(10)(A)
	Social Security	703.140 (b)(10)(A)
	Unemployment compensation	703.140 (b)(10)(A)
	Veterans' benefits	703.140 (b)(10)(B)
tools of trade	Implements, books & tools of trade to $1,500	703.140 (b)(6)
wages	None	
wild card	$800 of any property	703.140 (b)(5)
	Unused portion of homestead or burial exemption, of any property	703.140 (b)(5)

Colorado

Federal Bankruptcy Exemptions not available. All law references are to Colorado Revised Statutes.

ASSET	EXEMPTION	LAW
homestead	Real property, mobile home or manufactured home (mobile or manufactured home if loan incurred after 1/1/83) you occupy to $30,000; sale proceeds exempt 1 year after received (husband & wife may double)	38-41-201, 38-41-201.6, 38-41-203, 38-41-207 *In re Pastrana*, 216 B.R. 948 (Colo. 1998)
	Spouse or child of deceased owner may claim homestead exemption	38-41-204
	House trailer or coach used as residence to $3,500	13-54-102(1)(o)(I)
	Mobile home used as residence to $6,000	13-54-102(1)(o)(II)
insurance	Disability benefits to $200 per month; if receive lump sum, entire amount exempt	10-8-114
	Fraternal benefit society benefits	10-14-122
	Group life insurance policy or proceeds	10-7-205
	Homeowners' insurance proceeds for 1 year after received, to homestead exemption amount	38-41-209
	Life insurance avails to $25,000	13-54-102(1)(l)
	Life insurance proceeds if clause prohibits proceeds from being used to pay beneficiary's creditors	10-7-106
miscellaneous	Child support	13-54-102.5
	Property of business partnership	7-60-125
pensions *see also wages*	ERISA-qualified benefits, including IRAs	13-54-102(1)(s)
	Firefighters	31-30-412, 518
	Police officers	31-30-313,31-30-616
	Public employees	24-51-212
	Teachers	22-64-120
	Veterans	13-54-102(1)(h)
personal property	1 burial plot per person and dependent	13-54102(1)(d)
	Clothing to $1,500	13-54-102(1)(a)
	Food & fuel to $600	13-54-102(1)(f)
	Health aids	13-54-102(1)(p)
	Household goods to $3,000	13-54-102(1)(e)
	Jewelry & articles of adornment to $1,000	13-54-102(1)(b)
	Motor vehicles or bicycles used for work to $3,000; to $6,000 if used by a debtor or by a dependent who is disabled or 65 or over	13-54-102(j)(I), (II)
	Personal injury recoveries	13-54-102(1)(n)
	Family pictures & books to $1,500	13-54-102(1)(c)
	Proceeds for damaged exempt property	13-54-102(1)(m)
	Security deposits	13-54-102(1)(r)
public benefits	Aid to blind, aged, disabled, public assistance	26-2-131
	Crime victims' compensation	13-54-102(1)(q); 24-4.1-114
	Unemployment compensation	8-80-103
	Veterans' benefits for veteran, spouse or child if veteran served in war	13-54-102(1)(h)
	Workers' compensation	8-42-124
tools of trade	Livestock or other animals, machinery, tools, equipment & seed of person engaged in agriculture, to $25,000 total	13-54-102(1)(g)
	Professional's library to $3,000 (if not claimed under other tools of trade exemption)	13-54-102(1)(k)
	Stock in trade, supplies, fixtures, tools, machines, electronics, equipment, books & other business materials, to $10,000 total	13-54-102(1)(i)
wages	Minimum 75% of earned but unpaid wages, pension payments	13-54-104
wild card	None	

Connecticut

Federal Bankruptcy Exemptions available. All law references are to Connecticut General Statutes Annotated.

ASSET	EXEMPTION	LAW
homestead	Real property, including mobile or manufactured home, to $75,000 (husband & wife may double)	52-352b
insurance	Disability benefits paid by association for its members	52-352b(p)
	Fraternal benefit society benefits	38a-637
	Health or disability benefits	52-352b(e)
	Life insurance proceeds if clause prohibits proceeds from being used to pay beneficiary's creditors	38a-454
	Life insurance proceeds or avails	38a-453
	Unmatured life insurance policy loan value to $4,000	52-352b(s)
miscellaneous	Alimony, to extent wages exempt	52-352b(n)
	Child support	52-352b(h)
	Farm partnership animals and livestock feed reasonably required to run farm where at least 50% of partners are members of same family	52-352d
	Property of business partnership	34-63
pensions	ERISA-qualified benefits, including IRAs and Keoghs, to extent wages exempt	52-321a 52-352b(m)
	Medical savings account	52-321(a)
	Municipal employees	7-446
	Probate judges & employees	45-29o
	State employees	5-171, 5-192w
	Teachers	10-183q
personal property	Appliances, food, clothing, furniture, bedding	52-352b(a)
	Burial plot	52-352b(c)
	Health aids needed	52-352b(f)
	Motor vehicle to $1,500	52-352b(j)
	Proceeds for damaged exempt property	52-352b(q)
	Residential utility & security deposits for 1 residence	52-352b(l)
	Wedding & engagement rings	52-352b(k)
public benefits	Aid to blind, aged, disabled, public assistance	52-352b(d)
	Crime victims' compensation	52-352b(o); 54-213
	Social Security	52-352b(g)
	Unemployment compensation	31-272(c); 52-352b(g)
	Veterans' benefits	52-352b(g)
	Vietnam veterans' death benefits	27-140i
	Wages from earnings incentive program	52-352b(d)
	Workers' compensation	52-352b(g)
tools of trade	Arms, military equipment, uniforms, musical instruments of military personnel	52-352b(i)
	Tools, books, instruments & farm animals needed	52-352b(b)
wages	Minimum 75% of earned but unpaid wages	52-361a(f)
wild card	$1,000 of any property	52-352b(r)

Delaware

Federal Bankruptcy Exemptions not available. All law references are to Delaware Code Annotated unless otherwise noted.

Note: A single person may exempt no more than $5,000 total in all exemptions; a husband & wife may exempt no more than $10,000 total (10-4914).

ASSET	EXEMPTION	LAW
homestead	None, however, property held as tenancy by the entirety may be exempt against debts owed by only one spouse	*In re Hovatter*, 25 B.R. 123 (D. Del. 1982)
insurance	Annuity contract proceeds to $350 per month	18-2728
	Fraternal benefit society benefits	18-6118
	Group life insurance policy or proceeds	18-2727
	Health or disability benefits	18-2726
	Life insurance proceeds if clause prohibits proceeds from being used to pay beneficiary's creditors	18-2729
	Life insurance proceeds or avails	18-2725
miscellaneous	Property of business partnership	6-1525
pensions	IRAs	*In re Yuhas*, 104 F.3d 612 (3rd Cir. 1997)
	Kent County employees	9-4316
	Police officers	11-8803
	State employees	29-5503
	Volunteer firefighters	16-6653
personal property	Bible, books & family pictures	10-4902(a)
	Burial plot	10-4902(a)
	Church pew or any seat in public place of worship	10-4902(a)
	Clothing, includes jewelry	10-4902(a)
	Pianos and leased organs	10-4902(d)
	Sewing machines	10-4902(c)
public benefits	Aid to blind	31-2309
	Aid to aged, disabled, general assistance	31-513
	Unemployment compensation	19-3374
	Workers' compensation	19-2355
tools of trade	Tools, implements & fixtures to $75 in New Castle & Sussex Counties; to $50 in Kent County	10-4902(b)
wages	85% of earned but unpaid wages	10-4913
wild card	$500 of any personal property, except tools of trade, if head of family	10-4903

District of Columbia

Federal Bankruptcy Exemptions available. All law references are to District of Columbia Code unless otherwise noted.

ASSET	EXEMPTION	LAW
homestead	None, however, property held as tenancy by the entirety may be exempt against debts owed by only one spouse	*Estate of Wall,* 440 F.2d 215 (D.C. Cir. 1971)
insurance	Disability benefits	35-522
	Fraternal benefit society benefits	35-1211
	Group life insurance policy or proceeds	35-523
	Life insurance proceeds if clause prohibits proceeds from being used to pay beneficiary's creditors	35-525
	Life insurance proceeds or avails	35-521
	Other insurance proceeds to $200 per month, maximum 2 months, for head of family; else $60 per month	15-503
miscellaneous	Property of business partnership	41-124
pensions	ERISA-qualified benefits, IRAs, Keoghs, etc. to maximum deductible contribution	15-501(a)(9)
	Judges	11-1570(d)
also see wages	Public school teachers	31-1217, 31-1238
personal property	Beds, bedding, radios, cooking utensils, stoves, furniture, furnishings & sewing machines to $300 total	15-501(a)(2)
	Books to $400	15-501(a)(8)
	Clothing to $300 per person for immediate family	15-501(a)(1), 15-503(b)
	Cooperative association holdings to $50	29-1128
	Family pictures	15-501(a)(8)
	Food & fuel to last 3 months	15-501(a)(3),(4)
	Residential condominium deposit	45-1869
	Uninsured motorist benefits	35-2114(h)
	Wrongful death damages	16-2703
public benefits	Aid to blind, aged, disabled, general assistance	3-215.1
	Crime victims' compensation	3-407
	Unemployment compensation	46-119
	Workers' compensation	36-317
tools of trade	Library, furniture, tools of professional or artist to $300	15-501(a)(6)
	Mechanic's tools; tools of trade or business to $200	15-501(a)(5), 15-503(b)
	Motor vehicle, cart, wagon or dray, & horse or mule harness to $500	15-501(a)(7)
	Seal & documents of notary public	1-806
	Stock & materials to $200	15-501(a)(5)
wages	Minimum 75% of earned but unpaid wages, pension payments; bankruptcy judge may authorize more for low-income debtors	16-572
	Non-wage (including pension & retirement) earnings to $200 per month for head of family; else $60 per month for a maximum of two months	15-503
wild card	None	

Florida

Federal Bankruptcy Exemptions not available. All law references are to Florida Statutes Annotated unless otherwise noted.

ASSET	EXEMPTION	LAW
homestead	Real or personal property including mobile or modular home to unlimited value; cannot exceed $1/2$ acre in municipality or 160 acres elsewhere; spouse or child of deceased owner may claim homestead exemption (husband & wife may double)	222.01, 222.02, 222.03, 222.05; Constitution 10-4 *In re Colwell,*196 F. 3d (11th Cir. 1999)
	May file homestead declaration	222.01
	Property held as tenancy by the entirety may be exempt against debts owed by only one spouse	*In re Avins,* 19 B.R. 736 (S.D. Fla. 1982)
insurance	Annuity contract proceeds; does not include lottery winnings	222.14; *In re Pizzi,* 153 B.R. 357 (S.D. Fla. 1993)
	Death benefits payable to a specific beneficiary, not the deceased's estate	222.13
	Disability or illness benefits	222.18
	Fraternal benefit society benefits,	632.619
	Life insurance cash surrender value	222.14
miscellaneous	Alimony, child support needed for support	222.201
	Damages to employees for injuries in hazardous occupations	769.05
	Property of business partnership	620.68
pensions	County officers, employees	122.15
also see wages	ERISA-qualified benefits	222.21(2)
	Firefighters	175.241
	Highway patrol officers	321.22
	Police officers	185.25
	State officers, employees	121.131
	Teachers	238.15
personal property	Any personal property to $1,000 (husband & wife may double)	Constitution 10-4 *In re Hawkins,* 51 B.R. 348 (S.D. Fla. 1985)
	Health aids	222.25
	Motor vehicle to $1,000	222.25
	Pre-need funeral contract deposits	497.413(8)
	Pre-paid college education trust deposits	222.22(1)
	Pre-paid medical savings account deposits	222.22(2)
public benefits	Crime victims' compensation unless seeking to discharge debt for treatment of injury incurred during the crime	960.14
	Hazardous occupation injury recoveries	769.05
	Public assistance	222.201
	Social Security	222.201
	Unemployment compensation	222.201; 443.051(2),(3)
	Veterans' benefits	222.201; 744.626
	Workers' compensation	440.22
tools of trade	None	
wages	100% of wages for heads of family up to $500 per week either unpaid or paid and deposited into bank account for up to 6 months	222.11
	Federal government employees pension payments needed for support & received 3 months prior	222.21
wild card	See personal property	

Georgia

Federal Bankruptcy Exemptions not available. All law references are to the Official Code of Georgia Annotated, not to the Georgia Code Annotated.

ASSET	EXEMPTION	LAW
homestead	Real or personal property, including co-op, used as residence to $5,000 (husband & wife may double); unused portion of homestead may be applied to any property	44-13-100(a)(1)
insurance	Annuity & endowment contract benefits	33-28-7
	Disability or health benefits to $250 per month	33-29-15
	Fraternal benefit society benefits	33-15-20
	Group insurance	33-30-10
	Industrial life insurance if policy owned by someone you depended on, needed for support	33-26-5
	Life insurance proceeds if policy owned by someone you depended on, needed for support	44-13-100(a)(11)(C)
	Unmatured life insurance contract	44-13-100(a)(8)
	Unmatured life insurance dividends, interest, loan value or cash value to $2,000 if beneficiary is you or someone you depend on	44-13-100(a)(9)
miscellaneous	Alimony, child support needed for support	44-13-100(a)(2)(D)
pensions	Employees of non-profit corporations	44-13-100(a)(2.1)(B)
	ERISA-qualified benefits	18-4-22
	Public employees	44-13-100(a)(2.1)(A); 47-2-332
	Other pensions needed for support	18-4-22; 44-13-100(a)(2)(E), 44-13-100(a)(2.1)(C)
personal property	Animals, crops, clothing, appliances, books, furnishings, household goods, musical instruments to $200 per item, $3,500 total	44-13-100(a)(4)
	Burial plot, in lieu of homestead	44-13-100(a)(1)
	Health aids	44-13-100(a)(10)
	Jewelry to $500	44-13-100(a)(5)
	Lost future earnings needed for support	44-13-100(a)(11)(E)
	Motor vehicles to $1,000 (husband & wife may double)	44-13-100(a)(3)
	Personal injury recoveries to $7,500	44-13-100(a)(11)(C)
	Wrongful death recoveries needed for support	44-13-100(a)(11)(B)
public benefits	Aid to blind	49-4-58
	Aid to disabled	49-4-84
	Crime victims' compensation	44-13-100(a)(11)(A)
	Local public assistance	44-13-100(a)(2)(A)
	Old age assistance	49-4-35
	Social Security	44-13-100(a)(2)(A)
	Unemployment compensation	44-13-100(a)(2)(A)
	Veterans' benefits	44-13-100(a)(2)(B)
	Workers' compensation	34-9-84
tools of trade	Implements, books & tools of trade to $500	44-13-100(a)(7)
wages	Minimum 75% of earned but unpaid wages for private & federal workers; bankruptcy judge may authorize more for low-income debtors	18-4-20, 18-4-21
wild card	$400 of any property	44-13-100(a)(6)
	Unused portion of homestead exemption	44-13-100(a)(6)

Hawaii

Federal Bankruptcy Exemptions available. All law references are to Hawaii Revised Statutes unless otherwise noted.

ASSET	EXEMPTION	LAW
homestead	Head of family or over 65 to $30,000; all others to $20,000; property cannot exceed 1 acre; sale proceeds exempt for 6 months after sale (husband & wife may not double)	651-91, 651-92,651-96
	Property held as tenancy by the entirety may be exempt against debts owed by only one spouse	*Security Pacific Bank v. Chang,* 818 F.Supp. 1343 (D. Ha. 1993)
insurance	Annuity contract or endowment policy if beneficiary is insured's spouse, child or parent	431:10-232(b)
	Disability benefits	431:10-231
	Fraternal benefit society benefits	432:2-403
	Group life insurance policy or proceeds	431:10-233
	Life or health insurance policy for spouse or child	431:10-234
	Life insurance proceeds if clause prohibits proceeds from being used to pay beneficiary's creditors	431:10D-112
miscellaneous	Property of business partnership	425-125
pensions	ERISA-qualified benefits deposited over 3 years before filing bankruptcy	651-124
	Firefighters	88-169
	Police officers	88-169
	Public officers & employees	88-91; 36-653-3
personal property	Appliances & furnishings	651-121(1)
	Books	651-121(1)
	Burial plot to 250 sq. ft. plus tombstones, monuments & fencing	651-121(4)
	Clothing	651-121(1)
	Down payments for home in state housing project	20-359-104
	Jewelry, watches & articles of adornment to $1,000	651-121(1)
	Motor vehicle to wholesale value of $2,575	651-121(2)
	Proceeds for sold or damaged exempt property; sale proceeds exempt for 6 months after sale	651-121(5)
public benefits	Public assistance paid by Dept. of Health Services for work done in home or workshop	346-33
	Unemployment compensation	383-163
	Unemployment work relief funds to $60 per month	653-4
	Workers' compensation	386-57
tools of trade	Tools, implements, books, instruments, uniforms, furnishings, fishing boat, nets, motor vehicle & other property needed for livelihood	651-121(3)
wages	Unpaid wages due for services of past 31 days	651-121(6)
	Prisoner's wages held by Dept. of Public Safety	353-22
wild card	None	

Idaho

Federal Bankruptcy Exemptions not available. All law references are to Idaho Code.

ASSET	EXEMPTION	LAW
homestead	Real property or mobile home to $50,000; sale proceeds exempt for 6 months (husband & wife may not double)	55-1003, 55-1113
	Must record homestead exemption for property that is not yet occupied	55-1004
insurance	Annuity contract proceeds to $350 per month	41-1836
	Death or disability benefits	11-604(1)(a); 41-1834
	Fraternal benefit society benefits	41-3218
	Group life insurance benefits	41-1835
	Homeowners' insurance proceeds to amount of homestead exemption	55-1008
	Life insurance proceeds if clause prohibits proceeds from being used to pay beneficiary's creditors	41-1930
	Life insurance proceeds or avails for beneficiary other than the insured	11-604(d); 41-1833
	Medical, surgical or hospital care benefits	11-603(5)
	Unmatured life insurance contract, other than credit life insurance, owned by debtor	11-605(8)
	Unmatured life insurance contract interest or dividends to $5,000 owned by debtor or person debtor depends on	11-605(9)
miscellaneous	Alimony, child support	11-604(1)(b)
	Liquor licenses	23-514
	Property of business partnership	53-325
pensions *also see wages*	ERISA-qualified benefits	55-1011
	Firefighters	72-1422
	Government and private pensions and retirement plans, IRAs, Keoghs, etc.	11-604A
	Police officers	50-1517
	Public employees	59-1317
personal property	Appliances, furnishings, books, clothing, pets, musical instruments, 1 firearm, family portraits & sentimental heirlooms to $500 per item, $5,000 total	11-605(1)
	Building materials	45-514
	Burial plot	11-603(1)
	Crops cultivated on maximum of 50 acres, to $1,000; water rights to 160 inches	11-605(6)
	Health aids	11-603(2)
	Jewelry to $1,000	11-605(2)
	Motor vehicle to $3,000	11-605(3)
	Personal injury recoveries	11-604(1)(c)
	Proceeds for damaged exempt property for 3 months after proceeds received	11-606
	Wrongful death recoveries	11-604(1)(c)
public benefits	Aid to blind, aged, disabled	56-223
	Federal, state & local public assistance	11-603(4)
	General assistance	56-223
	Social Security	11-603(3)
	Unemployment compensation	11-603(6)
	Veterans' benefits	11-603(3)
	Workers' compensation	72-802
tools of trade	Arms, uniforms & accoutrements that peace officer, national guard or military personnel is required to keep	11-605(5)
	Implements, books & tools of trade to $1,500	11-605(3)
wages	Minimum 75% of earned but unpaid wages, pension payments; bankruptcy judge may authorize more for low-income debtors	11-207
wild card	$800 in any tangible personal property	11-605(10)

Illinois

Federal Bankruptcy Exemptions not available. All law references are to Illinois Annotated Statutes.

ASSET	EXEMPTION	LAW
homestead	Real or personal property including a farm, lot & buildings, condo, co-op or mobile home to $7,500 (husband and wife may double); sale proceeds exempt for 1 year	735-5/12-901, 735-5/12-906
	Spouse or child of deceased owner may claim homestead exemption	735-5/12-902
insurance	Fraternal benefit society benefits	215-5/299.1a
	Health or disability benefits	735-5/12-1001(g)(3)
	Homeowners proceeds if home destroyed, to $7,500	735-5/12-907
	Life insurance, annuity proceeds or cash value if beneficiary is insured's child, parent, spouse or other dependent	215-5/238
	Life insurance policy if beneficiary is insured's spouse or child	735-5/12-1001(f)
	Life insurance proceeds if clause prohibits proceeds from being used to pay beneficiary's creditors	215-5/238
	Life insurance proceeds needed for support	735-5/12-1001(f),(g)(3)
miscellaneous	Alimony, child support	735-5/12-1001(g)(4)
	Property of business partnership	805-205/25
pensions	Civil service employees	40-5/11-223
	County employees	40-5/9-228
	Disabled firefighters; widows & children of firefighters	40-5/22-230
	ERISA-qualified benefits	735-5/12-1006
	Firefighters	40-5/4-135, 40-5/6-213
	General assembly members	40-5/2-154
	House of correction employees	40-5/19-117
	Judges	40-5/18-161
	Municipal employees	40-5/7-217(a), 40-5/8-244
	Park employees	40-5/12-190
	Police officers	40-5/3-144.1, 40-5/5-218
	Public employees	735-5/12-1006
	Public library employees	40-5/19-218
	Sanitation district employees	40-5/13-808
	State (and state university) employees	40-5/14-147, 40-5/15-185
	Teachers	40-5/16-190, 40-5/17-151
personal property	Bible, family pictures, schoolbooks & clothing	735-5/12-1001(a)
	Health aids	735-5/12-1001(e)
	Motor vehicle to $1,200	735-5/12-1001(c)
	Personal injury recoveries to $7,500	735-5/12-1001(g)(4)
	Proceeds of sold exempt property	735-5/12-1001
	Title certificate for boat over 12 ft.	652-45/3A-7
	Wrongful death recoveries	735-5/12-1001(h)(2)
public benefits	Aid to aged, blind, disabled, public assistance	305-5/11-3
	Crime victims' compensation	735-5/12-1001(h)(1)
	Restitution payments for WWII relocation of Aleuts & Japanese Americans	735-5/12-1001(12)(h)(5)
	Social Security	735-5/12-1001(g)(1)
	Unemployment compensation	735-5/12-1001(g) (1),(3)
	Veterans' benefits	735-5/12-1001(g)(2)
	Workers' compensation	820-305/21
	Workers' occupational disease compensation	820-310/21
tools of trade	Implements, books & tools of trade to $750	735-5/12-1001(d)
wages	Minimum 85% of earned but unpaid wages; bankruptcy judge may authorize more for low-income debtors	740-170/4
wild card	$2,000 of any personal property (includes wages)	735-5/12-1001(b); *In re Johnson,* 57 B.R. 635 (N.D. Ill. 1986)

Indiana

Federal Bankruptcy Exemptions not available. All law references are to Indiana Statutes Annotated.

ASSET	EXEMPTION	LAW
homestead *also see wild card*	Real or personal property used as residence to $7,500 (homestead plus personal property —except health aids—can't exceed $10,000)	34-55-10-2(b)(1) 34-55-10-2(c)
	Property held as tenancy by the entirety may be exempt against debts incurred by only one spouse	34-55-10-2(b)(5)
insurance	Employer's life insurance policy on employee	27-1-12-17.1
	Fraternal benefit society benefits	27-11-6-3
	Group life insurance policy	27-1-12-29
	Life insurance policy, proceeds, cash value or avails if beneficiary is insured's spouse or dependent	27-1-12-14
	Life insurance proceeds if clause prohibits proceeds to be used to pay beneficiary's creditors	27-2-5-1
	Mutual life or accident proceeds	27-8-3-23
miscellaneous	Property of business partnership	23-4-1-25
pensions	Firefighters	36-8-7-22, 36-8-8-17
	Police officers	10-1-2-9; 36-8-8-17
	Public employees	5-10.3-8-9
	Public or private retirement benefits	34-55-10-2(b)(6)
	Sheriffs	36-8-10-19
	State teachers	21-6.1-5-17
personal property *also see wild card*	Health aids	34-55-10-2(b)(4)
	Money in medical care savings account	34-55-10-2(b)(10)
	$100 of any intangible personal property, except money owed to you	34-55-10-2(b)(3)
public benefits	Crime victims' compensation unless seeking to discharge debt for treatment of injury incurred during the crime	12-18-6-36
	Unemployment compensation	22-4-33-3
	Workers' compensation	22-3-2-17
tools of trade	National guard uniforms, arms & equipment	10-2-6-3
wages	Minimum 75% of earned but unpaid wages; bankruptcy judge may authorize more for low-income debtors	24-4.5-5-105
wild card	$4,000 of any real estate or tangible personal property	34-55-10-2(b)(2)

Iowa

Federal Bankruptcy Exemptions not available. All law references are to Iowa Code Annotated.

ASSET	EXEMPTION	LAW
homestead	Real property or an apartment to an unlimited value; property cannot exceed ½ acre in town or city, 40 acres elsewhere (husband & wife may not double)	499A.18; 561.2, 561.16
	May record homestead declaration	561.4
insurance	Accident, disability, health, illness or life proceeds or avails to $15,000, paid to surviving spouse, child or other dependent	627.6(6)
	Disability or illness benefit	627.6(8)(c)
	Employee group insurance policy or proceeds	509.12
	Life insurance proceeds to $10,000, acquired within 2 years of filing for bankruptcy, paid to spouse, child or other dependent	627.6(6)
	Life insurance proceeds if clause prohibits proceeds from being used to pay beneficiary's creditors	508.32
miscellaneous	Alimony, child support needed for support	627.6(8)(d)
	Liquor licenses	123.38
	Property of business partnership	486.25(2)(c)
pensions *also see wages*	Disabled firefighters, police officers (only payments being received)	410.11
	Federal government pension (only payments being received)	627.8
	Firefighters	411.13
	Peace officers	97A.12
	Police officers	411.13
	Public employees	97B.39
	Other pension payments needed for support, contributions must have been made 1 year prior to filing for bankruptcy	627.6(8)(e)
	Retirement plans, Keoghs, IRAs, ERISA qualified benefits	627.6(8)(f)
personal property	Appliances, furnishings & household goods to $2,000 total	627.6(5)
	Bibles, books, portraits, pictures & paintings to $1,000 total	627.6(3)
	Burial plot to 1 acre	627.6(4)
	Clothing and its storage containers to $1,000	627.6(1)
	Health aids	627.6(7)
	Motor vehicle, musical instruments & tax refund to $5,000 total, no more than $1,000 from tax refund	627.6(9)
	Residential security or utility deposit, or rent, to $500	627.6(14)
	Rifle or musket; shotgun	627.6(2)
	Wedding or engagement rings	627.6(1)
public benefits	Adopted child assistance	627.19
	Local public assistance	627.6(8)(a)
	Social Security	627.6(8)(a)
	Unemployment compensation	627.6(8)(a)
	Veterans' benefits	627.6(8)(b)
	Workers' compensation	627.13
tools of trade	Farming equipment; includes livestock, feed to $10,000	627.6(11)
	Non-farming equipment to $10,000	627.6(10)
wages	Minimum 75% of earned but unpaid wages, pension payments; bankruptcy judge may authorize more for low-income debtors	642.21
wild card	$100 of any personal property, including cash	627.6(13)

Kansas

Federal Bankruptcy Exemptions not available. All law references are to Kansas Statutes Annotated unless otherwise noted.

ASSET	EXEMPTION	LAW
homestead	Real property or mobile home you occupy or intend to occupy to unlimited value; property cannot exceed 1 acre in town or city, 160 acres on farm	60-2301; Constitution 15-9
insurance	Disability and illness benefits	60-2313(a)
	Fraternal life insurance benefits	40-711
	Life insurance forfeiture value if file for bankruptcy over 1 year after policy issued	40-414(b)
	Life insurance proceeds if clause prohibits proceeds from being used to pay beneficiary's creditors	40-414(a)
miscellaneous	Alimony, maintenance and support	60-2312(b)
	Liquor licenses	41-326
	Property of business partnership	60-2313(b)
pensions	Elected & appointed officials in cities with populations between 120,000 & 200,000	13-14,102
	ERISA-qualified benefits	60-2308(b)
	Federal government pension needed for support & paid within 3 months of filing for bankruptcy (only payments being received)	60-2308(a)
	Firefighters	12-5005(e); 14-10a10
	Judges	20-2618
	Police officers	12-5005(e); 13-14a10
	Public employees	74-4923, 74-49,105
	State highway patrol officers	74-4978g
	State school employees	72-5526
personal property	Burial plot or crypt	60-2304(d)
	Clothing to last 1 year	60-2304(a)
	Food & fuel to last 1 year	60-2304(a)
	Funeral plan prepayments	16-310(d)
	Furnishings & household equipment	60-2304(a)
	Jewelry & articles of adornment to $1,000	60-2304(b)
	Motor vehicle to $20,000; if designed or equipped for disabled person, no limit	60-2304(c)
public benefits	Crime victims' compensation	74-7313(d)
	General assistance	39-717
	Social Security	60-2312(b)
	Unemployment compensation	44-718(c)
	Veteran's benefits	60-2312(b)
	Workers' compensation	44-514
tools of trade	Books, documents, furniture, instruments, equipment, breeding stock, seed, grain & stock to $7,500 total	60-2304(e)
	National Guard uniforms, arms & equipment	48-245
wages	Minimum 75% of earned but unpaid wages; bankruptcy judge may authorize more for low-income debtors	60-2310
wild card	None	

Kentucky

Federal Bankruptcy Exemptions not available. All law references are to Kentucky Revised Statutes.

ASSET	EXEMPTION	LAW
homestead	Real or personal property used as residence to $5,000; sale proceeds exempt	427.060, 427.090
insurance	Annuity contract proceeds to $350 per month	304.14-330
	Cooperative life or casualty insurance benefits	427.110(1)
	Fraternal benefit society benefits	427.110(2)
	Group life insurance proceeds	304.14-320
	Health or disability benefits	304.14-310
	Life insurance policy if beneficiary is a married woman	304.14-340
	Life insurance proceeds if clause prohibits proceeds from being used to pay beneficiary's creditors	304.14-350
	Life insurance proceeds or cash value if beneficiary is someone other than insured	304.14-300
miscellaneous	Alimony, child support needed for support	427.150(1)
	Property of business partnership	362.270
pensions	Firefighters,	67A.620; 95.878
	Police officers	427.120, 427.125
	ERISA-qualified benefits, including IRAs, SEPs, and Keoghs deposited more than 120 days before filing	427.150
	State employees	61.690
	Teachers	161.700
	Urban county government employees	67A.350
personal property	Burial plot to $5,000, in lieu of homestead	427.060
	Clothing, jewelry, articles of adornment & furnishings to $3,000 total	427.010(1)
	Health aids	427.010(1)
	Lost earnings payments needed for support	427.150(2)(d)
	Medical expenses paid & reparation benefits received under motor vehicle reparation law	304.39-260
	Motor vehicle to $2,500	427.010(1)
	Personal injury recoveries to $7,500 (not to include pain & suffering or pecuniary loss)	427.150(2)(c)
	Prepaid tuition payment fund account	164A.707(3)
	Wrongful death recoveries for person you depended on, needed for support	427.150(2)(b)
public benefits	Aid to blind, aged, disabled, public assistance	205.220
	Crime victims' compensation	427.150(2)(a)
	Unemployment compensation	341.470
	Workers' compensation	342.180
tools of trade	Library, office equipment, instruments & furnishings of minister, attorney, physician, surgeon, chiropractor, veterinarian or dentist to $1,000	427.040
	Motor vehicle of auto mechanic, mechanical or electrical equipment servicer, minister, attorney, physician, surgeon, chiropractor, veterinarian or dentist to $2,500	427.030
	Tools, equipment, livestock & poultry of farmer to $3,000	427.010(1)
	Tools of non-farmer to $300	427.030
wages	Minimum 75% of earned but unpaid wages; bankruptcy judge may authorize more for low-income debtors	427.010(2),(3)
wild card	$1,000 of any property	427.160

Louisiana

Federal Bankruptcy Exemptions not available. All law references are to Louisiana Revised Statutes Annotated unless otherwise noted.

ASSET	EXEMPTION	LAW
homestead	Property you occupy to $25,000 (if debt is result of catastrophic or terminal illness or injury, limit is full value of property as of 1 year before filing); cannot exceed 5 acres in city or town, 200 acres elsewhere (husband & wife may not double)	20:1(A)(1),(2),(3)
	Spouse or child of deceased owner may claim homestead exemption; spouse given home in divorce gets homestead	20:1(B)
insurance	Annuity contract proceeds and avails	22:647
	Fraternal benefit society benefits	22:558
	Group insurance policies or proceeds	22:649
	Health, accident or disability proceeds or avails	22:646
	Life insurance proceeds or avails; if policy issued within 9 months of filing, exempt only to $35,000	22:647
miscellaneous	Property of minor child	13:3881(A)(3); Civil Code Art.223
pensions	Assessors	11:1401
	Court clerks	11:1526
	District attorneys	11:1583
	ERISA-qualified benefits, including IRAs and Keoghs, if contributions made over 1 year before filing for bankruptcy	13:3881(D)(1); 20:33(1)
	Firefighters	11:2263
	Gift or bonus payments from employer to employee or heirs whenever paid	20:33(2)
	Judges	11:1378
	Louisiana University employees	17:1613
	Municipal employees	11:1735
	Parochial employees	11:1905
	Police officers	11:3513
	School employees	11:1003
	Sheriffs	11:2182
	State employees	11:405
	Teachers	11:704
	Voting registrars	11:2033
personal property	Arms, military accoutrements; bedding; dishes, glassware, utensils, silverware (non-sterling); clothing, family portraits, musical instruments; bedroom, living room & dining room furniture; poultry, 1 cow, household pets; heating & cooling equipment, refrigerator, freezer, stove, washer & dryer, iron, sewing machine	13:3881(A)(4)
	Cemetery plot, monuments	8:313
	Engagement & wedding rings to $5,000	13:3881(A)(5)
public benefits	Aid to blind, aged, disabled, public assistance	46:111
	Crime victims' compensation	46:1811
	Unemployment compensation	23:1693
	Workers' compensation	23:1205
tools of trade	Tools, instruments, books, pickup truck (maximum 3 tons) or non-luxury auto & utility trailer, needed to work	13:3881(A)(2)
wages	Minimum 75% of earned but unpaid wages; bankruptcy judge may authorize more for low-income debtors	13:3881(A)(1)
wild card	None	

Maine

Federal Bankruptcy Exemptions not available. All law references are to Maine Revised Statutes Annotated.

ASSET	EXEMPTION	LAW
homestead	Real or personal property (including cooperative) used as residence to $12,500; if debtor has minor dependents in residence, to $25,000; if debtor over age 60 or physically or mentally disabled, $60,000 (joint debtors in this category may double); proceeds of sale exempt for six months	14-4422(1)
insurance	Annuity proceeds to $450 per month	24-A-2431
	Disability or health proceeds, benefits or avails	14-4422(13)(A),(C); 24-A-2429
	Fraternal benefit society benefits	24-A-4118
	Group health or life policy or proceeds	24-A-2430
	Life, endowment, annuity or accident policy, proceeds or avails	14-4422(14)(C); 24-A-2428
	Life insurance policy, interest, loan value or accrued dividends for policy from person you depended on, to $4,000	14-4422(11)
	Unmatured life insurance policy, except credit insurance policy	14-4422(10)
miscellaneous	Alimony & child support needed for support	14-4422(13)(D)
	Property of business partnership	31-305
pensions	ERISA-qualified benefits	14-4422(13)(E)
	Judges	4-1203
	Legislators	3-703
	State employees	5-17054
personal property	Animals, crops, musical instruments, books, clothing, furnishings, household goods, appliances to $200 per item	14-4422(3)
	Balance due on repossessed goods; total amount financed can't exceed $2,000	9-A-5-103
	Burial plot in lieu of homestead exemption	14-4422(1)
	Cooking stove; furnaces & stoves for heat	14-4422(6)(A),(B)
	Food to last 6 months	14-4422(7)(A)
	Fuel not to exceed 10 cords of wood, 5 tons of coal or 1,000 gal. of heating oil	14-4422(6)(C)
	Health aids	14-4422(12)
	Jewelry to $750; no limit for one wedding & one engagement ring	14-4422(4)
	Lost earnings payments needed for support	14-4422(14)(E)
	Military clothes, arms & equipment	37-B-262
	Motor vehicle to $2,500	14-4422(2)
	Personal injury recoveries to $12,500	14-4422(14)(D)
	Seeds, fertilizers & feed to raise & harvest food for one season	14-4422(7)(B)
	Tools & equipment to raise & harvest food	14-4422(7)(C)
	Wrongful death recoveries needed for support	14-4422(14)(B)
public benefits	Crime victims' compensation	14-4422(14)(A)
	Public assistance	22-3753
	Social Security	14-4422(13)(A)
	Unemployment compensation	14-4422(13)(A),(C)
	Veterans' benefits	14-4422(13)(B)
	Workers' compensation	39-67
tools of trade	Commercial fishing boat, 5 ton limit	14-4422(9)
	Books, materials & stock to $5,000	14-4422(5)
	One of each farm implement (and its maintenance equipment) needed to harvest and raise crops	14-4422(8)
wages	None	
wild card	Unused portion of exemption in homestead to $6,000; or unused exemption in animals, crops, musical instruments, books, clothing, furnishings, household goods, appliances, tools of the trade & personal injury recoveries	14-4422(15)
	$400 of any property	14-4422(15)

Maryland

Federal Bankruptcy Exemptions not available. All law references are to Annotated Code of Maryland unless otherwise noted.

ASSET	EXEMPTION	LAW
homestead *also see wild card*	None, however, property held as tenancy by the entirety may be exempt against debts owed by only one spouse	*In re Sefren,* 41 B.R. 747 (D. Md. 1984)
insurance	Disability or health benefits, including court awards, arbitrations & settlements	Courts & Jud. Proc. 11-504(b)(2)
	Fraternal benefit society benefits	48A-328; Estates & Trusts 8-115
	Life insurance or annuity contract proceeds or avails if beneficiary is insured's dependent, child or spouse	48A-385; Estates & Trusts 8-115
	Medical benefits deducted from wages	Commercial Law 15-601.1(3)
miscellaneous	Property of business partnership	Corps. & Ass'ns. 9-502
pensions	Deceased Baltimore police officers (only benefits building up)	73B-49
	ERISA-qualified benefits, except IRAs	Courts & Jud. Proc. 11-504(h)(1)
	State employees	73B-17, 73B-125
	State police	88B-60
	Teachers	73B-96, 73B-152
personal property	Appliances, furnishings, household goods, books, pets & clothing to $500 total	Courts & Jud. Proc. 11-504(b)(4)
	Burial plot	23-164
	Health aids	Courts & Jud. Proc. 11-504(b)(3)
	Lost future earnings recoveries	Courts & Jud. Proc. 11-504(b)(2)
public benefits	Crime victims' compensation	26A-13
	General assistance	88A-73
	Unemployment compensation	Labor & Employment 8-106
	Workers' compensation	Labor & Employment 9-732
tools of trade	Clothing, books, tools, instruments & appliances to $2,500; can't include car	Courts & Jud. Proc. 11-504(b)(1)
wages	Earned but unpaid wages, the greater of 75% or $145 per week; in Kent, Caroline, & Queen Anne's of Worcester Counties, the greater of 75% or 30 times Federal minimum hourly wage	Commercial Law 15-601.1
wild card	$5,500 of any property (may include up to $3,000 in cash)	Courts & Jud. Proc. 11-504(b)(5),(f)

Massachusetts

Federal Bankruptcy Exemptions available. All law references are to Massachusetts General Laws Annotated.

ASSET	EXEMPTION	LAW
homestead	Property you occupy or intend to occupy to $100,000; if over 65 or disabled, $200,000 (joint owners may not double)	188-1, 188-1A
	Must record homestead declaration before filing bankruptcy	188-2
	Spouse or child of deceased owner may claim homestead exemption	188-4
	Property held as tenancy by the entirety may be exempt against non-necessity debts	209-1
insurance	Disability benefits to $400 per week	175-110A
	Fraternal benefit society benefits	176-22
	Group annuity policy or proceeds	175-132C
	Group life insurance policy	175-135
	Life or endowment policy, proceeds or cash value	175-125
	Life insurance annuity contract	175-125
	Life insurance policy if beneficiary is married woman	175-126
	Life insurance proceeds if clause prohibits proceeds from being used to pay beneficiary's creditors	175-119A
	Medical malpractice self-insurance	175F-15
miscellaneous	Property of business partnership	108A-25
pensions *also see wages*	Credit union employees	171-84
	ERISA-qualified benefits, including IRAs	235-34A; 246-28
	Private retirement benefits	32-41
	Public employees	32-19
	Savings bank employees	168-41, 168-44
personal property	Bank deposits to $125; food or cash for food to $300	235-34
	Beds & bedding; heating unit; clothing	235-34
	Bibles & books to $200 total; sewing machine to $200	235-34
	Burial plots, tombs & church pew	235-34
	Cash for fuel, heat, water or light to $75 per month	235-34
	Cash to $200/month for rent, in lieu of homestead	235-34
	Cooperative association shares to $100	235-34
	2 cows, 12 sheep, 2 swine, 4 tons of hay	235-34
	Furniture to $3,000; motor vehicle to $700	235-34
	Moving expenses for eminent domain	79-6A
	Trust company, bank or credit union deposits to $500	246-28A
public benefits	Aid to aged, disabled	235-34
	Public assistance	118-10
	Unemployment compensation	151A-36
	Veterans' benefits	115-5
	Workers' compensation	152-47
tools of trade	Arms, accoutrements & uniforms required	235-34
	Fishing boats, tackle & nets to $500	235-34
	Materials you designed & procured to $500	235-34
	Tools, implements & fixtures to $500 total	235-34
wages	Earned but unpaid wages to $125 per week	246-28
wild card	None	

Michigan

Federal Bankruptcy Exemptions available. All law references are to Michigan Compiled Laws Annotated unless otherwise noted.

ASSET	EXEMPTION	LAW
homestead	Real property including condo to $3,500; property cannot exceed 1 lot in town, village, city, or 40 acres elsewhere; spouse or child of deceased owner may claim homestead exemption	559.214; 600.6023(1)(h),(i) 600.6023(3)
	Property held as tenancy by the entirety may be exempt against debts owed by only one spouse	*SNB Bank & Trust v. Kensey*, 378 N.W. 2d 594 (Ct. App. Mich. 1985)
insurance	Disability, mutual life or health benefits	600.6023(1)(f)
	Fraternal benefit society benefits	500.8181
	Life, endowment or annuity proceeds if clause prohibits proceeds from being used to pay beneficiary's creditors	500.4054
miscellaneous	Property of business partnership	449.25
pensions	Firefighters, police officers	38.559(6)
	ERISA-qualified benefits	600.6023(1)(l)
	IRAs	600.6023(1)(k)
	Judges	38.826
	Legislators	38.1057
	Probate judges	38.927
	Public school employees	38.1346
	State employees	38.40
personal property	Appliances, utensils, books, furniture & household goods to $1,000 total	600.6023(1)(b)
	Building & loan association shares to $1,000 par value, in lieu of homestead	600.6023(1)(g)
	Burial plots, cemeteries; church pew, slip, seat	600.6023(1)(c)
	Clothing; family pictures	600.6023(1)(a)
	2 cows, 100 hens, 5 roosters, 10 sheep, 5 swine & feed to last 6 months	600.6023(1)(d)
	Food & fuel to last 6 months	600.6023(1)(a)
public benefits	Crime victims' compensation	18.362
	Social welfare benefits	400.63
	Unemployment compensation	421.30
	Veterans' benefits for Korean War veterans	35.977
	Veterans' benefits for Vietnam veterans	35.1027
	Veterans' benefits for WWII veterans	35.926
	Workers' compensation	418.821
tools of trade	Arms & accoutrements required	600.6023(1)(a)
	Tools, implements, materials, stock, apparatus, team, motor vehicle, horse & harness to $1,000 total	600.6023(1)(e)
wages	head of household may keep 60% of earned but unpaid wages (no less than $15/week), plus $2/week per non-spouse dependent; if not head of household may keep 40% (no less than $10/week)	600.5311
wild card	None	

Minnesota

Federal Bankruptcy Exemptions available. All law references are to Minnesota Statutes Annotated. **Note:** Section 550.37(4)(a) requires certain exemptions to be adjusted for inflation on July 1 of even-numbered years; this table includes all changes through July 1, 2000. Exemptions are published in the May 1 issue of the *Minnesota State Register*, http://www.comm.media.state.mn.us/bookstore/stateregister.asp, or Minnesota Dept. of Commerce at 651-296-7977.

ASSET	EXEMPTION	LAW
homestead	Real property, mobile home or manufactured home to $200,000; if homestead is used for agricultural purposes, $500,000; cannot exceed 1/2 acre in city, 160 acres elsewhere; manufactured home to an unlimited value	510.01, 510.02; 550.37 subd. 12
insurance	Accident or disability proceeds	550.39
	Fraternal benefit society benefits	64B.18
	Life insurance proceeds to $36,000, if beneficiary is spouse or child of insured, plus $9,000 per dependent	550.37 subd. 10
	Police, fire or beneficiary association benefits	550.37 subd. 11
	Unmatured life insurance contract dividends, interest or loan value to $7,200 if insured is debtor or person debtor depends on	550.37 subd. 23
miscellaneous	Earnings of minor child	550.37 subd. 15
	Property of business partnership	323.24
pensions	ERISA-qualified benefits or needed for support, up to $54,000 in present value	550.37 subd. 24
	IRAs needed for support, up to $54,000 in present value	550.37 subd. 24
	Private retirement benefits (only benefits building up)	181B.16
	Public employees	353.15
	State employees	352.96
	State troopers	352B.071
personal property	Appliances, furniture, jewelry, radio, phonographs & TV to $8,100 total	550.37 subd. 4(b)
	Bible and books	550.37 subd. 2
	Burial plot; church pew or seat	550.37 subd. 3
	Clothing, one watch, food & utensils	550.37 subd. 4(a)
	Motor vehicle to $3,600 (up to $36,000 if vehicle has been modified for disability)	550.37 subd. 12(a)
	Personal injury recoveries	550.37 subd. 22
	Proceeds for damaged exempt property	550.37 subds. 9, 16
	Wrongful death recoveries	550.37 subd. 22
public benefits	Crime victims' compensation	611A.60
	Supplemental & general assistance, Social Security & Supplemental Security Income	550.37 subd. 14
	Unemployment compensation	268.17 subd. 2
	Veterans' benefits	550.38
	Workers' compensation	176.175
tools of trade *total tools of trade (except teaching materials) can't exceed $13,000*	Farm machines, implements, livestock, produce & crops	550.37 subd. 5
	Teaching materials of college, university, public school or public institution teacher	550.37 subd. 8
	Tools, machines, instruments, stock in trade, furniture & library to $9,000 total	550.37 subd. 6
wages	Earned but unpaid wages, paid within 6 mos. of returning to work, if you received welfare	550.37 subd. 13
	Minimum 75% of earned but unpaid wages	571.922
	Wages deposited into bank accounts for 20 days after depositing	550.37 subd. 13
	Wages of released inmates paid within 6 months of release	550.37 subd. 14
wild card	None	

Note: Some courts have held "unlimited" exemptions unconstitutional under the Minnesota Constitution, which allows debtors to exempt only a "reasonable amount" of property. See *In re Tveten*, 402 N.W. 2d 551 (Minn. 1987) and *In re Medill*, 119 B.R. 685, (D. Minn. 1990).

Mississippi

Federal Bankruptcy Exemptions not available. All law references are to Mississippi Code.

ASSET	EXEMPTION	LAW
homestead	Property you occupy to $75,000; if over 60, and married or widowed, may claim former residence; property cannot exceed 160 acres; sale proceeds exempt.	85-3-1(b)(i), 85-3-21, 85-3-23
	Mobile home does not qualify as homestead unless you own land on which it is located.	In re Cobbins, 234 B.R. 882 (S.D. Miss.1999)
	May file homestead declaration	85-3-27, 85-3-31
insurance	Disability benefits	85-3-1(b)(ii)
	Fraternal benefit society benefits	83-29-39
	Homeowners' insurance proceeds to $75,000	85-3-23
	Life insurance proceeds if clause prohibits proceeds from being used to pay beneficiary's creditors	83-7-5
miscellaneous	Property of business partnership	79-12-49
pensions	ERISA-qualified benefits, IRAs, Keoghs deposited over 1 yr. before filing bankruptcy	85-3-1(b)(iii)
	Firefighters	21-29-257
	Highway patrol officers	25-13-31
	Private retirement benefits to extent tax-deferred	71-1-43
	Police officers	21-29-257
	Public employees retirement & disability benefits	25-11-129
	State employees	25-14-5
	Teachers	25-11-201(1)(d)
personal property	Tangible personal property: furniture, dishes, kitchenware, household goods, appliances, 1 radio & 1 TV, clothing, wedding rings, motor vehicles, tools of the trade, books, crops, health aids, domestic animals to $10,000 (does not include works of art, antiques, jewelry or electronic entertainment equipment)	85-3-1(a)
	Personal injury judgments to $10,000	85-3-17
	Sale or insurance proceeds for exempt property	85-3-1(b)(i)
public benefits	Assistance to aged	43-9-19
	Assistance to blind	43-3-71
	Assistance to disabled	43-29-15
	Crime victims' compensation	99-41-23
	Social Security	25-11-129
	Unemployment compensation	71-5-539
	Workers' compensation	71-3-43
tools of trade	See personal property	
wages	Earned but unpaid wages owed for 30 days; after 30 days, minimum 75% (bankruptcy judge may authorize more for low-income debtors)	85-3-4
wild card	See personal property	

Missouri

Federal Bankruptcy Exemptions not available. All law references are to Annotated Missouri Statutes unless otherwise noted.

ASSET	EXEMPTION	LAW
homestead	Real property to $8,000 or mobile home to $1,000 (joint owners may not double)	513.430(6), 513.475 In re Smith, 254 B.R. 71 (W.D. Mo. 2000)
	Property held as tenancy by the entirety may be exempt against debts owed by only one spouse	In re Anderson, 12 B.R. 483 (W.D. Mo. 1981)
insurance	Assessment or insurance premium proceeds	377.090
	Disability or illness benefits	513.430(10)(c)
	Fraternal benefit society benefits to $5,000, bought over 6 months before filing	513.430(8)
	Life insurance dividends, loan value or interest to $5,000, bought over 6 months before filing	513.430(8)
	Life insurance proceeds if policy owned by a woman & insures her husband	376.530
	Life insurance proceeds if policy owned by unmarried woman & insures her father or brother	376.550
	Stipulated insurance premiums	377.330
	Unmatured life insurance policy	513.430(7)
miscellaneous	Alimony, child support to $500 per month	513.430(10)(d)
	Property of business partnership	358.250
pensions	Employees of cities with 100,000 or more people	71.207
	ERISA-qualified benefits needed for support (only payments being received)	513.430(10)(e)
	Firefighters	87.090, 87.365, 87.485
	Highway & transportation employees	104.250
	Police department employees	86.190, 86.353, 86.493, 86.780
	Public officers & employees	70.695, 70.755
	State employees	104.540
	Teachers	169.090
personal property	Appliances, household goods, furnishings, clothing, books, crops, animals & musical instruments to $1,000 total	513.430(1)
	Burial grounds to 1 acre or $100	214.190
	Health aids	513.430(9)
	Jewelry to $500	513.430(2)
	Motor vehicle to $1,000	513.430(5)
	Personal injury causes of action	In re Mitchell, 73 B.R. 93 (E.D. Mo. 1987)
	Wrongful death recoveries for person you depended on	513.430(11)
public benefits	Public assistance	513.430(10)(a)
	Social Security	513.430(10)(a)
	Unemployment compensation	288.380(10)(l); 513.430(10)(c)
	Veterans' benefits	513.430(10)b)
	Workers' compensation	287.260
tools of trade	Implements, books & tools of trade to $2,000	513.430(4)
wages	Minimum 75% of earned but unpaid wages (90% for head of family); bankruptcy judge may authorize more for low-income debtors	525.030
	Wages of servant or common laborer to $90	513.470
wild card	$1,250 of any property if head of family, else $400; head of family may claim additional $250 per child	513.430(3), 513.440

Montana

Federal Bankruptcy Exemptions not available. All law references are to Montana Code Annotated.

ASSET	EXEMPTION	LAW
homestead	Real property or mobile home you occupy to $60,000; sale, condemnation or insurance proceeds exempt 18 months	70-32-104, 70-32-201, 70-32-213
	Must record homestead declaration before filing for bankruptcy	70-32-105
insurance	Annuity contract proceeds to $350 per month	33-15-514
	Disability or illness proceeds, avails or benefits	25-13-608(1)(d); 33-15-513
	Fraternal benefit society benefits	33-7-522
	Group life insurance policy or proceeds	33-15-512
	Hail insurance benefits	80-2-245
	Life insurance proceeds if clause prohibits proceeds from being used to pay beneficiary's creditors	33-20-120
	Medical, surgical or hospital care benefits	25-13-608(1)(f)
	Unmatured life insurance contracts to $4,000	25-13-609(4)
miscellaneous	Alimony, child support	25-13-608(1)(g)
	Property of business partnership	35-10-502
pensions	ERISA-qualified benefits deposited over 1 year before filing bankruptcy in excess of 15% of debtor's yearly income	31-2-106
	Firefighters	19-11-612(1)
	Game wardens	19-8-805(2)
	Highway patrol officers	19-6-705(2)
	IRA contributions & earnings made before judgment filed	25-13-608(1)(e)
	Judges	19-5-704
	Police officers	19-10-504(1)
	Public employees	19-2-1004
	Sheriffs	19-7-705(2)
	Teachers	19-4-706(2)
	University system employees	19-21-212
personal property	Appliances, household furnishings, goods, animals with feed, crops, musical instruments, books, firearms, sporting goods, clothing & jewelry to $600 per item, $4,500 total	25-13-609(1)
	Burial plot	25-13-608(1)(h)
	Cooperative association shares to $500 value	35-15-404
	Health aids	25-13-608(1)(a)
	Motor vehicle to $2,500	25-13-609(2)
	Proceeds from sale or for damage or loss of exempt property for 6 mos. after received	25-13-610
public benefits	Aid to aged, disabled	53-2-607
	Crime victims' compensation	53-9-129
	Local public assistance	25-13-608(1)(b)
	Silicosis benefits	39-73-110
	Social Security	25-13-608(1)(b)
	Subsidized adoption payments	53-2-607
	Unemployment compensation	31-2-106(2); 39-51-3105
	Veterans' benefits	25-13-608(1)(c)
	Vocational rehabilitation to the blind	53-2-607
	Workers' compensation	39-71-743
tools of trade	Implements, books & tools of trade to $3,000	25-13-609(3)
	Uniforms, arms, accoutrements needed to carry out government functions	25-13-613(b)
wages	Minimum 75% of earned but unpaid wages; bankruptcy judge may authorize more for low-income debtors	25-13-614
wild card	None	

Nebraska

Federal Bankruptcy Exemptions not available. All law references are to Revised Statutes of Nebraska.

ASSET	EXEMPTION	LAW
homestead	$12,500 for married debtor or head of household; cannot exceed 2 lots in city or village, 160 acres elsewhere; sale proceeds exempt 6 months after sale (husband & wife may not double)	40-101, 40-111, 40-113
	May record homestead declaration	40-105
insurance	Fraternal benefit society benefits to $10,000 loan value unless beneficiary convicted of a crime related to benefits	44-1089
	Life insurance or annuity contract proceeds to $10,000 loan value	44-371
miscellaneous	Property of business partnership	67-325
pensions *also see wages*	County employees	23-2322
	ERISA-qualified benefits needed for support	25-1563.01
	Military disability benefits	25-1559
	School employees	79-1060, 79-1552
	State employees	84-1324
personal property	Burial plot	12-517
	Clothing	25-1556(2)
	Crypts, lots, tombs, niches, vaults	12-605
	Furniture, household goods & appliances, household electronics, personal computers, books & musical instruments to $1,500	25-1556(3)
	Health aids	25-1556(5)
	Perpetual care funds	12-511
	Personal injury recoveries	25-1563.02
	Personal possessions	25-1556
public benefits	Aid to disabled, blind, aged, public assistance	68-1013
	Unemployment compensation	48-647
	Workers' compensation	48-149
tools of trade	Equipment or tools including a vehicle used in/or for commuting to principal place of business to $2,400 (husband & wife may double)	25-1556(4) *In re Keller*, 50 B.R. 23 (D. Neb. 1985)
wages	Minimum 85% of earned but unpaid wages or pension payments for head of family; 75% for all others; bankruptcy judge may authorize more for low-income debtors	25-1558
wild card	$2,500 of any personal property, except wages, in lieu of homestead	25-1552

Nevada

Federal Bankruptcy Exemptions not available. All law references are to Nevada Revised Statutes Annotated.

ASSET	EXEMPTION	LAW
homestead	Real property or mobile home to $125,000 (husband & wife may not double)	21.090(1)(m), 115.010
	Must record homestead declaration before filing for bankruptcy	115.020
insurance	Annuity contract proceeds to $350 per month	687B.290
	Fraternal benefit society benefits	695A.220
	Group life or health policy or proceeds	687B.280
	Health proceeds or avails	687B.270
	Life insurance policy or proceeds if annual premiums not over $1,000 (husband & wife may double)	21.090(1)(k) *In re Bower,* 234 B.R. 109 (Nev. 1999)
	Life insurance proceeds if you're not the insured	687B.260
miscellaneous	Alimony and child support	21.090(1)(r)
	Property of business partnership	87.250
pensions	ERISA-qualified benefits or IRAs to $500,000	21.090(1)(q)
	Public employees	286.670
personal property	Appliances, household goods, furniture, home & yard equipment to $3,000 total	21.090(1)(b)
	Books to $1,500	21.090(1)(a)
	Burial plot purchase money held in trust	452.550
	Funeral service contract money held in trust	689.700
	Health aids	21.090(1)(p)
	Keepsakes & pictures	21.090(1)(a)
	Metal-bearing ores, geological specimens, art curiosities or paleontological remains; must be arranged, classified, catalogued & numbered in reference books	21.100
	Mortgage impound accounts	645B.180
	Motor vehicle to $4,500; no limit on vehicle equipped for disabled person	21.090(1)(f),(o)
	One gun	21.090(1)(i)
public benefits	Aid to blind, aged, disabled, public assistance	422.291
	Industrial insurance (workers' compensation)	616.550
	Unemployment compensation	612.710
	Vocational rehabilitation benefits	615.270
tools of trade	Arms, uniforms & accoutrements you're required to keep	21.090(1)(j)
	Cabin or dwelling of miner or prospector; mining claim, cars, implements & appliances to $4,500 total (for working claim only)	21.090(1)(e)
	Farm trucks, stock, tools, equipment & seed to $4,500	21.090(1)(c)
	Library, equipment, supplies, tools & materials to $4,500	21.090(1)(d)
wages	Minimum 75% of earned but unpaid wages; bankruptcy judge may authorize more for low-income debtors	21.090(1)(g)
wild card	None	

New Hampshire

Federal Bankruptcy Exemptions available. All law references are to New Hampshire Revised Statutes Annotated.

ASSET	EXEMPTION	LAW
homestead	Real property or manufactured housing (and the land it's on if you own it) to $30,000	480:1
insurance	Firefighters' aid insurance	402:69
	Fraternal benefit society benefits	418:24
	Homeowners' insurance proceeds to $5,000	512:21(VIII)
miscellaneous	Child support	161-C-11
	Jury, witness fees	512:21(VI)
	Property of business partnership	304A:25
	Wages of minor child	512:21(III)
pensions	Federally created pension (only benefits building up)	512:21(IV)
	Firefighters	102:23
	Police officers	103:18
	Public employees	100A:26
personal property	Beds, bedding & cooking utensils	511:2(II)
	Bibles & books to $800	511:2(VIII)
	Burial plot, lot	511:2(XIV)
	Church pew	511:2(XV)
	Clothing	511:2(I)
	Cooking & heating stoves, refrigerator	511:2(IV)
	1 cow, 6 sheep & their fleece, 4 tons of hay	511:2(XI), (XII)
	Domestic fowl to $300	511:2(XIII)
	Food & fuel to $400	511:2(VI)
	Furniture to $3,500	511:2(III)
	1 hog or pig or its meat (if slaughtered)	511:2(X)
	Jewelry to $500	511:2(XVII)
	Motor vehicle to $4,000	511:2(XVI)
	Proceeds for lost or destroyed exempt property	512:21(VIII)
	Sewing machine	511:2(V)
public benefits	Aid to blind, aged, disabled, public assistance	167:25
	Unemployment compensation	282A:159
	Workers' compensation	281A:52
tools of trade	Tools of your occupation to $5,000	511:2(IX)
	Uniforms, arms & equipment of military member	511:2(VII)
	Yoke of oxen or horse needed for farming or teaming	511:2(XII)
wages	Earned but unpaid wages; judge decides amount exempt based on a percentage of the federal minimum wage	512:21(II)
	Earned but unpaid wages of spouse	512:21(III)
wild card	$1,000 of any property	511:2(XVIII)
	Unused portion of bibles & books, food & fuel, furniture, jewelry, motor vehicle and tools of trade exemptions to $7,000	511:2(XVIII)

New Jersey

Federal Bankruptcy Exemptions available. All law references are to New Jersey Statutes Annotated.

ASSET	EXEMPTION	LAW
homestead	None	
insurance	Annuity contract proceeds to $500 per month	17B:24-7
	Disability or death benefits for military member	38A:4-8
	Disability, death, medical or hospital benefits for civil defense workers	App. A:9-57.6
	Fraternal benefit society benefits	17:44A-19
	Group life or health policy or proceeds	17B:24-9
	Health or disability benefits	17:18-12, 17B:24-8
	Life insurance proceeds if clause prohibits proceeds from being used to pay beneficiary's creditors	17B:24-10
	Life insurance proceeds or avails if you're not the insured	17B:24-6b
miscellaneous	Property of business partnership	42:1-25
pensions	Alcohol beverage control officers	43:8A-20
	City boards of health employees	43:18-12
	Civil defense workers	App. A:9-57.6
	County employees	43:10-57, 43:10-105
	ERISA-qualified benefits for city employees	43:13-9
	Firefighters, police officers, traffic officers	43:16-7, 43:16A-17
	IRAs	In re Yuhas, 104 F.3d 612 (3rd Cir. 1997)
	Judges	43:6A-41
	Municipal employees	43:13-44
	Prison employees	43:7-13
	Public employees	43:15A-53
	School district employees	18A:66-116
	State police	53:5A-45
	Street & water department employees	43:19-17
	Teachers	18A:66-51
	Trust containing personal property created pursuant to federal tax law	25:2-1
personal property	Personal property & possessions of any kind, stock or interest in corporations to $1,000 total	2A:17-19
	Burial plots	8A:5-10
	Clothing	2A:17-19
	Furniture & household goods to $1,000	2A:26-4
public benefits	Crime victims' compensation	52:4B-30
	Old age, permanent disability assistance	44:7-35
	Unemployment compensation	43:21-53
	Workers' compensation	34:15-29
tools of trade	None	
wages	90% of earned but unpaid wages if income under $7,500; if income over $7,500, judge decides amount that is exempt	2A:17-56
	Wages or allowances received by military personnel	38A:4-8
wild card	None	

New Mexico

Federal Bankruptcy Exemptions available. All law references are to New Mexico Statutes Annotated.

ASSET	EXEMPTION	LAW
homestead	$30,000 (joint owners may double)	42-10-9
insurance	Benevolent association benefits to $5,000	42-10-4
	Fraternal benefit society benefits	59A-44-18
	Life, accident, health or annuity benefits, withdrawal or cash value, if beneficiary is a New Mexico resident	42-10-3
	Life insurance proceeds	42-10-5
miscellaneous	Ownership interest in unincorporated association	53-10-2
	Property of business partnership	54-1-25
pensions	Pension or retirement benefits	42-10-1, 42-10-2
	Public school employees	22-11-42A
personal property	Books & furniture	42-10-1, 42-10-2
	Building materials	48-2-15
	Clothing	42-10-1, 42-10-2
	Cooperative association shares, minimum amount needed to be member	53-4-28
	Health aids	42-10-1, 42-10-2
	Jewelry to $2,500	42-10-1, 42-10-2
	Materials, tools & machinery to dig, drill, complete, operate or repair oil line, gas well or pipeline	70-4-12
	Motor vehicle to $4,000	42-10-1, 42-10-2
public benefits	Crime victims' compensation to $20,000	31-22-15
	General assistance	27-2-21
	Occupational disease disablement benefits	52-3-37
	Unemployment compensation	51-1-37
	Workers' compensation	52-1-52
tools of trade	$1,500	42-10-1, 42-10-2
wages	Minimum 75% of earned but unpaid wages; bankruptcy judge may authorize more for low-income debtors	35-12-7
wild card	$500 of any personal property	42-10-1
	$2,000 of any real or personal property, in lieu of homestead	42-10-10

New York

Federal Bankruptcy Exemptions not available. Law references to Consolidated Laws of New York; Civil Practice Law & Rules, are abbreviated C.P.L.R.

ASSET	EXEMPTION	LAW
homestead	Real property including co-op, condo or mobile home, to $10,000	C.P.L.R. 5206(a)
	Husband & wife may double	*In re Pearl,* 723 F.2d 193 (2nd Cir. 1983)
insurance	Annuity contract benefits due the debtor, if debtor paid for the contract; $5,000 limit if purchased within 6 mos. prior to filing & not tax-deferred	Ins. 3212(d); Debt. & Cred. 283(1)
	Disability or illness benefits to $400/month	Ins. 3212(c)
	Life insurance proceeds left at death with the insurance company, if clause prohibits proceeds from being used to pay beneficiary's creditors	Est. Powers & Trusts 7-1.5(a)(2)
	Life insurance proceeds and avails if the beneficiary is not the debtor, or if debtor's spouse has taken out policy	Ins. 3212(b)
miscellaneous	Alimony, child support	C.P.L.R. 5205 (d)(3); Debt. & Cred. 282(2)(d)
	Property of business partnership	Partnership 51
pensions	ERISA-qualified benefits, IRAs, & Keoghs needed for support	C.P.L.R. 5205(c); Debt. & Cred. 282(2)(e)
	Public retirement benefits	Ins. 4607
	State employees	Ret. & Soc. Sec. 110
	Teachers	Educ. 524
	Village police officers	Unconsol. 5711-o
personal property	Bible, schoolbooks, other books to $50; pictures; clothing; church pew or seat; sewing machine, refrigerator, TV, radio; furniture, cooking utensils & tableware, dishes; food to last 60 days; stoves with fuel to last 60 days; domestic animal with food to last 60 days, to $450; wedding ring; watch to $35; exemptions may not exceed $5,000 total (including tools of trade & limited annuity)	C.P.L.R. 5205(1)-(6); Debt. & Cred. 283(1)
	Burial plot, without structure to ¼ acre	C.P.L.R. 5206(f)
	Cash (including savings bonds, tax refunds, bank & credit union deposits) to $2,500, or to $5,000 after exemptions for personal property taken, whichever amount is less (for debtors who do not claim homestead)	Debt. & Cred. 283(2)
	College tuition savings program trust fund	C.P.L.R. 5205(j)
	Health aids, including service animals with food	C.P.L.R. 5205(h)
	Lost future earnings recoveries needed for support	Debt. & Cred. 282(3)(iv)
	Motor vehicle to $2,400 (husband & wife may double)	Debt. & Cred. 282(1); *In re Miller,* 167 B.R. 782 (S.D. N.Y. 1994)
	Personal injury recoveries up to 1 year after receiving	Debt. & Cred. 282(3)(iii)
	Security deposit to landlord, utility company	C.P.L.R. 5205(g)
	Trust fund principal, 90% of income	C.P.L.R. 5205(c),(d)
	Wrongful death recoveries for person you depended on	Debt. & Cred. 282(3)(ii)

ASSET	EXEMPTION	LAW
public benefits	Aid to blind, aged, disabled	Debt. & Cred. 282(2)(c)
	Crime victims' compensation	Debt. & Cred. 282(3)(i)
	Home relief, local public assistance	Debt. & Cred. 282(2)(a)
	Social Security, unemployment compensation	Debt. & Cred. 282(2)(a)
	Veterans' benefits	Debt. & Cred. 282(2)(b)
	Workers' compensation	Debt. & Cred. 282(2)(c)
tools of trade	Farm machinery, team & food for 60 days; professional furniture, books & instruments to $600 total	C.P.L.R. 5205(b)
	Uniforms, medals, emblems, equipment, horse, arms & sword of member of military	C.P.L.R. 5205(e)
wages	90% of earned but unpaid wages received within 60 days before & any time after filing	C.P.L.R. 5205(d)
	90% of earnings from dairy farmer's sales to milk dealers	C.P.L.R. 5205(f)
	100% of pay of non-commissioned officer, private or musician in U.S. or N.Y. state armed forces	C.P.L.R. 5205(e)
wild card	None	

North Carolina

Federal Bankruptcy Exemptions not available. All law references are to General Statutes of North Carolina unless otherwise noted.

ASSET	EXEMPTION	LAW
homestead	Real or personal property, including co-op, used as residence to $10,000; up to $3,500 of unused portion of homestead may be applied to any property (husband & wife may double)	1C-1601(a)(1),(2)
	Property held as tenancy by the entirety may be exempt against debts owed by only one spouse	In re Crouch, 33 B.R. 271 (E.D. N.C. 1983)
insurance	Employee group life policy or proceeds	58-58-165
	Fraternal benefit society benefits	58-24-85
miscellaneous	Property of business partnership	59-55
	Support received by a surviving spouse for 1 year, up to $10,000	30-15
pensions	Firefighters & rescue squad workers	58-86-90
	IRAs	1C-1601(a)(9)
	Law enforcement officers	143-166.30(g)
	Legislators	120-4.29
	Municipal, city & county employees	128-31
	Teachers & state employees	135-9, 135-95
personal property	Animals, crops, musical instruments, books, clothing, appliances, household goods & furnishings to $3,500 total; may add $750 per dependent, up to $3,000 total additional (all property must have been purchased at least 90 days before filing)	1C-1601(a)(4),(d)
	Burial plot to $10,000, in lieu of homestead	1C-1601(a)(1)
	Health aids	1C-1601(a)(7)
	Motor vehicle to $1,500	1C-1601(a)(3)
	Personal injury and wrongful death recoveries for person you depended on	1C-1601(a)(8)
public benefits	Aid to blind	111-18
	Crime victims' compensation	15B-17
	Special adult assistance	108A-36
	Unemployment compensation	96-17
	Workers' compensation	97-21
tools of trade	Implements, books & tools of trade to $750	1C-1601(a)(5)
wages	Earned but unpaid wages received 60 days before filing for bankruptcy, needed for support	1-362
wild card	$3,500 less any amount claimed for homestead or burial exemption, of any property	1C-1601(a)(2)
	$500 of any personal property	Constitution Art. X §1

North Dakota

Federal Bankruptcy Exemptions not available. All law references are to North Dakota Century Code.

ASSET	EXEMPTION	LAW
homestead	Real property, house trailer or mobile home to $80,000 (husband & wife may not double)	28-22-02(10); 47-18-01
insurance	Fraternal benefit society benefits	26.1-15.1-18, 26.1-33-40
	Life insurance proceeds payable to deceased's estate, not to a specific beneficiary	26.1-33-40
	Life insurance surrender value to $100,000 per policy, if beneficiary is insured's dependent & policy was owned over 1 year before filing for bankruptcy; limit does not apply if more needed for support	28-22-03.1(3)
miscellaneous	Property of business partnership	45-08-02
pensions	Disabled veterans' benefits, except military retirement pay	28-22-03.1(4)(d)
	ERISA-qualified benefits, IRAs & Keoghs to $100,000 per plan; limit does not apply if more needed for support; total (with life insurance surrender value exemption) cannot exceed $200,000	28-22-03.1(3)
	Public employees	28-22-19 (1)
personal property	1. All debtors may exempt:	
	Bible, schoolbooks; other books to $100	28-22-02 (4)
	Burial plots, church pew	28-22-02 (2),(3)
	Cash to $7,500, in lieu of homestead	28-22-03.1(1)
	Clothing & family pictures	28-22-02 (1),(5)
	Crops or grain raised by debtor on 1 tract 160 acres	28-22-02 (8)
	Food & fuel to last 1 year	28-22-02 (6)
	Insurance proceeds for exempt property	28-22-02 (9)
	Motor vehicle to $1,200	28-22-03.1(2)
	Personal injury recoveries to $7,500	28-22-03.1(4)(b)
	Wrongful death recoveries to $7,500	28-22-03.1(4)(a)
	2. Head of household not claiming crops or grain may claim $5,000 of any personal property or:	28-22-03
	Books & musical instruments to $1,500	28-22-04(1)
	Household & kitchen furniture, beds & bedding, to $1,000	28-22-04(2)
	Library & tools of professional, tools of mechanic & stock in trade, to $1,000	28-22-04(4)
	Livestock & farm implements to $4,500	28-22-04(3)
	3. Non-head of household not claiming crops or grain, may claim $2,500 of any personal property	28-22-05
public benefits	Crime victims' compensation	28-22-19(2)
	Public assistance	28-22-19(3)
	Social Security	28-22-03.1(4)(c)
	Unemployment compensation	52-06-30
	Vietnam veterans' adjustment compensation	37-25-07
	Workers' compensation	65-05-29
tools of trade	See personal property, option 2	
wages	Minimum 75% of earned but unpaid wages; bankruptcy judge may authorize more for low-income debtors	32-09.1-.03
wild card	See personal property, options 2 or 3	

Ohio

Federal Bankruptcy Exemptions not available. All law references are to Ohio Revised Code unless otherwise noted.

ASSET	EXEMPTION	LAW
homestead	Real or personal property used as residence to $5,000	2329.66(A)(1)(b)
	Property held as tenancy by the entirety may be exempt against debts owed by only one spouse	In re Thomas, 14 B.R. 423 (N.D. Ohio 1981)
insurance	Benevolent society benefits to $5,000	2329.63, 2329.66(A)(6)(a)
	Disability benefits to $600 per month	2329.66(A)(6)(e), 3923.19
	Fraternal benefit society benefits	2329.66(A)(6)(d), 3921.18
	Group life insurance policy or proceeds	2329.66(A)(6)(c), 3917.05
	Life, endowment or annuity contract avails for your spouse, child or dependent	2329.66(A)(6)(b), 3911.10
	Life insurance proceeds for a spouse	3911.12
	Life insurance proceeds if clause prohibits proceeds from being used to pay beneficiary's creditors	3911.14
miscellaneous	Alimony, child support needed for support	2329.66(A)(11)
	Property of business partnership	1775.24; 2329.66(A)(14)
pensions	ERISA-qualified benefits needed for support	2329.66(A)(10)(b)
	Firefighters, police officers	742.47
	Firefighters', police officers' death benefits	2329.66(A)(10)(a)
	IRAs & Keoghs needed for support	2329.66(A)(10)(c)
	Public employees	145.56
	Public school employees	3307.71, 3309.66
	State highway patrol employees	5505.22
	Volunteer firefighters' dependents	146.13
personal property	Animals, crops, books, musical instruments, appliances, household goods, furnishings, firearms, hunting & fishing equipment to $200 per item; jewelry to $400 for 1 item, $200 for all others; $1,500 total ($2,000 if no homestead exemption claimed) (husband & wife may double)	2329.66(A)(4)(b),(c),(d); In re Szydlowski, 186 B.R. 907 (N.D. Ohio 1995)
	Beds, bedding, clothing to $200 per item	2329.66(A)(3)
	Burial plot	517.09, 2329.66(A)(8)
	Cash, money due within 90 days, tax refund, bank, security & utility deposits to $400 total (husband & wife may double)	2329.66(A)(4)(a); In re Szydlowski, 186 B.R. 907 (N.D. Ohio 1995)
	Cooking unit & refrigerator to $300 each	2329.66(A)(3)
	Health aids	2329.66(A)(7)
	Lost future earnings needed for support, received during 12 months before filing	2329.66(A)(12)(d)
	Motor vehicle to $1,000	2329.66(A)(2)(b)
	Personal injury recoveries to $5,000, received during 12 months before filing	2329.66(A)(12)(c)
	Tuition credit or payment	2329.66(A)(16)
	Wrongful death recoveries for person debtor depended on, needed for support, received during 12 months before filing	2329.66(A)(12)(b)
public benefits	Crime victim's compensation, received during 12 months before filing	2329.66(A)(12)(a); 2743.66
	Disability assistance payments	2329.66(A)(9)(f); 5113.07
	Public assistance	2329.66(A)(9)(d); 5107.12
	Unemployment compensation	2329.66(A)(9)(c); 4141.32
	Vocational rehabilitation benefits	2329.66(A)(9)(a); 3304.19
	Workers' compensation	2329.66(A)(9)(b); 4123.67
tools of trade	Implements, books & tools of trade to $750	2329.66(A)(5)
wages	Minimum 75% of earned but unpaid wages due for 30 days; bankruptcy judge may authorize more for low-income debtors	2329.66(A)(13)
wild card	$400 of any property	2329.66(A)(17)

Oklahoma

Federal Bankruptcy Exemptions not available. All law references are to Oklahoma Statutes Annotated.

ASSET	EXEMPTION	LAW
homestead	Real property or manufactured home to unlimited value; property cannot exceed 1 acre in city, town or village, or 160 acres elsewhere; $5,000 limit if more than 25% of total sq. ft. area used for business purposes; okay to rent homestead as long as no other residence is acquired	31-1(A)(1), 31-1(A)(2), 31-2
insurance	Annuity benefits & cash value	36-3631.1
	Assessment or mutual benefits	36-2410
	Fraternal benefit society benefits	36-2720
	Funeral benefits prepaid & placed in trust	36-6125
	Group life policy or proceeds	36-3632
	Life, health, accident & mutual benefit insurance proceeds & cash value, if clause prohibits proceeds from being used to pay beneficiary's creditors	36-3631.1
	Limited stock insurance benefits	36-2510
miscellaneous	Alimony, child support	31-1(A)(19)
	Property of business partnership	54-225
pensions	County employees	19-959
	Disabled veterans	31-7
	ERISA-qualified benefits, IRAs & Keoghs	31-1(A)(20),(23),(24)
	Firefighters	11-49-126
	Judges	20-1111
	Law enforcement employees	47-2-303.3
	Police officers	11-50-124
	Public employees	74-923
	Tax exempt benefits	60-328
	Teachers	70-17-109
personal property	Books, portraits & pictures	31-1(A)(7)
	Burial plots	31-1(A)(4); 8-7
	Clothing to $4,000	31-1(A)(8)
	Federal earned income tax credit	31-1(A)(25)
	Food & seed for growing to last 1 year	31-1(A)(17)
	1 gun	31-1(A)(14)
	Health aids	31-1(A)(9)
	Household & kitchen furniture	31-1(A)(3)
	Livestock for personal or family use: 5 dairy cows & calves under 6 months; 100 chickens; 20 sheep; 10 hogs; 2 horses, bridles & saddles; forage & feed to last 1 year	31-1(A)(10),(11),(12), (15),(16),(17)
	Motor vehicle to $3,000	31-1(A)(13)
	Personal injury & wrongful death recoveries to $50,000	31-1(A)(21)
	Prepaid funeral benefits	36-6125(H)
	War bond payroll savings account	51-42
public benefits	Crime victims' compensation	21-142.13
	Public assistance	56-173
	Social Security	56-173
	Unemployment compensation	40-2-303
	Workers' compensation	85-48
tools of trade	Implements needed to farm homestead, tools, books & apparatus to $5,000 total	31-1(A)(5),(6), 31-1(C)
wages	75% of wages earned in 90 days before filing bankruptcy; bankruptcy judge may allow more if you show hardship	12-1171.1; 31-1(A)(18), 31-1.1
wild card	None	

Oregon

Federal Bankruptcy Exemptions not available. All law references are to Oregon Revised Statutes.

ASSET	EXEMPTION	LAW
homestead	Real property you occupy or intend to occupy to $25,000 ($33,000 for joint owners); mobile home or houseboat to $23,000 ($30,000 for joint owners); property cannot exceed 1 block in town or city or 160 acres elsewhere; sale exempt 1 year from sale, if you intend to purchase another home	proceeds 23.164, 23.240, 23.250
	Real property of a soldier or sailor during time of war	408.440
insurance	Annuity contract benefits to $500 per month	743.049
	Fraternal benefit society benefits	748.207
	Group life policy or proceeds not payable to insured	743.047
	Health or disability proceeds or avails	743.050
	Life insurance proceeds or cash value if you are not the insured	743.046
miscellaneous	Alimony, child support needed for support	23.160(1)(i)
	Liquor licenses	471.301(1)
	Property of business partnership	68.420
pensions	ERISA-qualified benefits, including IRAs and SEPs	23.170
	Public officers, employees	237.201
	School district employees	239.261
personal property	Bank deposits to $7,500; cash for sold exempt property	23.166
	Books, pictures & musical instruments to $600 total (husband & wife may double)	23.160(1)(a)
	Burial plot	65.870
	Clothing, jewelry & other personal items to $1,800 total (husband & wife may double)	23.160(1)(b)
	Domestic animals, poultry & pets to $1,000 plus food to last 60 days	23.160(1)(e)
	Food & fuel to last 60 days if debtor is householder	23.160(1)(f)
	Furniture, household items, utensils, radios & TVs to $3,000 total	23.160(1)(f)
	Health aids	23.160(1)(h)
	Lost earnings payments for debtor or someone debtor depended on, to extent needed (husband & wife may double)	23.160(1)(L),(3)
	Motor vehicle to $1,700 (husband & wife may double)	23.160(1)(d),(3)
	Personal injury recoveries to $10,000 (husband & wife may double)	23.160(1)(k),(3)
	1 pistol and 1 rifle or shotgun (owned by person over 16) to $1,000	23.200
public benefits	Aid to blind	412.115
	Aid to disabled	412.610
	Civil defense & disaster relief	401.405
	Crime victims' compensation (husband & wife may double)	23.160(1)(j)(A), (3); 147.325
	General assistance	411.760
	Injured inmates' benefits	655.530
	Medical assistance	414.095
	Old-age assistance	413.130
	Unemployment compensation	657.855
	Veterans' benefits	407.125
	Vocational rehabilitation	344.580
	Workers' compensation	656.234
tools of trade	Tools, library, team with food to last 60 days, to $3,000 (husband & wife may double)	23.160(1)(c),(3)
wages	75% of earned but unpaid wages; bankruptcy judge may authorize more for low-income debtors	23.185
	Wages withheld in state employee's bond savings accounts	292.070
wild card	$400 of any personal property not already covered by existing exemption	23.160(1)(n)

Pennsylvania

Federal Bankruptcy Exemptions available. All law references are to Pennsylvania Consolidated Statutes Annotated.

ASSET	EXEMPTION	LAW
homestead	None, however, property held as tenancy by the entirety may be exempt against debts owed by only one spouse	*Keystone Savings Ass'n v. Kitsock,* 633 A.2d 165 (Pa. Super. Ct. 1993)
insurance	Accident or disability benefits	42-8124(c)(7)
	Fraternal benefit society benefits	42-8124(c)(1),(8)
	Group life policy or proceeds	42-8124(c)(5)
	Insurance policy or annuity contract payments, where insured is the beneficiary, cash value or proceeds to $100 per month	42-8124(c)(3)
	Life insurance annuity policy cash value or proceeds if beneficiary is insured's dependent, child or spouse	42-8124(c)(6)
	Life insurance proceeds if clause prohibits proceeds from being used to pay beneficiary's creditors	42-8214(c)(4)
	No-fault automobile insurance proceeds	42-8124(c)(9)
miscellaneous	Property of business partnership	15-8341
pensions	City employees	53-13445, 53-23572, 53-39383
	County employees	16-4716
	Municipal employees	53-881.115
	Police officers	53-764, 53-776, 53-23666
	Private retirement benefits to extent tax-deferred, if clause prohibits proceeds from being used to pay beneficiary's creditors; exemption limited to deposits of $15,000/year made at least 1 year before filing (does not apply to rollovers from other exempt funds or accounts)	42-8124(b)(1)(viii),(ix)
	Public school employees	24-8533
	State employees	71-5953
personal property	Bibles & schoolbooks	42-8124(a)(2)
	Clothing	42-8124(a)(1)
	Military uniforms & accoutrements	42-8124(a)(4)
	Sewing machines	42-8124(a)(3)
public benefits	Crime victims' compensation	18-11.708
	Korean conflict veterans' benefits	51-20098
	Unemployment compensation	42-8124(a)(10); 43-863
	Veterans' benefits	51-20012
	Workers' compensation	42-8124(c)(2)
tools of trade	Seamstress's sewing machine	42-8124(a)(3)
wages	Earned but unpaid wages	42-8127
wild card	$300 of any property, including cash, real property, securities or proceeds from sale of exempt property	42-8123

Rhode Island

Federal Bankruptcy Exemptions available. All law references are to General Laws of Rhode Island.

ASSET	EXEMPTION	LAW
homestead	$100,000 in land & buildings you occupy or intend to occupy as a principal residence (husband & wife may not double)	9-26-4.1
insurance	Accident or sickness proceeds, avails or benefits	27-18-24
	Fraternal benefit society benefits	27-25-18
	Life insurance proceeds if clause prohibits proceeds from being used to pay beneficiary's creditors	27-4-12
	Temporary disability insurance	28-41-32
miscellaneous	Earnings of a minor child	9-26-4(9)
	Property of business partnership	7-12-36
pensions	ERISA-qualified benefits	9-26-4(12)
	Firefighters	9-26-5
	IRAs	9-26-4(11)
	Police officers	9-26-5
	Private employees	28-17-4
	State & municipal employees	36-10-34
personal property	Beds, bedding, furniture, household goods & supplies, to $1,000 total (husband & wife may not double)	9-26-4(3); *In re Petrozella*, 247 B.R. 591 (R.I. 2000)
	Bibles & books to $300	9-26-4(4)
	Burial plot	9-26-4(5)
	Clothing	9-26-4(1)
	Consumer cooperative association holdings to $50	7-8-25
	Debt secured by promissory note or bill of exchange	9-26-4(7)
public benefits	Aid to blind, aged, disabled, general assistance	40-6-14
	State disability benefits	28-41-32
	Unemployment compensation	28-44-58
	Veterans' disability or survivors' death benefits	30-7-9
	Workers' compensation	28-33-27
tools of trade	Library of practicing professional	9-26-4(2)
	Working tools to $500	9-26-4(2)
wages	Earned but unpaid wages to $50	9-26-4(8)(iii)
	Earned but unpaid wages due military member on active duty	30-7-9
	Earned but unpaid wages due seaman	9-26-4(6)
	Wages of any person who had been receiving public assistance are exempt for 1 year after going off of relief	9-26-4(8)(ii)
	Wages of spouse & minor children	9-26-4(9)
	Wages paid by charitable organization or fund providing relief to the poor	9-26-4(8)(i)
wild card	None	

South Carolina

Federal Bankruptcy Exemptions not available. All law references are to Code of Laws of South Carolina.

ASSET	EXEMPTION	LAW
homestead	Real property, including co-op, to $5,000 (joint owners may double)	15-41-30(1)
insurance	Accident & disability benefits	38-63040(D)
	Benefits accruing under life insurance policy after death of insured, where proceeds left with insurance company pursuant to agreement; benefits not exempt from action to recover necessaries if parties so agree	38-63-50
	Disability or illness benefits	15-41-30(10)(C)
	Fraternal benefit society benefits	38-37-870
	Group life insurance proceeds; cash value to $50,000	38-63-40(C), 38-65-90
	Life insurance avails from policy for person you depended on to $4,000	15-41-30(8)
	Life insurance proceeds from policy for person you depended on, needed for support	15-41-30(11)(C)
	Proceeds & cash surrender value of life insurance payable to beneficiary other than insured's estate and for the express benefit of insured's spouse, children or dependents (must be purchased 2 years before filing)	38-63-40(A)
	Proceeds of life insurance or annuity contract	38-63-40(B)
	Unmatured life insurance contract, except credit insurance policy	15-41-30(7)
miscellaneous	Alimony, child support	15-41-30(10)(D)
	Property of business partnership	33-41-720
pensions	ERISA-qualified benefits; your share of the pension plan fund	15-41-30(10)(E),(13)
	Firefighters	9-13-230
	General assembly members	9-9-180
	IRAs	15-41-30(12)
	Judges, solicitors	9-8-190
	Police officers	9-11-270
	Public employees	9-1-1680
personal property	Animals, crops, appliances, books, clothing, household goods, furnishings, musical instruments to $2,500 total	15-41-30(3)
	Burial plot to $5,000, in lieu of homestead (joint owners may double)	15-41-30(1)
	Cash & other liquid assets to $1,000, in lieu of burial or homestead exemption	15-41-30(5)
	Health aids	15-41-30(9)
	Jewelry to $500	15-41-30(4)
	Motor vehicle to $1,200	15-41-30(2)
	Personal injury & wrongful death recoveries for person you depended on for support	15-41-30(11)(B)
public benefits	Crime victims' compensation	15-41-30(11)(A); 16-3-1300
	General relief, aid to aged, blind, disabled	43-5-190
	Local public assistance	15-41-30(10)(A)
	Social Security	15-41-30(10)(A)
	Unemployment compensation	15-41-30(10)(A)
	Veterans' benefits	15-41-30(10)(B)
	Workers' compensation	42-9-360
tools of trade	Implements, books & tools of trade to $750	15-41-30(6)
wages	None	
wild card	None	

South Dakota

Federal Bankruptcy Exemptions not available. All law references are to South Dakota Codified Laws.

ASSET	EXEMPTION	LAW
homestead	Real property to unlimited value or mobile home (larger than 240 sq. ft. at its base and registered in the state at least 6 months before filing) to unlimited value; property cannot exceed 1 acre in town or 160 acres elsewhere; sale proceeds to $30,000 (no limit if over age 70 or widow or widower who hasn't remarried) exempt for 1 year after sale (husband & wife may not double) (Gold or silver mine, mill or smelter not exempt, 43-31-5.)	43-31-1, 43-31-2, 43-31-3, 43-31-4
	Spouse or child of deceased owner may claim homestead exemption	43-31-13
	May file homestead declaration	43-31-6
insurance	Annuity contract proceeds to $250 per month	58-12-6, 58-12-8
	Endowment, life insurance, policy proceeds to $20,000; if policy issued by mutual aid or benevolent society, cash value to $20,000	58-12-4
	Fraternal benefit society benefits	58-37-68
	Health benefits to $20,000	58-12-4
	Life insurance proceeds, if clause prohibits proceeds from being used to pay beneficiary's creditors	58-15-70
	Life insurance proceeds to $10,000, if beneficiary is surviving spouse or child	43-45-6
miscellaneous	Property of business partnership	48-4-14
pensions	City employees	9-16-47
	ERISA-qualified benefits, limited to income & distribution on $250,000	43-45-16
	Public employees	3-12-115
personal property	Bible, schoolbooks; other books to $200	43-45-2(4)
	Burial plots, church pew	43-45-2(2),(3)
	Clothing	43-45-2(5)
	Family pictures	43-45-2(1)
	Food & fuel to last 1 year	43-45-2(6)
public benefits	Crime victim's compensation	23A-28B-24
	Public assistance	28-7-16
	Unemployment compensation	61-6-28
	Workers' compensation	62-4-42
tools of trade	None	
wages	Earned wages owed 60 days before filing bankruptcy, needed for support of family	15-20-12
	Wages of prisoners in work programs	24-8-10
wild card	Head of family may claim $6,000 or non-head of family may claim $4,000 of any personal property	43-45-4

Tennessee

Federal Bankruptcy Exemptions not available. All law references are to Tennessee Code Annotated unless otherwise noted.

ASSET	EXEMPTION	LAW
homestead	$5,000; $7,500 for joint owners	26-2-301
	Life estate	26-2-302
	2-15 year lease	26-2-303
	Spouse or child of deceased owner may claim homestead exemption	26-2-301
	Property held as tenancy by the entirety may be exempt against debts owed by only one spouse	In re Arango, 136 B.R. 740, aff'd, 992 F.2d 611 (6th Cir. 1993)
insurance	Accident, health or disability benefits for resident & citizen of Tennessee	26-2-110
	Disability or illness benefits	26-2-111(1)(C)
	Fraternal benefit society benefits	56-25-1403
	Homeowners' insurance proceeds to $5,000	26-2-304
miscellaneous	Alimony, child support owed for 30 days before filing for bankruptcy	26-2-111(1)(E)
	Property of business partnership	61-1-124
pensions	ERISA-qualified benefits	26-2-111(1)(D)
	Public employees	8-36-111
	State & local government employees	26-2-104
	Teachers	49-5-909
personal property	Bible, schoolbooks, family pictures & portraits	26-2-103
	Burial plot to 1 acre	26-2-305, 46-2-102
	Clothing & storage containers	26-2-103
	Health aids	26-2-111(5)
	Lost future earnings payments for you or person you depended on	26-2-111(3)
	Personal injury recoveries to $7,500; wrongful death recoveries to $10,000 ($15,000 total for personal injury, wrongful death & crime victims' compensation)	26-2-111(2)(B),(C)
public benefits	Aid to blind	71-4-117
	Aid to disabled	71-4-1112
	Crime victims' compensation to $5,000 (see personal property)	26-2-111(2)(A), 29-13-111
	Local public assistance	26-2-111(1)(A)
	Old-age assistance	71-2-216
	Social Security	26-2-111(1)(A)
	Unemployment compensation	26-2-111(1)(A)
	Veterans' benefits	26-2-111(1)(B)
	Workers' compensation	50-6-223
tools of trade	Implements, books & tools of trade to $1,900	26-2-111(4)
wages	Minimum 75% of earned but unpaid wages, plus $2.50 per week per child; bankruptcy judge may authorize more for low-income debtors	26-2-106,107
wild card	$4,000 of any personal property including deposits on account with any bank or financial institution	26-2-102

Texas

Federal Bankruptcy Exemptions available. All law references are to Texas Revised Civil Statutes Annotated unless otherwise noted.

ASSET	EXEMPTION	LAW
homestead	Unlimited; property cannot exceed 10 acres in town, village, city or 100 acres (200 for families) elsewhere; sale proceeds exempt for 6 months after sale (renting okay if another home not acquired, Prop. 41.003)	Prop. 41.001, 41.002
	Must file homestead declaration	Prop. 41.005
insurance	Church benefit plan benefits	1407a-6
	Fraternal benefit society benefits	Ins. 10.28
	Life, health, accident or annuity benefits, monies, policy proceeds & cash values due or paid to beneficiary or insured	Ins. 21.22
	Texas employee uniform group insurance	Ins. 3.50-2(10)(a)
	Texas public school employees group insurance	Ins. 3.50-4(11)(a)
	Texas state college or university employee benefits	Ins. 3.50-3(9)(a)
miscellaneous	Alimony and child support	Prop. 42.001(b)(3)
	Property of business partnership	6132b-2.05
pensions	County & district employees	Gov't. 811.006
	ERISA-qualified government or church benefits, including Keoghs and IRAs	Prop. 42.0021
	Firefighters	6234a(8.03)(a), 6243e(5)
	Judges	Gov't. 831.004, .006
	Law enforcement officers', firefighters' and emergency medical personnel survivors	Gov't. 615.003
	Police officers	6243d-1(17), 6243j(20), 6234a(8.03)(a)
	Retirement benefits to extent tax-deferred	Prop. 42.0021
	State & municipal employees	Gov't. 811.005
	Teachers	Gov't. 821.005
personal property *$60,000 total if head of family, $30,000 if single; includes tools of trade & unpaid commissions*	Athletic and sporting equipment, including bicycles; 2 firearms	Prop. 42.002(a)(1),(7)
	Clothing & food	Prop. 42.002(a)(2),(5)
	Home furnishings including family heirlooms	Prop. 42.002(a)(1)
	Jewelry (limited to 25% of total exemption)	Prop. 42.002(a)(6)
	1 two-, three- or four-wheeled motor vehicle per family member or per single adult who holds a driver's license; or, if not licensed, who relies on someone else to operate vehicle	Prop. 42.002(9)
	Pets & domestic animals plus their food: 2 horses, mules or donkeys & tack; 12 head of cattle; 60 head of other livestock; 120 fowl	Prop. 42.002(10)(11)
	Burial plots (exempt from total)	Prop. 41.001
	Health aids (exempt from total)	Prop. 42.001(b)(2)
public benefits	Crime victims' compensation	Crim. Proc. 56.49
	Medical assistance	Hum. Res. 32.036
	Public assistance	Hum. Res. 31.040
	Unemployment compensation	Labor 207.075
	Workers' compensation	Labor 408.201
tools of trade *see note under personal property*	Farming or ranching vehicles & implements	Prop. 42.002(a)(3)
	Tools, equipment (includes boat & motor vehicles used in trade) & books	Prop. 42.002(a)(4)
wages	Earned but unpaid wages	Prop. 42.001(b)(1)
	Unpaid commissions not to exceed 25% of total personal property exemptions	Prop. 42.001(d)
wild card	None	

Utah

Federal Bankruptcy Exemptions not available. All law references are to Utah Code.

ASSET	EXEMPTION	LAW
homestead	Real property, mobile home or water rights to $20,000 if primary residence; $5,000 if not primary residence (joint owners may double)	78-23-3(1),(2),(4)
	Must file homestead declaration before attempted sale of home	78-23-4
	Sale proceeds exempt for 1 year	78-23-3(5)(b)
insurance	Disability, illness, medical or hospital benefits	78-23-5(1)(a)(iii)
	Fraternal benefit society benefits	31A-9-603
	Life insurance policy cash surrender value to $1,500	78-23-7
	Life insurance proceeds if beneficiary is insured's spouse or dependent, as needed for support	78-23-6(2)
	Medical, surgical and hospital benefits	78-23-5(1)(a)(iv)
miscellaneous	Alimony needed for support	78-23-5(1)(a)(vi), 78-23-6(1)
	Child support	78-23-5(1)(f), (k)
	Property of business partnership	48-1-22
pensions	ERISA-qualified benefits, IRAs, Keoghs (benefits that have accrued & contributions that have been made at least 1 year prior to filing for bankruptcy)	78-23-5(1)(a)(x)
	Public employees	49-1-609
	Other pensions & annuities needed for support	78-23-6(3)
personal property	Animals, books & musical instruments to $500	78-23-8(1)(c)
	Artwork depicting, or done by, a family member	78-23-5(1)(a)(viii)
	Bed, bedding, carpets	78-23-5(1)(a)(vii)
	Burial plot	78-23-5(1)(a)(i)
	Clothing (cannot claim furs or jewelry)	78-23-5(1)(a)(vii)
	Dining & kitchen tables & chairs to $500	78-23-8(1)(b)
	Food to last 12 months	78-23-5(1)(a)(vii)
	Health aids	78-23-5(1)(a)(ii)
	Heirlooms to $500	78-23-8(1)(d)
	Personal injury, wrongful death recoveries for you or person you depended on	78-23-5(1)(a)(ix)
	Proceeds for sold, lost or damaged exempt property	78-23-9
	Refrigerator, freezer, microwave, stove, sewing machine, washer & dryer	78-23-5(1)(a)(vii)
	Sofas, chairs & related furnishings to $500	78-23-8(1)(a)
public benefits	Crime victims' compensation	63-25a-421(4)
	General assistance	55-15-32
	Occupational disease disability benefits	34A-3-107
	Unemployment compensation	35A-4-103(4)(b)
	Veterans' benefits	78-23-5(1)(a)(v)
	Workers' compensation	34A-2-422
tools of trade	Implements, books & tools of trade to $3,500	78-23-8(2)
	Military property of National Guard member	39-1-47
	Motor vehicle used for profession to $2,500	78-23-8(3)
wages	Minimum 75% of earned but unpaid wages; bankruptcy judge may authorize more for low-income debtors	70C-7-103
wild card	None	

Vermont

Federal Bankruptcy Exemptions available. All law references are to Vermont Statutes Annotated unless otherwise noted.

ASSET	EXEMPTION	LAW
homestead	Real property or mobile home to $75,000; may also claim rents, issues, profits & out-buildings	27-101
	Spouse of deceased owner may claim homestead exemption	27-105
	Property held as tenancy by the entirety may be exempt against debts owed by only one spouse	In re McQueen, 21 B.R. 736 (D. Ver. 1982)
insurance	Annuity contract benefits to $350 per month	8-3709
	Disability benefits that supplement life insurance or annuity contract	8-3707
	Disability or illness benefits needed for support	12-2740(19)(C)
	Fraternal benefit society benefits	8-4478
	Group life or health benefits	8-3708
	Health benefits to $200 per month	8-4086
	Life insurance proceeds if beneficiary is not the insured	8-3706
	Life insurance proceeds for person you depended on	12-2740(19)(H)
	Life insurance proceeds if clause prohibits proceeds from being used to pay beneficiary's creditors	8-3705
	Unmatured life insurance contract other than credit	12-2740(18)
miscellaneous	Alimony, child support	12-2740(19)(D)
	Property of business partnership	11-1282
pensions	Municipal employees	24-5066
	Self-directed accounts (IRAs, Keoghs); contributions must be made 1 year before filing	12-2740(16)
	State employees	3-476
	Teachers	16-1946
	Other pensions	12-2740(19)(J)
personal property	Appliances, furnishings, goods, clothing, books, crops, animals, musical instruments to $2,500 total	12-2740(5)
	Bank deposits to $700	12-2740(15)
	Cow, 2 goats, 10 sheep, 10 chickens & feed to last 1 winter; 3 swarms of bees plus honey; 5 tons coal or 500 gal. heating oil, 10 cords of firewood; 500 gal. bottled gas; growing crops to $5,000; yoke of oxen or steers, plow & ox yoke; 2 horses with harnesses, halters & chains	12-2740(6), (9)-(14)
	Health aids	12-2740(17)
	Jewelry to $500; wedding ring unlimited	12-2740(3),(4)
	Motor vehicles to $2,500	12-2740(1)
	Personal injury, lost future earnings, wrongful death recoveries for you or person you depended on	12-2740(19)(F), (G),(I)
	Stove, heating unit, refrigerator, freezer, water heater & sewing machines	12-2740(8)
public benefits	Aid to blind, aged, disabled, general assistance	33-124
	Crime victims' compensation needed for support	12-2740(19)(E)
	Social Security needed for support	12-2740(19)(A)
	Unemployment compensation	21-1367
	Veterans' benefits needed for support	12-2740(19)(B)
	Workers' compensation	21-681
tools of trade	Books & tools of trade to $5,000	12-2740(2)
wages	Minimum 75% of earned but unpaid wages; bankruptcy judge may authorize more for low-income debtors	12-3170
	Entire wages, if you received welfare during 2 months before filing	12-3170
wild card	Unused exemptions for motor vehicle, tools of trade, jewelry, household furniture, appliances, clothing & crops to $7,000	12-2740(7)
	$400 of any property	12-2740(7)

Virginia

Federal Bankruptcy Exemptions not available. All law references are to Code of Virginia unless otherwise noted.

ASSET	EXEMPTION	LAW
homestead	$5,000 plus $500 per dependent; rents & profits; sale proceeds exempt to $5,000 (husband & wife may double, Cheeseman v. Nachman, 656 F.2d 60 (4th Cir. 1981)); unused portion of homestead may be applied to any personal property	34-4,34-18,34-20
	May include mobile home	In re Goad, 161 B.R. 161 (W.D. Va. 1993)
	Must file homestead declaration before filing for bankruptcy	34-6
	Property held as tenancy by the entirety may be exempt against debts owed by only one spouse	In re Harris, 155 B.R. 948 (E.D. Va. 1993)
	Surviving spouse may claim $10,000; if no surviving spouse, minor children may claim exemption	64.1-151.3
insurance	Accident or sickness benefits	38.2-3406
	Burial society benefits	38.2-4021
	Cooperative life insurance benefits	38.2-3811
	Fraternal benefit society benefits	38.2-4118
	Group life or accident insurance for government officials	51.1-510
	Group life insurance policy or proceeds	38.2-3339
	Industrial sick benefits	38.2-3549
	Life insurance proceeds	38.2-3122
miscellaneous	Property of business partnership	50-73.108
pensions	City, town & county employees	51.1-802
	ERISA-qualified benefits to $17,500	34-34
also see wages	Judges	51.1-300
	State employees	51.1-124.4(A)
	State police officers	51.1-200
personal property	Bible	34-26(1)
	Burial plot	34-26(3)
	Clothing to $1,000	34-26(4)
	Family portraits & heirlooms to $5,000 total	34-26(2)
	Health aids	34-26(6)
	Household furnishings to $5,000	34-26(4a)
	Motor vehicle to $2,000	34-26(8)
	Personal injury causes of action & recoveries	34-28.1
	Pets	34-26(5)
	Wedding and engagement rings	34-26(1a)
public benefits	Aid to blind, aged, disabled, general relief	63.1-88
	Crime victims' compensation unless seeking to discharge debt for treatment of injury incurred during crime	19.2-368.12
	Unemployment compensation	60.2-600
	Workers' compensation	65.2-531
tools of trade	For farmer, pair of horses or mules with gear; one wagon or cart, one tractor to $3,000; 2 plows & wedges; one drag, harvest cradle, pitchfork, rake; fertilizer to $1,000	34-27
	Tools, books and instruments of trade, including motor vehicles, to $10,000, needed in your occupation or education	34-26(7)
	Uniforms, arms, equipment of military member	44-96
wages	Minimum 75% of earned but unpaid wages, pension payments; bankruptcy judge may authorize more for low-income debtors	34-29
wild card	Unused portion of homestead or personal property exemption	34-13
	$2,000 of any property for disabled veterans	34-4.1

Washington

Federal Bankruptcy Exemptions available. All law references are to Revised Code of Washington Annotated.

ASSET	EXEMPTION	LAW
homestead	Real property or mobile home to $40,000; unimproved property intended for residence to $15,000 (husband & wife may not double)	6.13.010, 6.13.030
	Must record homestead declaration before sale of home if property unimproved or home unoccupied	6.15.040
insurance	Annuity contract proceeds to $250 per month	48.18.430
	Disability proceeds, avails or benefits	48.18.400
	Fraternal benefit society benefits	48.36A.180
	Group life insurance policy or proceeds	48.18.420
	Life insurance proceeds or avails if beneficiary is not the insured	48.18.410
miscellaneous	Property of business partnership	25.04.250
pensions	City employees	41.28.200, 41.44.240
	ERISA-qualified benefits, IRAs & Keoghs	6.15.020
	Judges	2.10.180, 2.12.090
	Law enforcement officials & firefighters	41.26.053
	Police officers	41.20.180
	Public & state employees	41.40.052
	State patrol officers	43.43.310
	Teachers	41.32.052
	Volunteer firefighters	41.24.240
personal property	Appliances, furniture, household goods, home & yard equipment to $2,700 total	6.15.010(3)(a)
	Books to $1,500	6.15.010(2)
	Burial plots sold by nonprofit cemetery association	68.20.120
	Clothing, no more than $1,000 in furs, jewelry, ornaments	6.15.010(1)
	Food & fuel for comfortable maintenance	6.15.010(3)(a)
	Fire insurance proceeds for lost, stolen or destroyed exempt property	6.15.030
	Keepsakes & family pictures	6.15.010(2)
	Two motor vehicles to $2,500 total	6.15.010(3)(c)
public benefits	Child welfare	74.13.070
	Crime victims' compensation	7.68.070
	General assistance	74.04.280
	Industrial insurance (workers' compensation)	51.32.040
	Old-age assistance	74.08.210
	Unemployment compensation	50.40.020
tools of trade	Commercial fishing license	75.28.011
	Farmer's trucks, stock, tools, seed, equipment & supplies to $5,000 total	6.15.010(4)(a)
	Library, office furniture, office equipment & supplies of physician, surgeon, attorney, clergy or other professional to $5,000 total	6.15.010(4)(b)
	Tools & materials used in any other trade to $5,000	6.15.010(4)(c)
wages	Minimum 75% of earned but unpaid wages; bankruptcy judge may authorize more for low-income debtors	6.27.150
wild card	$1,000 of any personal property (no more than $100 in cash, bank deposits, bonds, stocks & securities)	6.15.010(3)(b)

West Virginia

Federal Bankruptcy Exemptions not available. All law references are to West Virginia Code.

ASSET	EXEMPTION	LAW
homestead	Real or personal property used as residence to $15,000; unused portion of homestead may be applied to any property (husband & wife may double)	38-10-4(a)
insurance	Fraternal benefit society benefits	33-23-21
	Group life insurance policy or proceeds	33-6-28
	Health or disability benefits	38-10-4(j)(3)
	Life insurance payments from policy for person you depended on, needed for support	38-10-4(k)(3)
	Unmatured life insurance contract, except credit insurance policy	38-10-4(g)
	Unmatured life insurance contract's accrued dividend, interest or loan value to $8,000, if debtor owns contract & insured is either debtor or a person on whom debtor is dependent	38-10-4(h)
miscellaneous	Alimony, child support needed for support	38-10-4(j)(4)
	Property of business partnership	47-8A-25
pensions	ERISA-qualified benefits, IRAs needed for support	38-10-4(j)(5)
	Public employees	5-10-46
	Teachers	18-7A-30
personal property	Animals, crops, clothing, appliances, books, household goods, furnishings, musical instruments to $400 per item, $8,000 total	38-10-4(c)
	Burial plot to $15,000, in lieu of homestead	38-10-4(a)
	Health aids	38-10-4(i)
	Jewelry to $1,000	38-10-4(d)
	Lost earnings payments needed for support	38-10-4(k)(5)
	Motor vehicle to $2,400	38-10-4(b)
	Personal injury recoveries to $15,000	38-10-4(k)(4)
	Prepaid tuition trust fund payments	38-10-4(k)(6)
	Wrongful death recoveries for person you depended on, needed for support	38-10-4(k)(2)
public benefits	Aid to blind, aged, disabled, general assistance	9-5-1
	Crime victims' compensation	38-10-4(k)(1)
	Social Security	38-10-4(j)(1)
	Unemployment compensation	38-10-4(j)(1)
	Veterans' benefits	38-10-4(j)(2)
	Workers' compensation	23-4-18
tools of trade	Implements, books & tools of trade to $1,500	38-10-4(f)
wages	80% of earned but unpaid wages; bankruptcy judge may authorize more for low-income debtors	38-5A-3
wild card	$800 plus unused portion of homestead or burial exemption, of any property	38-10-4(e)

Wisconsin

Federal Bankruptcy Exemptions available. All law references are to Wisconsin Statutes Annotated.

ASSET	EXEMPTION	LAW
homestead	Property you occupy or intend to occupy to $40,000; sale proceeds exempt for 2 years if you intend to purchase another home (husband & wife's exemption may not exceed $40,000)	815.20
insurance	Federal disability insurance	815.18(3)(ds)
	Fraternal benefit society benefits	614.96
	Life insurance proceeds held in trust by insurer, if clause prohibits proceeds from being used to pay beneficiary's creditors	632.42
	Life insurance proceeds for someone debtor depended on, needed for support	815.18(3)(i)(a)
	Unmatured life insurance contract (except credit insurance contract) if debtor owns contract & insured is debtor or dependents, or someone debtor is dependent on	815.18(3)(f)
	Unmatured life insurance contract's accrued dividends, interest or loan value to $4,000 total, if debtor owns contract & insured is debtor or dependents, or someone debtor is dependent on	815.18(3)(f)
miscellaneous	Alimony, child support needed for support	815.18(3)(c)
	Property of business partnership	178.21(3)(c)
pensions	Certain municipal employees	66.81
	Firefighters, police officers who worked in city with population over 100,000	815.18(3)(ef)
	Military pensions	815.18(3)(n)
	Private or public retirement benefits	815.18(3)(j)
	Public employees	40.08(1)
personal property	Burial plot, tombstone, coffin (husband & wife may double)	815.18(3)(a)
	College savings account or tuition trust fund	14.64(7) 14.63(8)
	Deposit accounts to $1,000	815.18(3)(k)
	Fire & casualty proceeds for destroyed exempt property for 2 years from receiving	815.18(3)(e)
	Household goods and furnishings, clothing, keepsakes, jewelry, appliances, books, musical instruments, firearms, sporting animals goods, and other tangible personal property to $5,000 total (husband & wife may double)	815.18(3)(d)
	Lost future earnings recoveries, needed for support	815.18(3)(i)(d)
	Motor vehicles to $1,200 (husband & wife may double; unused portion of $5,000 personal property exemption may be added)	815.18(3)(g)
	Personal injury recoveries to $25,000	815.18(3)(i)(c)
	Tenant's lease or stock interest in housing co-op, to homestead amount	182.004(6)
	Wages used to purchase savings bonds	20.921(1)(e)
	Wrongful death recoveries, needed for support	815.18(3)(i)(b)
public benefits	Crime victims' compensation	949.07
	Social services payments	49.96
	Unemployment compensation	108.13
	Veterans' benefits	45.35(8)(b)
	Workers' compensation	102.27
tools of trade	Equipment, inventory, farm products, books and tools of trade to $7,500 total	815.18(3)(b)
wages	75% of earned but unpaid wages; bankruptcy judge may authorize more for low-income debtors	815.18(3)(h)
wild card	None	

Wyoming

Federal Bankruptcy Exemptions not available. All law references are to Wyoming Statutes Annotated unless otherwise noted.

ASSET	EXEMPTION	LAW
homestead	Real property you occupy to $10,000 or house trailer you occupy to $6,000 (joint owners may double)	1-20-101,102, 1-20-104
	Spouse or child of deceased owner may claim homestead exemption	1-20-103
	Property held as tenancy by the entirety may be exempt against debts owed by only one spouse	In re Anselmi, 52 B.R. 479 (D. Wy. 1985)
insurance	Annuity contract proceeds to $350 per month	26-15-132
	Disability benefits if clause prohibits proceeds from being used to pay beneficiary's creditors	26-15-130
	Fraternal benefit society benefits	26-29-218
	Group life or disability policy or proceeds	26-15-131
	Life insurance proceeds held by insurer, if clause prohibits proceeds from being used to pay beneficiary's creditors	26-15-133
miscellaneous	Liquor licenses & malt beverage permits	12-4-604
pensions	Criminal investigators, highway officers	9-3-620
	Firefighters' death benefits	15-5-209
	Game & fish wardens	9-3-620
	Police officers	15-5-313(c)
	Private or public retirement funds & accounts	1-20-110
	Public employees	9-3-426
personal property	Bedding, furniture, household articles & food to $2,000 per person in the home	1-20-106(a)(iii)
	Bible, schoolbooks & pictures	1-20-106(a)(i)
	Burial plot	1-20-106(a)(ii)
	Clothing & wedding rings to $1,000	1-20-105
	Motor vehicle to $2,400	1-20-106(a)(iv)
	Prepaid funeral contracts	26-32-102
public benefits	Crime victims' compensation	1-40-113
	General assistance	42-2-113(b)
	Unemployment compensation	27-3-319
	Workers' compensation	27-14-702
tools of trade	Library & implements of professional to $2,000 or tools, motor vehicle, implements, team & stock in trade to $2,000	1-20-106(b)
wages	Earnings of National Guard members	19-2-501
	Minimum 75% of earned but unpaid wages	1-15-511
	Wages of inmates on work release	7-16-308
wild card	None	

Federal Bankruptcy Exemptions

Married couples may double all exemptions. All references are to 11 U.S.C. § 522. These exemptions were last adjusted in 1998. Every three years ending on April 1, these amounts will be adjusted to reflect changes in the Consumer Price Index. The last scheduled adjustment took place April 1, 2001.

Debtors in the following states may select the Federal Bankruptcy Exemptions:

Arkansas	Massachusetts	New Jersey	Texas
Connecticut	Michigan	New Mexico	Vermont
District of Columbia	Minnesota	Pennsylvania	Washington
Hawaii	New Hampshire	Rhode Island	Wisconsin

ASSET	EXEMPTION	SUBSECTION
homestead	Real property, including co-op or mobile home, to $17,425; unused portion of homestead to $8,725 may be applied to any property	(d)(1)
insurance	Disability, illness or unemployment benefits	(d)(10)(C)
	Life insurance payments for person you depended on, needed for support	(d)(11)(C)
	Life insurance policy with loan value, in accrued dividends or interest, to $9,300	(d)(8)
	Unmatured life insurance contract, except credit insurance policy	(d)(7)
miscellaneous	Alimony, child support needed for support	(d)(10)(D)
pensions	ERISA-qualified benefits needed for support; may include IRAs	(d)(10)(E), *Carmichael v. Osherow*, 100 F.3d 375 (5th Cir. 1996)
personal property	Animals, crops, clothing, appliances, books, furnishings, household goods, musical instruments to $450 per item, $9,300 total	(d)(3)
	Health aids	(d)(9)
	Jewelry to $1,150	(d)(4)
	Lost earnings payments	(d)(11)(E)
	Motor vehicle to $2,775	(d)(2)
	Personal injury recoveries to $17,425 (not to include pain & suffering or pecuniary loss)	(d)(11)(D)
	Wrongful death recoveries for person you depended on	(d)(11)(B)
public benefits	Crime victims' compensation	(d)(11)(A)
	Public assistance	(d)(10)(A)
	Social Security	(d)(10)(A)
	Unemployment compensation	(d)(10)(A)
	Veterans' benefits	(d)(10)(A)
tools of trade	Implements, books & tools of trade to $1,750	(d)(6)
wages	None	
wild card	$925 of any property	(d)(5)
	$8,725 less any amount of homestead exemption claimed, of any property	(d)(5)

Federal Non-Bankruptcy Exemptions

These exemptions are available only if you select your state exemptions. You may use them for any exemptions in addition to those allowed by your state, but they cannot be claimed if you file using federal bankruptcy exemptions. All law references are to the United States Code.

ASSET	EXEMPTION	LAW
retirement benefits	CIA employees	50 § 403
	Civil service employees	5 § 8346
	Foreign Service employees	22 § 4060
	Military Medal of Honor roll pensions	38 § 1562(c)
	Military service employees	10 § 1440
	Railroad workers	45 § 231m
	Social Security	42 § 407
	Veterans' benefits	38 § 5301
survivor's benefits	Judges, U.S. court & judicial center directors, administrative assistants to U.S. Supreme Court Chief Justice	28 § 376
	Lighthouse workers	33 § 775
	Military service	10 § 1450
death & disability benefits	Government employees	5 § 8130
	Longshoremen & harbor workers	33 § 916
	War risk hazard death or injury compensation	42 § 1717
miscellaneous	Indian lands or homestead sales or lease proceeds	25 § 410
	Klamath Indian tribe benefits for Indians residing in Oregon	25 § 543, 545
	Military deposits in savings accounts while on permanent duty outside U.S.	10 § 1035
	Military group life insurance	38 § 1970(g)
	Railroad workers' unemployment insurance	45 § 352(e)
	Seamen's clothing	46 § 11110
	Seamen's wages (while on a voyage) pursuant to a written contract	46 § 11109
	75% of earned but unpaid wages; bankruptcy judge may authorize more for low-income debtors	15 § 1673

Appendix 2: Blank Forms

 Do not complete any of these forms until you have read the previous pages in this book.

Form 1—Voluntary Petition

Form 6, Schedule A—Real Property

Form 6, Schedule B—Personal Property

Form 6, Schedule C—Property Claimed As Exempt

Form 6, Schedule D—Creditors Holding Secured Claims

Form 6, Schedule E—Creditors Holding Unsecured Priority Claims

Form 6, Schedule F—Creditors Holding Unsecured Nonpriority Claims

Form 6, Schedule G—Executory Contracts and Unexpired Leases

Form 6, Schedule H—Codebtors

Form 6, Schedule I—Current Income of Individual Debtor(s)

Form 6, Schedule J—Current Expenditures of Individual Debtor(s)

Form 6, Summary of Schedules

Form 6, Declaration Concerning Debtor's Schedules

Form 7—Statement of Financial Affairs

Form 8—Chapter 7 Individual Debtor's Statement of Intention

Mailing Matrix

Form 3—Application and Order to Pay Filing Fee in Installments

Proof of Service by Mail

Amendment Cover Sheet

Notice of Change of Address

FORM 1. VOLUNTARY PETITION

United States Bankruptcy Court _____ District of _____	**Voluntary Petition**

Name of Debtor (if individual, enter Last, First, Middle):	Name of Joint Debtor (Spouse) (Last, First, Middle):
All Other Names used by the Debtor in the last 6 years (include married, maiden, and trade names):	All Other Names used by the Joint Debtor in the last 6 years (include married, maiden, and trade names):
Soc. Sec./Tax I.D. No. (if more than one, state all):	Soc. Sec./Tax I.D. No. (if more than one, state all):
Street Address of Debtor (No. & Street, City, State & Zip Code):	Street Address of Joint Debtor (No. & Street, City, State & Zip Code):
County of Residence or of the Principal Place of Business:	County of Residence or of the Principal Place of Business:
Mailing Address of Debtor (if different from street address):	Mailing Address of Joint Debtor (if different from street address):

Location of Principal Assets of Business Debtor
(if different from street address above):

Information Regarding the Debtor (Check the Applicable Boxes)

Venue (Check any applicable box)

☐ Debtor has been domiciled or has had a residence, principal place of business, or principal assets in this District for 180 days immediately preceding the date of this petition or for a longer part of such 180 days than in any other District.

☐ There is a bankruptcy case concerning debtor's affiliate, general partner, or partnership pending in this District.

Type of Debtor (Check all boxes that apply)	**Chapter or Section of Bankruptcy Code Under Which the Petition is Filed** (Check one box)
☐ Individual(s) ☐ Railroad ☐ Corporation ☐ Stockbroker ☐ Partnership ☐ Commodity Broker ☐ Other _____	☐ Chapter 7 ☐ Chapter 11 ☐ Chapter 13 ☐ Chapter 9 ☐ Chapter 12 ☐ Sec. 304 – Case ancillary to foreign proceeding

Nature of Debts (Check one box)	**Filing Fee** (Check one box)
☐ Consumer/Non-Business ☐ Business	☐ Full Filing Fee attached ☐ Filing Fee to be paid in installments. (Applicable to individuals only.) Must attach signed application for the court's consideration certifying that the debtor is unable to pay fee except in installments. Rule 1006(b). See Official Form No. 3.
Chapter 11 Small Business (Check all boxes that apply) ☐ Debtor is a small business as defined in 11 U.S.C. § 101 ☐ Debtor is and elects to be considered a small business under 11 U.S.C. §1121(e) (Optional)	

Statistical/Administrative Information (Estimates only)	THIS SPACE FOR COURT USE ONLY

☐ Debtor estimates that funds will be available for distribution to unsecured creditors.

☐ Debtor estimates that, after any exempt property is excluded and administrative expenses paid, there will be no funds available for distribution to unsecured creditors.

Estimated Number of Creditors	1-15	16-49	50-99	100-199	200-999	1000-over
	☐	☐	☐	☐	☐	☐

Estimated Assets							
$0 to $50,000	$50,001 to $100,000	$100,001 to $500,000	$500,001 to $1 million	$1,000,001 to $10 million	$10,000,001 to $50 million	$50,000,001 $100 million	More than $100 million
☐	☐	☐	☐	☐	☐	☐	☐

Estimated Debts							
$0 to $50,000	$50,001 to $100,000	$100,001 to $500,000	$500,001 to $1 million	$1,000,001 to $10 million	$10,000,001 to $50 million	$50,000,001 $100 million	More than $100 million
☐	☐	☐	☐	☐	☐	☐	☐

Voluntary Petition
(This page must be completed and filed in every case.)

Name of Debtor(s):

Form 1, Page 2

Prior Bankruptcy Case Filed Within Last 6 Years (If more than one, attach additional sheet)

Location Where Filed:	Case Number:	Date Filed:

Pending Bankruptcy Case Filed by any Spouse, Partner or Affiliate of this Debtor (If more than one, attach additional sheet)

Name of Debtor:	Case Number:	Date Filed:
District:	Relationship:	Judge:

Signatures

Signature(s) of Debtor(s) (Individual/Joint)

I declare under penalty of perjury that the information provided in this petition is true and correct.

[If petitioner is an individual whose debts are primarily consumer debts and has chosen to file under chapter 7] I am aware that I may proceed under chapter 7, 11, 12 or 13 of title 11, United States Code, understand the relief available under each such chapter, and choose to proceed under chapter 7.

I request relief in accordance with the chapter of title 11, United States Code, specified in this petition.

X _____
Signature of Debtor

X _____
Signature of Joint Debtor

_____
Telephone Number (If not represented by attorney)

_____
Date

Signature of Debtor (Corporation/Partnership)

I declare under penalty of perjury that the information provided in this petition is true and correct and that I have been authorized to file this petition on behalf of the debtor.

The debtor requests relief in accordance with the chapter of title 11, United States Code, specified in this petition.

X _____
Signature of Authorized Individual

_____
Printed Name of Authorized Individual

_____
Title of Authorized Individual

_____
Date

Signature of Attorney

X _____
Signature of Attorney for Debtor(s)

_____
Printed Name of Attorney for Debtor(s)

_____
Firm Name

_____
Address

_____

_____
Telephone Number

_____
Date

Signature of Non-Attorney Petition Preparer

I certify that I am a bankruptcy petition preparer as defined in 11 U.S.C. § 110, that I prepared this document for compensation, and that I have provided the debtor with a copy of this document.

_____
Printed Name of Bankruptcy Petition Preparer

_____
Social Security Number

_____
Address

_____

Names and Social Security numbers of all other individuals who prepared or assisted in preparing this document:

Exhibit A

(To be completed if debtor is required to file periodic reports (e.g., forms 10K and 10Q) with the Securities and Exchange Commission pursuant to Section 13 or 15(d) of the Securities Exchange Act of 1934 and is requesting relief under chapter 11.)

☐ Exhibit A is attached and made a part of this petition.

If more than one person prepared this document, attach additional sheets conforming to the appropriate official form for each person.

Exhibit B

(To be completed if debtor is an individual whose debts are primarily consumer debts.)

I, the attorney for the petitioner named in the foregoing petition, declare that I have informed the petitioner that [he or she] may proceed under chapter 7, 11, 12, or 13 of title 11, United States Code, and have explained the relief available under each such chapter.

X _____
Signature of Attorney for Debtor(s)   Date

X _____
Signature of Bankruptcy Petition Preparer

_____
Date

A bankruptcy petition preparer's failure to comply with the provisions of title 11 and the Federal Rules of Bankruptcy Procedure may result in fines or imprisonment or both. 11 U.S.C. § 110; 18 U.S.C. § 156.

In re _____,   Case No._____
                        Debtor   (If known)

SCHEDULE A—REAL PROPERTY

Except as directed below, list all real property in which the debtor has any legal, equitable, or future interest, including all property owned as a co-tenant, community property, or in which the debtor has a life estate. Include any property in which the debtor holds rights and powers exercisable for the debtor's own benefit. If the debtor is married, state whether husband, wife, or both own the property by placing an "H," "W," "J," or "C" in the column labeled "Husband, Wife, Joint, or Community." If the debtor holds no interest in real property, write "None" under "Description and Location of Property."

Do not include interests in executory contracts and unexpired leases on this schedule. List them in Schedule G—Executory Contracts and Unexpired Leases.

If an entity claims to have a lien or hold a secured interest in any property, state the amount of the secured claim. See Schedule D. If no entity claims to hold a secured interest in the property, write "None" in the column labeled "Amount of Secured Claim."

If the debtor is an individual or if a joint petition is filed, state the amount of any exception claimed in the property only in Schedule C—Property Claimed as Exempt.

DESCRIPTION AND LOCATION OF PROPERTY	NATURE OF DEBTOR'S INTEREST IN PROPERTY	HUSBAND, WIFE, JOINT, OR COMMUNITY	CURRENT MARKET VALUE OF DEBTOR'S INTEREST IN PROPERTY WITHOUT DEDUCTING ANY SECURED CLAIM OR EXEMPTION	AMOUNT OF SECURED CLAIM

Total ➡ $ _____

(Report also on Summary of Schedules.)

In re _____, Case No._____
　　　　　　　　　Debtor　　　　　　　　　　　　　　　　　　　　　　　　(If known)

SCHEDULE B—PERSONAL PROPERTY

Except as directed below, list all personal property of the debtor of whatever kind. If the debtor has no property in one or more of the categories, place an "X" in the appropriate position in the column labeled "None." If additional space is needed in any category, attach a separate sheet properly identified with the case name, case number, and the number of the category. If the debtor is married, state whether husband, wife, or both own the property by placing an "H," "W," "J," or "C" in the column labeled "Husband, Wife, Joint, or Community." If the debtor is an individual or a joint petition is filed, state the amount of any exemptions claimed only in Schedule C—Property Claimed as Exempt.

Do not include interests in executory contracts and unexpired leases on this schedule. List them in Schedule G—Executory Contracts and Unexpired Leases.

If the property is being held for the debtor by someone else, state that person's name and address under "Description and Location of Property."

TYPE OF PROPERTY	NONE	DESCRIPTION AND LOCATION OF PROPERTY	HUSBAND, WIFE, JOINT, OR COMMUNITY	CURRENT MARKET VALUE OF DEBTOR'S INTEREST IN PROPERTY, WITHOUT DEDUCTING ANY SECURED CLAIM OR EXEMPTION

In re _____,   Case No._____
                              Debtor   (If known)

SCHEDULE B—PERSONAL PROPERTY
(Continuation Sheet)

TYPE OF PROPERTY	NONE	DESCRIPTION AND LOCATION OF PROPERTY	HUSBAND, WIFE, JOINT, OR COMMUNITY	CURRENT MARKET VALUE OF DEBTOR'S INTEREST IN PROPERTY, WITHOUT DEDUCTING ANY SECURED CLAIM OR EXEMPTION
5. Books, pictures and other art objects, antiques, stamp, coin, record, tape, compact disc, and other collections or collectibles.				
6. Wearing apparel.				
7. Furs and jewelry.				
8. Firearms and sports, photo-graphic, and other hobby equipment.				
9. Interests in insurance policies. Name insurance company of each policy and itemize surrender or refund value of each.				
10. Annuities. Itemize and name each issuer.				
11. Interests in IRA, ERISA, Keogh, or other pension or profit sharing plans. Itemize.				
12. Stock and interests in incor-porated and unincorporated businesses. Itemize.				
13. Interests in partnerships or joint ventures. Itemize.				

In re _____,   Case No. _____
               Debtor   (If known)

SCHEDULE B—PERSONAL PROPERTY
(Continuation Sheet)

TYPE OF PROPERTY	NONE	DESCRIPTION AND LOCATION OF PROPERTY	HUSBAND, WIFE, JOINT, OR COMMUNITY	CURRENT MARKET VALUE OF DEBTOR'S INTEREST IN PROPERTY, WITHOUT DEDUCTING ANY SECURED CLAIM OR EXEMPTION
14. Government and corporate bonds and other negotiable and non-negotiable instruments.				
15. Accounts receivable.				
16. Alimony, maintenance, support, and property settlements to which the debtor is or may be entitled. Give particulars.				
17. Other liquidated debts owing debtor including tax refunds. Give particulars.				
18. Equitable or future interest, life estates, and rights or powers exercisable for the benefit of the debtor other than those listed in Schedule of Real Property.				
19. Contingent and noncontingent interests in estate of a decedent, death benefit plan, life insurance policy, or trust.				
20. Other contingent and unliquidated claims of every nature, including tax refunds, counterclaims of the debtor, and rights to setoff claims. Give estimated value of each.				
21. Patents, copyrights, and other intellectual property. Give particulars.				
22. Licenses, franchises, and other general intangibles. Give particulars.				

In re _____,   Case No._____
            Debtor   (If known)

SCHEDULE B—PERSONAL PROPERTY
(Continuation Sheet)

TYPE OF PROPERTY	NONE	DESCRIPTION AND LOCATION OF PROPERTY	HUSBAND, WIFE, JOINT, OR COMMUNITY	CURRENT MARKET VALUE OF DEBTOR'S INTEREST IN PROPERTY, WITHOUT DEDUCTING ANY SECURED CLAIM OR EXEMPTION
23. Automobiles, trucks, trailers, and other vehicles and accessories.				
24. Boats, motors, and accessories.				
25. Aircraft and accessories.				
26. Office equipment, furnishings, and supplies.				
27. Machinery, fixtures, equipment, and supplies used in business.				
28. Inventory.				
29. Animals.				
30. Crops—growing or harvested. Give particulars.				
31. Farming equipment and implements.				
32. Farm supplies, chemicals, and feed.				
33. Other personal property of any kind not already listed, such as season tickets. Itemize.				
			Total ➡	$

_____ continuation sheets attached

(Include amounts from any continuation sheets attached. Report total also on Summary of Schedules.)

In re _____, Case No._____
                        Debtor   (If known)

SCHEDULE C—PROPERTY CLAIMED AS EXEMPT

Debtor elects the exemptions to which debtor is entitled under:

(Check one box)

☐ 11 U.S.C. § 522(b)(1): Exemptions provided in 11 U.S.C. § 522(d). **Note: These exemptions are available only in certain states.**

☐ 11 U.S.C. § 522(b)(2): Exemptions available under applicable nonbankruptcy federal laws, state or local law where the debtor's domicile has been located for the 180 days immediately preceding the filing of the petition, or for a longer portion of the 180-day period than in any other place, and the debtor's interest as a tenant by the entirety or joint tenant to the extent the interest is exempt from process under applicable nonbankruptcy law.

DESCRIPTION OF PROPERTY	SPECIFY LAW PROVIDING EACH EXEMPTION	VALUE OF CLAIMED EXEMPTION	CURRENT MARKET VALUE OF PROPERTY WITHOUT DEDUCTING EXEMPTIONS

In re _____,   Case No._____
                     Debtor   (If known)

SCHEDULE D—CREDITORS HOLDING SECURED CLAIMS

State the name, mailing address, including zip code, and account number, if any, of all entities holding claims secured by property of the debtor as of the date of filing of the petition. List creditors holding all types of secured interest such as judgment liens, garnishments, statutory liens, mortgages, deeds of trust, and other security interests. List creditors in alphabetical order to the extent practicable. If all secured creditors will not fit on this page, use the continuation sheet provided.

If any entity other than a spouse in a joint case may be jointly liable on a claim, place an "X" in the column labeled "Codebtor," include the entity on the appropriate schedule of creditors, and complete Schedule H—Codebtors. If a joint petition is filed, state whether husband, wife, both of them, or the marital community may be liable on each claim by placing an "H," "W," "J," or "C" in the column labeled "Husband, Wife, Joint, or Community."

If the claim is contingent, place an "X" in the column labeled "Contingent." If the claim is unliquidated, place an "X" in the column labeled "Unliquidated." If the claim is disputed, place an "X" in the column labeled "Disputed." (You may need to place an "X" in more than one of these three columns.)

Report the total of all claims listed on this schedule in the box labeled "Total" on the last sheet of the completed schedule. Report this total also on the Summary of Schedules.

☐   Check this box if debtor has no creditors holding secured claims to report on this Schedule D.

CREDITOR'S NAME AND MAILING ADDRESS INCLUDING ZIP CODE	CODEBTOR	HUSBAND, WIFE, JOINT, OR COMMUNITY	DATE CLAIM WAS INCURRED, NATURE OF LIEN, AND DESCRIPTION AND MARKET VALUE OF PROPERTY SUBJECT TO LIEN	CONTINGENT	UNLIQUIDATED	DISPUTED	AMOUNT OF CLAIM WITHOUT DEDUCTING VALUE OF COLLATERAL	UNSECURED PORTION, IF ANY
ACCOUNT NO.								
			VALUE $					
ACCOUNT NO.								
			VALUE $					
ACCOUNT NO.								
			VALUE $					
ACCOUNT NO.								
			VALUE $					

_____ continuation sheets attached

Subtotal ➡ $_____
(Total of this page)

Total ➡ $_____
(Use only on last page)
(Report total also on Summary of Schedules)

In re _____ ,   Case No._____
                                    Debtor   (If known)

SCHEDULE D—CREDITORS HOLDING SECURED CLAIMS
(Continuation Sheet)

CREDITOR'S NAME AND MAILING ADDRESS INCLUDING ZIP CODE	CODEBTOR	HUSBAND, WIFE, JOINT, OR COMMUNITY	DATE CLAIM WAS INCURRED, NATURE OF LIEN, AND DESCRIPTION AND MARKET VALUE OF PROPERTY SUBJECT TO LIEN	CONTINGENT	UNLIQUIDATED	DISPUTED	AMOUNT OF CLAIM WITHOUT DEDUCTING VALUE OF COLLATERAL	UNSECURED PORTION, IF ANY
ACCOUNT NO.								
			VALUE $					
ACCOUNT NO.								
			VALUE $					
ACCOUNT NO.								
			VALUE $					
ACCOUNT NO.								
			VALUE $					
ACCOUNT NO.								
			VALUE $					
ACCOUNT NO.								
			VALUE $					

Subtotal ➡ $ _____
(Total of this page)

Total ➡ $ _____
(Use only on last page)

Sheet no. _____ of _____ continuation sheets attached to
Schedule of Creditors Holding Secured Claims

(Report total also on Summary of Schedules)

In re _____,   Case No._____
                          Debtor   (If known)

SCHEDULE E—CREDITORS HOLDING UNSECURED PRIORITY CLAIMS

A complete list of claims entitled to priority, listed separately by type of priority, is to be set forth on the sheets provided. Only holders of unsecured claims entitled to priority should be listed in this schedule. In the boxes provided on the attached sheets, state the name and mailing address, including zip code, and account number, if any, of all entities holding priority claims against the debtor or the property of the debtor, as of the date of the filing of the petition.

If any entity other than a spouse in a joint case may be jointly liable on a claim, place an "X" in the column labeled "Codebtor," include the entity on the appropriate schedule of creditors, and complete Schedule H—Codebtors. If a joint petition is filed, state whether husband, wife, both of them, or the marital community may be liable on each claim by placing an "H," "W," "J," or "C" in the column labeled "Husband, Wife, Joint, or Community."

If the claim is contingent, place an "X" in the column labeled "Contingent." If the claim is unliquidated, place an "X" in the column labeled "Unliquidated." If the claim is disputed, place an "X" in the column labeled "Disputed." (You may need to place an "X" in more than one of these three columns.)

Report the total of all claims listed on each sheet in the box labeled "Subtotal" on each sheet. Report the total of all claims listed on this Schedule E in the box labeled "Total" on the last sheet of the completed schedule. Repeat this total also on the Summary of Schedules.

☐   **Check this box if debtor has no creditors holding unsecured priority claims to report on this Schedule E.**

TYPES OF PRIORITY CLAIMS (Check the appropriate box(es) below if claims in that category are listed on the attached sheets)

☐   **Extensions of credit in an involuntary case**

Claims arising in the ordinary course of the debtor's business or financial affairs after the commencement of the case but before the earlier of the appointment of a trustee or the order for relief. 11 U.S.C. § 507(a)(2).

☐   **Wages, salaries, and commissions**

Wages, salaries, and commissions, including vacation, severance, and sick leave pay owing to employees and commissions owing to qualifying independent sales representatives up to $4,000* per person, earned within 90 days immediately preceding the filing of the original petition, or the cessation of business, whichever occurred first, to the extent provided in 11 U.S.C. § 507(a)(3).

☐   **Contributions to employee benefit plans**

Money owed to employee benefit plans for services rendered within 180 days immediately preceding the filing of the original petition, or the cessation of business, whichever occurred first, to the extent provided in 11 U.S.C. § 507(a)(4).

☐   **Certain farmers and fishermen**

Claims of certain farmers and fishermen, up to a maximum of $4,000* per farmer or fisherman, against the debtor, as provided in 11 U.S.C. § 507(a)(5).

☐   **Deposits by individuals**

Claims of individuals up to a maximum of $1,800* for deposits for the purchase, lease, or rental of property or services for personal, family, or household use, that were not delivered or provided. 11 U.S.C. § 507(a)(6).

☐   **Alimony, Maintenance, or Support**

Claims of a spouse, former spouse, or child of the debtor for alimony, maintenance, or support, to the extent provided in 11 U.S.C. § 507(a)(7).

☐   **Taxes and Certain Other Debts Owed to Governmental Units**

Taxes, customs, duties, and penalties owing to federal, state, and local governmental units as set forth in 11 U.S.C. § 507(a)(8).

☐   **Commitments to Maintain the Capital of an Insured Depository Institution**

Claims based on commitments to the FDIC, RTC, Director of the Office of Thrift Supervision, Comptroller of the Currency, or Board of Governors of the Federal Reserve system, or their predecessors or successors, to maintain the capital of an insured depository institution. 11 U.S.C. § 507 (a)(9).

* Amounts are subject to adjustment on April 1, 2001, and every three years thereafter with respect to cases commenced on or after the date of adjustment.

_____ continuation sheets attached

In re _____,   Case No._____
                        Debtor   (If known)

SCHEDULE E—CREDITORS HOLDING UNSECURED PRIORITY CLAIMS
(Continuation Sheet)

TYPE OF PRIORITY

CREDITOR'S NAME AND MAILING ADDRESS INCLUDING ZIP CODE	CODEBTOR	HUSBAND, WIFE, JOINT, OR COMMUNITY	DATE CLAIM WAS INCURRED AND CONSIDERATION FOR CLAIM	CONTINGENT	UNLIQUIDATED	DISPUTED	TOTAL AMOUNT OF CLAIM	AMOUNT ENTITLED TO PRIORITY
ACCOUNT NO.								
ACCOUNT NO.								
ACCOUNT NO.								
ACCOUNT NO.								
ACCOUNT NO.								

Subtotal ➡ $
(Total of this page)

Total ➡ $
(Use only on last page)

Sheet no. _____ of _____ sheets attached to
Schedule of Creditors Holding Unsecured Priority Claims

(Report total also on Summary of Schedules)

In re _____,   Case No._____
                    Debtor   (If known)

SCHEDULE F—CREDITORS HOLDING UNSECURED NONPRIORITY CLAIMS

State the name, mailing address, including zip code, and account number, if any, of all entities holding unsecured claims without priority against the debtor or the property of the debtor as of the date of filing of the petition. Do not include claims listed in Schedules D and E. If all creditors will not fit on this page, use the continuation sheet provided.

If any entity other than a spouse in a joint case may be jointly liable on a claim, place an "X" in the column labeled "Codebtor," include the entity on the appropriate schedule of creditors, and complete Schedule H—Codebtors. If a joint petition is filed, state whether husband, wife, both of them, or the marital community may be liable on each claim by placing an "H," "W," "J," or "C" in the column labeled "Husband, Wife, Joint, or Community."

If the claim is contingent, place an "X" in the column labeled "Contingent." If the claim is unliquidated, place an "X" in the column labeled "Unliquidated." If the claim is disputed, place an "X" in the column labeled "Disputed." (You may need to place an "X" in more than one of these three columns.)

Report the total of all claims listed on this schedule in the box labeled "Total" on the last sheet of the completed schedule. Report this total also on the Summary of Schedules.

☐ Check this box if debtor has no creditors holding unsecured nonpriority claims to report on this Schedule F.

CREDITOR'S NAME AND MAILING ADDRESS INCLUDING ZIP CODE	CODEBTOR	HUSBAND, WIFE, JOINT, OR COMMUNITY	DATE CLAIM WAS INCURRED AND CONSIDERATION FOR CLAIM. IF CLAIM IS SUBJECT TO SETOFF, SO STATE	CONTINGENT	UNLIQUIDATED	DISPUTED	AMOUNT OF CLAIM
ACCOUNT NO.							
ACCOUNT NO.							
ACCOUNT NO.							
ACCOUNT NO.							

_____ continuation sheets attached

Subtotal ➡ $ _____
(Total of this page)

Total ➡ $ _____
(Use only on last page)

(Report total also on Summary of Schedules)

In re _____ ,   Case No._____
                              Debtor   (If known)

SCHEDULE F—CREDITORS HOLDING UNSECURED NONPRIORITY CLAIMS
(Continuation Sheet)

CREDITOR'S NAME AND MAILING ADDRESS INCLUDING ZIP CODE	CODEBTOR	HUSBAND, WIFE, JOINT, OR COMMUNITY	DATE CLAIM WAS INCURRED AND CONSIDERATION FOR CLAIM. IF CLAIM IS SUBJECT TO SETOFF, SO STATE	CONTINGENT	UNLIQUIDATED	DISPUTED	AMOUNT OF CLAIM
ACCOUNT NO.							
ACCOUNT NO.							
ACCOUNT NO.							
ACCOUNT NO.							
ACCOUNT NO.							

Subtotal ➡ $
(Total of this page)

Total ➡ $
(Use only on last page)

Sheet no. _____ of _____ continuation sheets attached to
Schedule of Creditors Holding Unsecured Nonpriorty Claims

(Report total also on Summary of Schedules)

In re _____,   Case No._____
                        Debtor   (If known)

SCHEDULE G—EXECUTORY CONTRACTS AND UNEXPIRED LEASES

Describe all executory contracts of any nature and all unexpired leases of real personal property. Include any timeshare interests.

State nature of debtor's interest in contract, i.e., "Purchaser," "Agent," etc. State whether debtor is the lessor or lessee of a lease.

Provide the names and complete mailing addresses of all other parties to each lease or contract described.

NOTE: A party listed on this schedule will not receive notice of the filing of this case unless the party is also scheduled in the appropriate schedule of creditors.

☐ Check this box if debtor has no executory contracts or unexpired leases.

NAME AND MAILING ADDRESS, INCLUDING ZIP CODE, OF OTHER PARTIES TO LEASE OR CONTRACT	DESCRIPTION OF CONTRACT OR LEASE AND NATURE OF DEBTOR'S INTEREST. STATE WHETHER LEASE IS FOR NONRESIDENTIAL REAL PROPERTY. STATE CONTRACT NUMBER OF ANY GOVERNMENT CONTRACT

In re _____,   Case No._____
                        Debtor   (If known)

SCHEDULE H—CODEBTORS

Provide the information requested concerning any person or entity, other than a spouse in a joint case, that is also liable on any debts listed by debtor in the schedules of creditors. Include all guarantors and co-signers. In community property states, a married debtor not filing a joint case should report the name and address of the nondebtor spouse on this schedule. Include all names used by the nondebtor spouse during the six years immediately preceding the commencement of this case.

☐ Check this box if debtor has no codebtors.

NAME AND ADDRESS OF CODEBTOR	NAME AND ADDRESS OF CREDITOR

In re _____,   Case No._____
                    Debtor   (If known)

SCHEDULE I—CURRENT INCOME OF INDIVIDUAL DEBTOR(S)

The column labled "Spouse" must be completed in all cases filed by joint debtors and by a married debtor in a Chapter 12 or 13 case whether or not a joint petition is filed, unless the spouses are separated and a joint petition is not filed.

DEBTOR'S MARITAL STATUS:	DEPENDENTS OF DEBTOR AND SPOUSE		
	NAMES	AGE	RELATIONSHIP

Employment:	DEBTOR	SPOUSE
Occupation		
Name of Employer		
How long employed		
Address of Employer		

INCOME: (Estimate of average monthly income)   DEBTOR   SPOUSE

Current monthly gross wages, salary, and commissions
   (pro rate if not paid monthly) $ _____ $ _____

Estimated monthly overtime $ _____ $ _____

SUBTOTAL $ _____ $ _____

   LESS PAYROLL DEDUCTIONS

   a. Payroll taxes and Social Security $ _____ $ _____

   b. Insurance $ _____ $ _____

   c. Union dues $ _____ $ _____

   d. Other (Specify: _____) $ _____ $ _____

   SUBTOTAL OF PAYROLL DEDUCTIONS $ _____ $ _____

TOTAL NET MONTHLY TAKE HOME PAY $ _____ $ _____

Regular income from operation of business or profession or farm
(attach detailed statement) $ _____ $ _____

Income from real property $ _____ $ _____

Interest and dividends $ _____ $ _____

Alimony, maintenance or support payments payable to the debtor for the debtor's use or
that of dependents listed above $ _____ $ _____

Social Security or other government assistance

(Specify:_____) $ _____ $ _____

Pension or retirement income $ _____ $ _____

Other monthly income $ _____ $ _____

(Specify:_____) $ _____ $ _____

       _____ $ _____ $ _____

TOTAL MONTHLY INCOME $ _____ $ _____

TOTAL COMBINED MONTHLY INCOME $ _____   (Report also on Summary of Schedules)

Describe any increase or decrease of more than 10% in any of the above categories anticipated to occur within the year following the filing of this document:

In re _____,   Case No._____
                          Debtor   (If known)

SCHEDULE J—CURRENT EXPENDITURES OF INDIVIDUAL DEBTOR(S)

Complete this schedule by estimating the average monthly expenses of the debtor and the debtor's family. Pro rate any payments made bi-weekly, quarterly, semi-annually, or annually to show monthly rate.

☐ Check this box if a joint petition is filed and debtor's spouse maintains a separate household. Complete a separate schedule of expenditures labeled "Spouse."

Rent or home mortgage payment (include lot rented for mobile home) $ _____

Are real estate taxes included?   Yes _____   No _____

Is property insurance included?   Yes _____   No _____

Utilities: Electricity and heating fuel $ _____

        Water and sewer $ _____

        Telephone $ _____

        Other _____ $ _____

Home maintenance (repairs and upkeep) $ _____

Food $ _____

Clothing $ _____

Laundry and dry cleaning $ _____

Medical and dental expenses $ _____

Transportation (not including car payments) $ _____

Recreation, clubs and entertainment, newspapers, magazines, etc. $ _____

Charitable contributions $ _____

Insurance (not deducted from wages or included in home mortgage payments)

        Homeowner's or renter's $ _____

        Life $ _____

        Health $ _____

        Auto $ _____

        Other _____ $ _____

Taxes (not deducted from wages or included in home mortgage payments)

(Specify: _____) $ _____

Installment payments: (In Chapter 12 and 13 cases, do not list payments to be included in the plan)

        Auto $ _____

        Other _____ $ _____

        Other _____ $ _____

Alimony, maintenance, and support paid to others $ _____

Payments for support of additional dependents not living at your home $ _____

Regular expenses from operation of business, profession, or farm (attach detailed statement) $ _____

Other _____ $ _____

TOTAL MONTHLY EXPENSES (Report also on Summary of Schedules) $ _____

[FOR CHAPTER 12 AND CHAPTER 13 DEBTORS ONLY]
Provide the information requested below, including whether plan payments are to be made bi-weekly, monthly, annually, or at some other regular interval.

A. Total projected monthly income $ _____

B. Total projected monthly expenses $ _____

C. Excess income (A minus B) $ _____

D. Total amount to be paid into plan each_____ $ _____

                            (interval)

United States Bankruptcy Court

_____ District of _____

In re _____,   Case No._____
                    Debtor   (If known)

SUMMARY OF SCHEDULES

Indicate as to each schedule whether that schedule is attached and state the number of pages in each. Report the totals from Schedules A, B, D, E, F, I and J in the boxes provided. Add the amounts from Schedules A and B to determine the total amount of the debtor's assets. Add the amounts from Schedules D, E and F to determine the total amount of the debtor's liabilities.

NAME OF SCHEDULE		ATTACHED (YES/NO)	NUMBER OF SHEETS	AMOUNTS SCHEDULED		
				ASSETS	LIABILITIES	OTHER
A	Real Property			$		
B	Personal Property			$		
C	Property Claimed as Exempt					
D	Creditors Holding Secured Claims				$	
E	Creditors Holding Unsecured Priority Claims				$	
F	Creditors Holding Unsecured Nonpriority Claims				$	
G	Executory Contracts and Unexpired Leases					
H	Codebtors					
I	Current Income of Individual Debtor(s)					$
J	Current Expenditures of Individual Debtor(s)					$
Total Number of Sheets of All Schedules ➡						
Total Assets ➡				$		
Total Liabilities ➡					$	

In re _____ ,   Case No._____
           Debtor   (If known)

DECLARATION CONCERNING DEBTOR'S SCHEDULES

DECLARATION UNDER PENALTY OF PERJURY BY INDIVIDUAL DEBTOR

I declare under penalty of perjury that I have read the foregoing summary and schedules consisting of _____
sheets, and that they are true and correct to the best of my knowledge, information, and belief.   (Total shown on summary page plus 1)

Date_____   Signature _____
                                                            Debtor

Date_____   Signature _____
                                                     (Joint Debtor, if any)

[If joint case, both spouses must sign.]

CERTIFICATION AND SIGNATURE OF NON-ATTORNEY BANKRUPTCY PETITION PREPARER (See 11 U.S.C. § 110)

I certify that I am a bankruptcy petition preparer as defined in 11 U.S.C. § 110, that I prepared this document for compensation, and that I have provided the debtor with a copy of this document.

_____   _____
Printed or Typed Name of Bankruptcy Petition Preparer   Social Security No.

_____

Address

Names and Social Security numbers of all other individuals who prepared or assisted in preparing this document:

If more than one person prepared this document, attach additional signed sheets conforming to the appropriate Official Form for each person.

X _____   _____
Signature of Bankruptcy Petition Preparer   Date

A bankruptcy petition preparer's failure to comply with the provisions of Title 11 and the Federal Rules of Bankruptcy Procedure may result in fine or imprisonment or both. 11 U.S.C. § 110; 18 U.S.C. § 156.

DECLARATION UNDER PENALTY OF PERJURY ON BEHALF OF CORPORATION OR PARTNERSHIP

I, the _____ [the president or other officer or an authorized agent of the corporation or a member or an authorized agent of the partnership] of the _____ [corporation or partnership] named as debtor in this case, declare under penalty of perjury that I have read the foregoing summary and schedules, consisting of _____ sheets, and that they are true and correct to the best of my knowledge, information, and belief.
(Total shown on summary page plus 1)

Date_____   Signature _____

                                               _____
                                             [Print or type name of individual signing on behalf of debtor]

[An individual signing on behalf of a partnership or corporation must indicate position or relationship to debtor.]

Penalty for making a false statement or concealing property: Fine of up to $500,000, imprisonment for up to 5 years, or both. 18 U.S.C. §§ 152 and 3571.

FORM 7. STATEMENT OF FINANCIAL AFFAIRS

UNITED STATES BANKRUPTCY COURT

_____ DISTRICT OF _____

In re: _____,   Case No. _____
         (Name)   (if known)
           Debtor

STATEMENT OF FINANCIAL AFFAIRS

This statement is to be completed by every debtor. Spouses filing a joint petition may file a single statement on which the information for both spouses is combined. If the case is filed under chapter 12 or chapter 13, a married debtor must furnish information for both spouses whether or not a joint petition is filed, unless the spouses are separated and a joint petition is not filed. An individual debtor engaged in business as a sole proprietor, partner, family farmer, or self-employed professional, should provide the information requested on this statement concerning all such activities as well as the individual's personal affairs.

Questions 1 - 18 are to be completed by all debtors. Debtors that are or have been in business, as defined below, also must complete Questions 19 - 25. **If the answer to an applicable question is "None," mark the box labeled "None."** If additional space is needed for the answer to any question, use and attach a separate sheet properly identified with the case name, case number (if known), and the number of the question.

DEFINITIONS

"In business." A debtor is "in business" for the purpose of this form if the debtor is a corporation or partnership. An individual debtor is "in business" for the purpose of this form if the debtor is or has been, within the six years immediately preceding the filing of this bankruptcy case, any of the following: an officer, director, managing executive, or owner of 5 percent or more of the voting or equity securities of a corporation; a partner, other than a limited partner, of a partnership; a sole proprietor or self-employed.

"Insider." The term "insider" includes but is not limited to: relatives of the debtor; general partners of the debtor and their relatives; corporations of which the debtor is an officer, director, or person in control; officers, directors, and any owner of 5 percent or more of the voting or equity securities of a corporate debtor and their relatives; affiliates of the debtor and insiders of such affiliates; any managing agent of the debtor. 11 U.S.C. § 101.

_____

1. Income from employment or operation of business

None
☐

State the gross amount of income the debtor has received from employment, trade, or profession, or from operation of the debtor's business from the beginning of this calendar year to the date this case was commenced. State also the gross amounts received during the **two years** immediately preceding this calendar year. (A debtor that maintains, or has maintained, financial records on the basis of a fiscal rather than a calendar year may report fiscal year income. Identify the beginning and ending dates of the debtor's fiscal year.) If a joint petition is filed, state income for each spouse separately. (Married debtors filing under chapter 12 or chapter 13 must state income of both spouses whether or not a joint petition is filed, unless the spouses are separated and a joint petition is not filed.)

        AMOUNT   SOURCE (if more than one)

2. Income other than from employment or operation of business

None
☐

State the amount of income received by the debtor other than from employment, trade, profession, or operation of the debtor's business during the **two years** immediately preceding the commencement of this case. Give particulars. If a joint petition is filed, state income for each spouse separately. (Married debtors filing under chapter 12 or chapter 13 must state income for each spouse whether or not a joint petition is filed, unless the spouses are separated and a joint petition is not filed.)

AMOUNT   SOURCE

---

3. Payments to creditors

None
☐

a. List all payments on loans, installment purchases of goods or services, and other debts, aggregating more than $600 to any creditor, made within **90 days** immediately preceding the commencement of this case. (Married debtors filing under chapter 12 or chapter 13 must include payments by either or both spouses whether or not a joint petition is filed, unless the spouses are separated and a joint petition is not filed.)

NAME AND ADDRESS OF CREDITOR	DATES OF PAYMENTS	AMOUNT PAID	AMOUNT STILL OWING

None
☐

b. List all payments made within **one year** immediately preceding the commencement of this case to or for the benefit of creditors who are or were insiders. (Married debtors filing under chapter 12 or chapter 13 must include payments by either or both spouses whether or not a joint petition is filed, unless the spouses are separated and a joint petition is not filed.)

NAME AND ADDRESS OF CREDITOR AND RELATIONSHIP TO DEBTOR	DATE OF PAYMENT	AMOUNT PAID	AMOUNT STILL OWING

---

4. Suits and administrative proceedings, executions, garnishments and attachments

None
☐

a. List all suits and administrative proceedings to which the debtor is or was a party within **one year** immediately preceding the filing of this bankruptcy case. (Married debtors filing under chapter 12 or chapter 13 must include information concerning either or both spouses whether or not a joint petition is filed, unless the spouses are separated and a joint petition is not filed.)

CAPTION OF SUIT AND CASE NUMBER	NATURE OF PROCEEDING	COURT OR AGENCY AND LOCATION	STATUS OR DISPOSITION

3

None ☐   b.   Describe all property that has been attached, garnished or seized under any legal or equitable process within **one year** immediately preceding the commencement of this case. (Married debtors filing under chapter 12 or chapter 13 must include information concerning property of either or both spouses whether or not a joint petition is filed, unless the spouses are separated and a joint petition is not filed.)

NAME AND ADDRESS OF PERSON FOR WHOSE BENEFIT PROPERTY WAS SEIZED	DATE OF SEIZURE	DESCRIPTION AND VALUE OF PROPERTY

---

5. Repossessions, foreclosures and returns

None ☐   List all property that has been repossessed by a creditor, sold at a foreclosure sale, transferred through a deed in lieu of foreclosure or returned to the seller, within **one year** immediately preceding the commencement of this case. (Married debtors filing under chapter 12 or chapter 13 must include information concerning property of either or both spouses whether or not a joint petition is filed, unless the spouses are separated and a joint petition is not filed.)

NAME AND ADDRESS OF CREDITOR OR SELLER	DATE OF REPOSSESSION, FORECLOSURE SALE, TRANSFER OR RETURN	DESCRIPTION AND VALUE OF PROPERTY

---

6. Assignments and receiverships

None ☐   a.   Describe any assignment of property for the benefit of creditors made within **120 days** immediately preceding the commencement of this case. (Married debtors filing under chapter 12 or chapter 13 must include any assignment by either or both spouses whether or not a joint petition is filed, unless the spouses are separated and a joint petition is not filed.)

NAME AND ADDRESS OF ASSIGNEE	DATE OF ASSIGNMENT	TERMS OF ASSIGNMENT OR SETTLEMENT

None ☐   b.   List all property which has been in the hands of a custodian, receiver, or court-appointed official within **one year** immediately preceding the commencement of this case. (Married debtors filing under chapter 12 or chapter 13 must include information concerning property of either or both spouses whether or not a joint petition is filed, unless the spouses are separated and a joint petition is not filed.)

NAME AND ADDRESS OF CUSTODIAN	NAME AND LOCATION OF COURT CASE TITLE & NUMBER	DATE OF ORDER	DESCRIPTION AND VALUE OF PROPERTY

4

7. Gifts

None ☐

List all gifts or charitable contributions made within **one year** immediately preceding the commencement of this case except ordinary and usual gifts to family members aggregating less than $200 in value per individual family member and charitable contributions aggregating less than $100 per recipient. (Married debtors filing under chapter 12 or chapter 13 must include gifts or contributions by either or both spouses whether or not a joint petition is filed, unless the spouses are separated and a joint petition is not filed.)

NAME AND ADDRESS OF PERSON OR ORGANIZATION	RELATIONSHIP TO DEBTOR, IF ANY	DATE OF GIFT	DESCRIPTION AND VALUE OF GIFT

8. Losses

None ☐

List all losses from fire, theft, other casualty or gambling within **one year** immediately preceding the commencement of this case **or since the commencement of this case**. (Married debtors filing under chapter 12 or chapter 13 must include losses by either or both spouses whether or not a joint petition is filed, unless the spouses are separated and a joint petition is not filed.)

DESCRIPTION AND VALUE OF PROPERTY	DESCRIPTION OF CIRCUMSTANCES AND, IF LOSS WAS COVERED IN WHOLE OR IN PART BY INSURANCE, GIVE PARTICULARS	DATE OF LOSS

9. Payments related to debt counseling or bankruptcy

None ☐

List all payments made or property transferred by or on behalf of the debtor to any persons, including attorneys, for consultation concerning debt consolidation, relief under the bankruptcy law or preparation of a petition in bankruptcy within **one year** immediately preceding the commencement of this case.

NAME AND ADDRESS OF PAYEE	DATE OF PAYMENT, NAME OF PAYOR IF OTHER THAN DEBTOR	AMOUNT OF MONEY OR DESCRIPTION AND VALUE OF PROPERTY

10. Other transfers

None ☐

List all other property, other than property transferred in the ordinary course of the business or financial affairs of the debtor, transferred either absolutely or as security within **one year** immediately preceding the commencement of this case. (Married debtors filing under chapter 12 or chapter 13 must include transfers by either or both spouses whether or not a joint petition is filed, unless the spouses are separated and a joint petition is not filed.)

NAME AND ADDRESS OF TRANSFEREE, RELATIONSHIP TO DEBTOR	DATE	DESCRIBE PROPERTY TRANSFERRED AND VALUE RECEIVED

5

11. Closed financial accounts

None
☐

List all financial accounts and instruments held in the name of the debtor or for the benefit of the debtor which were closed, sold, or otherwise transferred within **one year** immediately preceding the commencement of this case. Include checking, savings, or other financial accounts, certificates of deposit, or other instruments; shares and share accounts held in banks, credit unions, pension funds, cooperatives, associations, brokerage houses and other financial institutions. (Married debtors filing under chapter 12 or chapter 13 must include information concerning accounts or instruments held by or for either or both spouses whether or not a joint petition is filed, unless the spouses are separated and a joint petition is not filed.)

NAME AND ADDRESS OF INSTITUTION	TYPE AND NUMBER OF ACCOUNT AND AMOUNT OF FINAL BALANCE	AMOUNT AND DATE OF SALE OR CLOSING

12. Safe deposit boxes

None
☐

List each safe deposit or other box or depository in which the debtor has or had securities, cash, or other valuables within **one year** immediately preceding the commencement of this case. (Married debtors filing under chapter 12 or chapter 13 must include boxes or depositories of either or both spouses whether or not a joint petition is filed, unless the spouses are separated and a joint petition is not filed.)

NAME AND ADDRESS OF BANK OR OTHER DEPOSITORY	NAMES AND ADDRESSES OF THOSE WITH ACCESS TO BOX OR DEPOSITORY	DESCRIPTION OF CONTENTS	DATE OF TRANSFER OR SURRENDER, IF ANY

13. Setoffs

None
☐

List all setoffs made by any creditor, including a bank, against a debt or deposit of the debtor within **90 days** preceding the commencement of this case. (Married debtors filing under chapter 12 or chapter 13 must include information concerning either or both spouses whether or not a joint petition is filed, unless the spouses are separated and a joint petition is not filed.)

NAME AND ADDRESS OF CREDITOR	DATE OF SETOFF	AMOUNT OF SETOFF

14. Property held for another person

None
☐

List all property owned by another person that the debtor holds or controls.

NAME AND ADDRESS OF OWNER	DESCRIPTION AND VALUE OF PROPERTY	LOCATION OF PROPERTY

6

15. Prior address of debtor

None
☐

If the debtor has moved within the **two years** immediately preceding the commencement of this case, list all premises which the debtor occupied during that period and vacated prior to the commencement of this case. If a joint petition is filed, report also any separate address of either spouse.

ADDRESS   NAME USED   DATES OF OCCUPANCY

16. Spouses and Former Spouses

None
☐

If the debtor resides or resided in a community property state, commonwealth, or territory (including Alaska, Arizona, California, Idaho, Louisiana, Nevada, New Mexico, Puerto Rico, Texas, Washington, or Wisconsin) within the **six-year period** immediately preceding the commencement of the case, identify the name of the debtor's spouse and of any former spouse who resides or resided with the debtor in the community property state.

NAME

17. Environmental Information.

For the purpose of this question, the following definitions apply:

"Environmental Law" means any federal, state, or local statute or regulation regulating pollution, contamination, releases of hazardous or toxic substances, wastes or material into the air, land, soil, surface water, groundwater, or other medium, including, but not limited to, statutes or regulations regulating the cleanup of these substances, wastes, or material.

"Site" means any location, facility, or property as defined under any Environmental Law, whether or not presently or formerly owned or operated by the debtor, including, but not limited to, disposal sites.

"Hazardous Material" means anything defined as a hazardous waste, hazardous substance, toxic substance, hazardous material, pollutant, or contaminant or similar term under an Environmental Law

None
☐

a. List the name and address of every site for which the debtor has received notice in writing by a governmental unit that it may be liable or potentially liable under or in violation of an Environmental Law. Indicate the governmental unit, the date of the notice, and, if known, the Environmental Law:

SITE NAME   NAME AND ADDRESS   DATE OF   ENVIRONMENTAL
AND ADDRESS   OF GOVERNMENTAL UNIT   NOTICE   LAW

None
☐

b. List the name and address of every site for which the debtor provided notice to a governmental unit of a release of Hazardous Material. Indicate the governmental unit to which the notice was sent and the date of the notice.

SITE NAME   NAME AND ADDRESS   DATE OF   ENVIRONMENTAL
AND ADDRESS   OF GOVERNMENTAL UNIT   NOTICE   LAW

None ☐ c. List all judicial or administrative proceedings, including settlements or orders, under any Environmental Law with respect to which the debtor is or was a party. Indicate the name and address of the governmental unit that is or was a party to the proceeding, and the docket number.

NAME AND ADDRESS OF GOVERNMENTAL UNIT	DOCKET NUMBER	STATUS OR DISPOSITION

---

18 . Nature, location and name of business

None ☐ a. If the debtor is an individual, list the names, addresses, taxpayer identification numbers, nature of the businesses, and beginning and ending dates of all businesses in which the debtor was an officer, director, partner, or managing executive of a corporation, partnership, sole proprietorship, or was a self-employed professional within the **six years** immediately preceding the commencement of this case, or in which the debtor owned 5 percent or more of the voting or equity securities within the **six years** immediately preceding the commencement of this case.

If the debtor is a partnership, list the names, addresses, taxpayer identification numbers, nature of the businesses, and beginning and ending dates of all businesses in which the debtor was a partner or owned 5 percent or more of the voting or equity securities, within the **six years** immediately preceding the commencement of this case.

If the debtor is a corporation, list the names, addresses, taxpayer identification numbers, nature of the businesses, and beginning and ending dates of all businesses in which the debtor was a partner or owned 5 percent or more of the voting or equity securities within the **six years** immediately preceding the commencement of this case.

NAME	TAXPAYER I.D. NUMBER	ADDRESS	NATURE OF BUSINESS	BEGINNING AND ENDING DATES

None ☐ b. Identify any business listed in response to subdivision a., above, that is "single asset real estate" as defined in 11 U.S.C. § 101.

NAME	ADDRESS

The following questions are to be completed by every debtor that is a corporation or partnership and by any individual debtor who is or has been, within the **six years** immediately preceding the commencement of this case, any of the following: an officer, director, managing executive, or owner of more than 5 percent of the voting or equity securities of a corporation; a partner, other than a limited partner, of a partnership; a sole proprietor or otherwise self-employed.

*(An individual or joint debtor should complete this portion of the statement **only** if the debtor is or has been in business, as defined above, within the six years immediately preceding the commencement of this case. A debtor who has not been in business within those six years should go directly to the signature page.)*

8

19. Books, records and financial statements

None ☐   a.   List all bookkeepers and accountants who within the **two years** immediately preceding the filing of this bankruptcy case kept or supervised the keeping of books of account and records of the debtor.

NAME AND ADDRESS   DATES SERVICES RENDERED

None ☐   b.   List all firms or individuals who within the **two years** immediately preceding the filing of this bankruptcy case have audited the books of account and records, or prepared a financial statement of the debtor.

NAME   ADDRESS   DATES SERVICES RENDERED

None ☐   c.   List all firms or individuals who at the time of the commencement of this case were in possession of the books of account and records of the debtor. If any of the books of account and records are not available, explain.

NAME   ADDRESS

None ☐   d.   List all financial institutions, creditors and other parties, including mercantile and trade agencies, to whom a financial statement was issued within the **two years** immediately preceding the commencement of this case by the debtor.

NAME AND ADDRESS   DATE ISSUED

---

20. Inventories

None ☐   a.   List the dates of the last two inventories taken of your property, the name of the person who supervised the taking of each inventory, and the dollar amount and basis of each inventory.

                                         DOLLAR AMOUNT OF INVENTORY

DATE OF INVENTORY   INVENTORY SUPERVISOR   (Specify cost, market or other basis)

None ☐   b.   List the name and address of the person having possession of the records of each of the two inventories reported in a., above.

                                         NAME AND ADDRESSES OF CUSTODIAN

DATE OF INVENTORY   OF INVENTORY RECORDS

9

21 . Current partners, officers, directors and shareholders

None ☐

a. If the debtor is a partnership, list the nature and percentage of partnership interest of each member of the partnership.

NAME AND ADDRESS   NATURE OF INTEREST   PERCENTAGE OF INTEREST

None ☐

b. If the debtor is a corporation, list all officers and directors of the corporation, and each stockholder who directly or indirectly owns, controls, or holds 5 percent or more of the voting or equity securities of the corporation.

NAME AND ADDRESS   TITLE   NATURE AND PERCENTAGE OF STOCK OWNERSHIP

22 . Former partners, officers, directors and shareholders

None ☐

a. If the debtor is a partnership, list each member who withdrew from the partnership within **one year** immediately preceding the commencement of this case.

NAME   ADDRESS   DATE OF WITHDRAWAL

None ☐

b. If the debtor is a corporation, list all officers, or directors whose relationship with the corporation terminated within **one year** immediately preceding the commencement of this case.

NAME AND ADDRESS   TITLE   DATE OF TERMINATION

23 . Withdrawals from a partnership or distributions by a corporation

None ☐

If the debtor is a partnership or corporation, list all withdrawals or distributions credited or given to an insider, including compensation in any form, bonuses, loans, stock redemptions, options exercised and any other perquisite during **one year** immediately preceding the commencement of this case.

NAME & ADDRESS
OF RECIPIENT,   DATE AND PURPOSE
RELATIONSHIP TO DEBTOR   OF WITHDRAWAL

AMOUNT OF MONEY
OR DESCRIPTION
AND VALUE OF PROPERTY

10

24. Tax consolidation group

None
☐

If the debtor is a corporation, list the name and federal taxpayer identification number of the parent corporation of any consolidated group for tax purposes of which the debtor has been a member at any time within the **six-year period** immediately preceding the commencement of the case.

NAME OF PARENT CORPORATION   TAXPAYER IDENTIFICATION NUMBER

---

25. Pension funds

None
☐

If the debtor is not an individual, list the name and federal taxpayer identification number of any pension fund to which the debtor, as an employer, has been responsible for contributing at any time within the **six-year period** immediately preceding the commencement of the case.

NAME OF PENSION FUND   TAXPAYER IDENTIFICATION NUMBER

---

* * * * * *

[If completed by an individual or individual and spouse]

I declare under penalty of perjury that I have read the answers contained in the foregoing statement of financial affairs and any attachments thereto and that they are true and correct.

Date _____ Signature _____
                                                        of Debtor

Date _____ Signature _____
                                                        of Joint Debtor
                                                        (if any)

[If completed on behalf of a partnership or corporation]

I, declare under penalty of perjury that I have read the answers contained in the foregoing statement of financial affairs and any attachments thereto and that they are true and correct to the best of my knowledge, information and belief.

Date _____ Signature _____

                                                        _____
                                                        Print Name and Title

[An individual signing on behalf of a partnership or corporation must indicate position or relationship to debtor.]

_____ continuation sheets attached

Penalty for making a false statement: Fine of up to $500,000 or imprisonment for up to 5 years, or both. 18 U.S.C. § 152 and 3571

CERTIFICATION AND SIGNATURE OF NON-ATTORNEY BANKRUPTCY PETITION PREPARER (See 11 U.S.C. § 110)

I certify that I am a bankruptcy petition preparer as defined in 11 U.S.C. § 110, that I prepared this document for compensation, and that I have provided the debtor with a copy of this document.

_____   _____
Printed or Typed Name of Bankruptcy Petition Preparer   Social Security No.

_____

_____
Address

Names and Social Security numbers of all other individuals who prepared or assisted in preparing this document:

If more than one person prepared this document, attach additional signed sheets conforming to the appropriate Official Form for each person.

X _____   _____
Signature of Bankruptcy Petition Preparer   Date

A bankruptcy petition preparer's failure to comply with the provisions of title 11 and the Federal Rules of Bankruptcy Procedure may result in fines or imprisonment or both. 18 U.S.C. § 156.

UNITED STATES BANKRUPTCY COURT

_____ DISTRICT OF _____

In re _____ ,   Case No. _____
                 (Name)   (If known)

Chapter _____

CHAPTER 7 INDIVIDUAL DEBTOR'S STATEMENT OF INTENTION (Form 8)

1. I have filed a schedule of assets and liabilities which includes consumer debts secured by property of the estate.
2. I intend to do the following with respect to the property of the estate which secures those consumer debts:

   a. Property to be surrendered.

Description of Property	Creditor's Name
1. _____	_____
2. _____	_____
3. _____	_____

   b.Property to be retained.   *[Check any applicable statement.]*

Description of property	Creditor's name	Property is claimed as exempt	Property will be redeemed pursuant to 11 USC § 772	Debt will bereaffirmed pursuant to 11 USC § 524(c)
1. _____	_____	_____	_____	_____
2. _____	_____	_____	_____	_____
3. _____	_____	_____	_____	_____
4. _____	_____	_____	_____	_____
5. _____	_____	_____	_____	_____

Date: _____   _____
                                       Signature of Debtor

CERTIFICATION AND SIGNATURE OF NON-ATTORNEY BANKRUPTCY PETITION PREPARER (See 11 U.S.C. § 110)

    I certify that I am a bankruptcy petition preparer as defined in 11 U.S.C. § 110, that I prepared this document for compensation, and that I have provided the debtor with a copy of this document.

_____   _____
Printed or Typed Name of Bankruptcy Petition Preparer   Social Security No.

_____

Address

Names and Social Security numbers of all other individuals who prepared or assisted in preparing this document:

If more than one person prepared this document, attach additional signed sheets conforming to the appropriate Official Form for each person.

X_____   _____
Signature of Bankruptcy Petition Preparer   Date

A bankruptcy petition preparer's failure to comply with the provisions of Title 11 and the Federal Rules of Bankruptcy Procedure may result in fine or imprisonment or both. 11 U.S.C. § 110; 18 U.S.C. § 156.

Form 3. APPLICATION AND ORDER TO PAY FILING FEE IN INSTALLMENTS
UNITED STATES BANKRUPTCY COURT
_____ DISTRICT OF _____

In re _____,
Debtor

Case No. _____

Chapter _____

APPLICATION TO PAY FILING FEE IN INSTALLMENTS

1.   In accordance with Fed. R. Bankr. P. 1006, I apply for permission to pay the Filing Fee amounting to $_____ in installments.

2.   I certify that I am unable to pay the Filing Fee except in installments.

3.   I further certify that I have not paid any money or transferred any property to an attorney for services in connection with this case and that I will neither make any payment nor transfer any property for services in connection with this case until the filing fee is paid in full.

4.   I propose the following terms for the payment of the Filing Fee.*

    $ _____   Check one ☐   With the filing of the petition, or
                                 ☐   On or before _____

    $ _____   on or before _____

    $ _____   on or before _____

    $ _____   on or before _____

*   The number of installments proposed shall not exceed four (4), and the final installment shall be payable not later than 120 days after filing the petition. For cause shown, the court may extend the time of any installment, provided the last installment is paid not later than 180 days after filing the petition. Fed. R. Bankr. P. 1006(b)(2).

5.   I understand that if I fail to pay any installment when due my bankruptcy case may be dismissed and I may not receive a discharge of my debts.

_____
Signature of Attorney   Date

_____
Name of Attorney

_____
Signature of Debtor   Date
(In a joint case, both spouses must sign.)

_____
Signature of Joint Debtor (if any)   Date

CERTIFICATION AND SIGNATURE OF NON-ATTORNEY BANKRUPTCY PETITION (See 11 U.S.C. § 110)

I certify that I am a bankruptcy petition preparer as defined in 11 U.S.C. § 110, that I prepared this document for compensation, and that I have provided the debtor with a copy of this document. I also certify that I will not accept money or any other property from the debtor before the filing fee is paid in full.

_____
Printed or Typed Name of Bankruptcy Petition Preparer

_____
Social Security No.

_____

_____
Address

Names and Social Security numbers of all other individuals who prepared or assisted in preparing this document:

If more than one person prepared this document, attach additional signed sheets conforming to the appropriate Official Form for each person.

x_____
Signature of Bankruptcy Petition Preparer

_____
Date

A bankruptcy petition preparer's failure to comply with the provisions of title 11 and the Federal Rules of Bankruptcy Procedure may result in fines or imprisonment or both. 11 U.S.C. § 110; 18 U.S.C. § 156.

UNITED STATES BANKRUPTCY COURT
_____ DISTRICT OF _____

In re _____,   Case No. _____

                     Debtor

                                                       Chapter _____

ORDER APPROVING PAYMENT OF FILING FEE IN INSTALLMENTS

        IT IS ORDERED that the debtor(s) may pay the filing fee in installments on the terms proposed in the foregoing application.

        IT IS FURTHER ORDERED that until the filing fee is paid in full the debtor shall not pay any money for services in connection with this case, and the debtor shall not relinquish any property as payment for services in connection with this case.

                                               BY THE COURT

Date: _____   _____
                                             United States Bankruptcy Judge

Your Name, Address & Phone Number:

In Pro Per

UNITED STATES BANKRUPTCY COURT FOR THE _____

DISTRICT OF _____

In re   )
) Case No. _____
)
)
                Debtor(s))
_____

PROOF OF SERVICE BY MAIL

I, _____, declare that:

I am over the age of 18 years and not a party to the within bankruptcy. I

reside in or am employed in the County of _____.

My residence/business address is _____

_____

On _____, I served the within _____

_____ by placing a true and correct copy of it in a

sealed envelope with first-class postage fully prepaid, in the United States

mail at _____

_____, addressed as follows:

I declare under penalty of perjury that the foregoing is true and correct.

Executed on _____, 20_____ at _____

_____.

_____
Signature

Your Name, Address & Phone Number:

In Pro Per

UNITED STATES BANKRUPTCY COURT _____

_____ DISTRICT OF _____

In re   )

)   Case No. _____

)   Chapter _____

)   AMENDMENT COVER SHEET

               Debtor(s))

Presented herewith are the original and one copy of the following:

☐ Voluntary Petition (Note: Spouse may not be added or deleted subsequent to initial filing.)

☐ Schedule A—Real Property

☐ Schedule B—Personal Property

☐ Schedule C—Property Claimed as Exempt

☐ Schedule D—Creditors Holding Secured Claims

☐ Schedule E—Creditors Holding Unsecured Priority Claims

☐ Schedule F—Creditors Holding Unsecured Nonpriority Claims

☐ Schedule G—Executory Contracts and Unexpired Leases

☐ Schedule H—Codebtors

☐ Schedule I—Current Income of Individual Debtor(s)

☐ Schedule J—Current Expenditures of Individual Debtor(s)

☐ Summary of Schedules

☐ Statement of Financial Affairs

☐ I have enclosed a $20 fee because I am adding new creditors or changing addresses after the original Meeting of Creditors Notice has been sent.

_____   _____
Signature of Debtor   Signature of Debtor's Spouse

I (we) _____

and _____,

the debtor(s) in this case, declare under penalty of perjury that the information set forth in the amendment attached hereto consisting of _____ pages is true and correct to the best of my (our) information and belief.

Dated: _____, 20_____

_____   _____
Signature of Debtor   Signature of Debtor's Spouse

Your Name, Address & Phone Number:

In Pro Per

UNITED STATES BANKRUPTCY COURT _____

_____ DISTRICT OF _____

In re   )
) Case No. _____
) Chapter _____
) NOTICE OF CHANGE OF ADDRESS
                          Debtor(s))
_____

Social Security Number (H): _____

Social Security Number (W): _____

MY (OUR) FORMER MAILING ADDRESS AND PHONE NUMBER WAS:

Name: _____

Street: _____

City: _____

State/Zip: _____

Phone: (_____) _____

PLEASE BE ADVISED THAT AS OF_____, 20____, MY (OUR) NEW
MAILING ADDRESS AND PHONE NUMBER IS:

Name: _____

Street: _____

City: _____

State/Zip: _____

Phone: (_____) _____

                          _____
                          Signature of Debtor

                          _____
                          Signature of Debtor's Spouse

Index

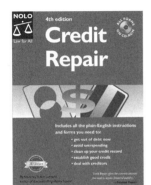
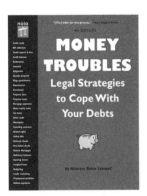